Including One, Including All

Including One, Including All

A Guide to Relationship-Based Early Childhood Inclusion

Leslie Roffman and Todd Wanerman
with Cassandra Britton

Redleaf Press®
www.redleafpress.org
800-423-8309

Published by Redleaf Press
10 Yorkton Court
St. Paul, MN 55117
www.redleafpress.org

First edition 2011
Cover design by Erin Kirk New
Cover photograph by Getty Images
Interior typeset in Sabon and Myriad and designed by Erin Kirk New
Interior photos by the authors
Developmental edit by Jeanne Engelmann
Printed in the United States of America
17 16 15 14 13 12 11 10   1 2 3 4 5 6 7 8

The excerpt on page 23 from "The Fourth R in Education—
Relationships" by Miriam W. Witmer was originally published by
Heldref Publications, 1319 Eighteenth Street NW, Washington, DC
20036, in *The Clearing House* 78 (5): 224–228. Copyright © 2005
by the Helen Dwight Reid Education Foundation. Reprinted with
permission.

Library of Congress Cataloging-in-Publication Data
Roffman, Leslie.
   Including one, including all : a guide to relationship-based early
childhood inclusion / Leslie Roffman and Todd Wanerman with
Cassandra Britton. — 1st ed.
      p. cm.
   Includes bibliographical references.
   ISBN 978-1-60554-013-9 (alk. paper)
   1. Inclusive education—United States. 2. Early childhood
education—United States. 3. Children with disabilities—Education
(Early childhood)—United States. I. Wanerman, Todd. II. Britton,
Cassandra. III. Title.
   LC1201.R64 2010
   371.9'046—dc22
                                                2009032121

Printed on acid-free paper

Including One, Including All

Foreword

We have all had moments of marveling at the qualities demonstrated by a young child. We admire the little boy who helps another child rebuild a knocked-over block tower, or the young girl who saves a place at the circle for the child who never seems to be able to settle in one spot, or the child with a raised fist and clenched jaw who manages to say "I feel like hitting you" but doesn't strike. What we admire in these children are the traits the teachers at The Little School, upon whose approach this book is based, focus on every day: engagement with others, internal discipline, self-awareness, curiosity, empathy, emotional range, self-esteem, flexibility, logical thinking and problem solving, creativity, and moral integrity. These qualities give a child the foundation he or she needs to navigate the increasingly global and complex society we live in.

The personal ingredients for success in life are learned in the preschool classroom. The authors of this book and all of the teachers at The Little School know that success in the modern world is not built on IQ or computer skills but on the internal resources one brings to the relationships that build satisfying experiences of family, community, and work. The relationship-based approach to education so skillfully executed at The Little School and beautifully illustrated in this volume grows out of the modern era of developmental research from studies of parent-child interaction to brain function. These have demonstrated that relationships are the central organizers of the child's experience and the foundation from which all learning unfolds. Modern employers are looking for young applicants who can do their job and function flexibly under pressure, provide self-reflective leadership, and take on responsibility with an organized and fluid interpersonal demeanor. As you read this insightful book, you will see these elements of success come to life in the daily experiences of students and teachers described on every page. A great contribution of this book resides in the detailed stories of life in the classroom that allow the reader to actively experience how the relationship-based approach works on the floor.

It is a privilege to write the foreword for this book. When I first met Leslie Roffman many years ago, she was starting a small preschool program with Tim Treadway in a local community center. Soon after, they were joined by other early childhood educators such as Cassandra Britton, Lisa Treadway, and Todd Wanerman. As a collaborative group, they formulated and sustained a theoretically rich, practical approach to the education of young children. They were committed to creating a learning environment for young children that valued relationships as the central organizer of development and emotional intelligence as the linchpin to learning in all domains. From the first days of The Little School, when it was truly little, they were committed to diversity in the student body. They welcomed children who learned differently, experienced a range of advantages and disadvantages in life, and came from diverse cultures.

From this beginning, their philosophy of early childhood education emphasized that the core principles of teaching and learning were good for all children. They were committed to viewing each child and parent as individuals with unique patterns of strengths and vulnerabilities that led them to respect each child and to create an individualized plan for the education of each child. They believed that social and emotional development is central to learning in every domain of development. And they recognized the strong connection between body and mind for integrated thought and self-expression. As The Little School grew and its programs matured, it also grew in size so many more children and families could benefit from the learning opportunities available through the school. The relationship-based approach to education thrived in San Francisco, and parents clamored to secure a place at the school for their children. The appreciation for an inclusive community was nurtured not just by the teachers but also by parents who understood the value of such an early experience for their child and for all children, and by the broader community, which worked to support inclusive learning opportunities.

Throughout this book, you will see evidence of teachers in an active role on the floor, respecting and acknowledging the internal life of the child, while promoting social thinking and behavior that nurture self-reflection and the capacity to hold others' needs and feelings in mind. As you read, you will learn the rationale, research, and theory behind the school's approach as well as the translation of theory into practice. This book gives all early childhood teachers the concrete and practical tools to implement inclusive practices in their settings. The suggestions interspersed throughout each chapter make handy guides for immediate use in the classroom.

Unique to The Little School is the focus on child development in the ecological context of school and family. Parents' participation in the school and in the maintenance of an inclusive community is thoroughly addressed by the authors. They don't shrink away from discussing the very complex feelings teachers as well as moms and dads experience when working together to understand the confusing behavior of a child or to interpret the meaning of a child's unusual behavior to other families. The sensitive descriptions of how to support the importance for all families of belonging to a community and the essential qualities of honesty and authenticity, respect for each child, and mutual compassion for each other as well as for oneself work together to describe how to create an accepting and nonjudgmental world of learners.

Fortunately for all the teachers and caregivers who pick up this book, the clear descriptions and guidelines on every page will enable them to prepare children and parents for the new and increasingly complex expectations facing children today. In the modern world of globalization, political conflicts, and needs for an environmentally unified planet, this book lays the foundation for how to instill in young children the qualities that enable them to thrive.

Barbara Kalmanson, PhD

Academic Dean

The Interdisciplinary Council on Developmental and Learning Disorders Graduate School in Infant Mental Health and Developmental Disorders

Preface

What inspired you to pick up this book? You are most likely looking for answers to the challenges posed by a certain child, or a certain group, or a program. You may be a family child care provider wondering how to manage an intense or puzzling assortment of children. You may be a teacher in a center or preschool looking to better understand certain children in your class. Perhaps you are an administrator who wants to respond to your staff's need for resources to support children with challenges. Or you may be an early childhood education teacher searching for informative yet readable sources for your students. We hope this book contains something useful and inspiring for each of you.

Several books have been published in recent years on the subject of inclusion. You may already know that inclusion is a model of education in which children with and without assessed special needs are educated together. But you may not consider yourself to be an inclusion teacher or the program in which you work to be an inclusion program. If you feel this way, you are in good company. You are also the very sort of practitioner to whom this book is addressed. If you are a more experienced inclusion professional, we think there is much in this book for you too. We have designed this book to speak to anyone who wants to improve their skills in supporting all children.

The three of us—Leslie, Todd, and Cassandra—have been working together at The Little School in San Francisco for over twenty years. Leslie cofounded the program with Tim Treadway in 1984. Cassie joined and became program director three years later. She continues in this role and coordinates the school's inclusion services. Todd has been the Head Teacher of a two- and three-year-old class since 1991. None of us entered the field of early childhood education with the express aim of working with children with special needs. Through our two decades of teaching together, we, along with the rest of The Little School staff, evolved into inclusion teachers in an inclusive setting. We simply wanted to serve each and every child to the best of our abilities.

Little by little, this commitment led us to make connections with therapists, special educators, parents, and resource and service organizations. With the help of these knowledgeable and dedicated partners, we learned about inclusion as we went along. We found that our relationship-based approach could work for a surprisingly high percentage of children in our community. Most of all, we found that bringing typically and atypically developing children together increased the quality of education and the integrity of the school community for *everyone*.

When we began, few of the people around us seemed to know what we meant when we talked about inclusion. But over the last fifteen years, while we were developing our approach to inclusion and learning, awareness and interest in this model have grown at an amazing pace. Today, every state and national conference catalog is brimming with presentations on the subject. And a quick Internet search of "inclusion education" will yield thousands of essays, books, Web sites, organizations, and support services.

For us, inclusion is a method of supporting all children, not just those with perplexing challenges or assessed special needs. It is also a means of creating an inclusive classroom and school community. We believe that these two elements are closely linked. Our inclusion program was developed in a mainstream preschool by teachers who had studied the basics of quality early childhood education. So for us, the part of the inclusion philosophy that sees all children united by their unique strengths and challenges is the heart of the matter—and the mission of our book.

This book offers you first and foremost a lens for viewing *all* children. We show you detailed ways to build effective relationships with all children and families in your care. We guide you through the process of learning each child's strengths and help you pursue questions or challenges that individual children present. Although you will see that we discourage teachers from focusing too much on quick answers or interpretations, we show you new ways of understanding all the children in your program. And throughout, we focus on the broad layer that we feel makes inclusion work: how to create an environment in which each child feels known and supported, in which each child, regardless of strengths and challenges, feels good.

Once you are equipped with a lens for viewing all children, we explore a framework for supporting all children. We describe and discuss an ongoing cycle we call *Engage-Reflect-Plan* that enables you to mold your understanding of children into detailed and effective plans. These plans use your understanding of children's strengths to help them address their challenges. You will find that this approach can fit into your child care or school setting regardless of how much time or how many resources you have. It is simple and flexible enough to work for family child care providers and preschool teachers, as well as elementary school teachers or aides.

Many very good books on inclusion try to present as many specific therapeutic techniques as can fit in a manageable volume. We take a slightly different approach. We share details and tools that we feel are central to successfully supporting children with different kinds of challenges. We know from our work that specific tools and skills are at the top layer of a successful approach. Without building your way up to the top layer from a strong foundation, a long list of details can be hard to understand and organize and even harder to remember and master. This idea that you must start by building a solid foundation and then go on to more sophisticated challenges is also a key theme in our approach to supporting children.

This book begins with an exploration of what inclusion is, where it came from, and what place it has found in the larger world of education. From that overview, we lead you through the process of building your own inclusion practice through stories and guiding principles. We feel the most effective way to share our ideas with you is through stories. We are confident that meaningful stories will illustrate the ideas and skills you need to learn. To help you pull out the important skills from the stories, we also want to make sure to provide the important ideas and approaches that guide us in our work.

Part 1, The Foundation of Relationship-Based Inclusion, is devoted to this part of your journey. Chapter 1 gives both a historical and philosophical summary of inclusion. It fleshes out the idea that general practitioners are poised to practice successful inclusion through their basic set of good teaching skills. Chapter 2 discusses relationship-based education, which we feel is the key to our success in inclusion education. Chapter 3 gives an overview of sensory integration and how understanding a child's unique sensory profile—how the child takes in sensations and responds with plans and actions—forms the most important building block of inclusion. These developmental frameworks offer new ways to view all learners and their various play styles and skills. Chapter 4 introduces the cycle of steps to support children that we call *Engage-Reflect-Plan*. This provides a simple framework for the detailed approaches that follow.

Part 2, Including All Children: Engage-Reflect-Plan, moves into the classroom to focus on teachers actually practicing inclusion. The separate chapters in this part follow the sequence of two children's experience in an inclusion program. Chapter 5 covers how to build an individual relationship with children and parents—how to use your powers of observation and partnership to gain insight into all children, identifying strengths and challenges. It also begins a discussion on how to partner with parents and other key adults. Chapter 6 looks at turning individualized understanding of children into an effective plan of action, setting the right goals, developing strategies, balancing individual plans with group needs, and integrating your own plans with outside services. Chapter 7 addresses the important elements of monitoring and updating your plans and nurturing the ongoing partnership among teachers, parents, and other important adults. Finally, chapter 8 discusses the often-overlooked process of supporting children as they transition out of your program and into new ones.

Throughout part 2, discussions of specific issues in inclusion will appear in boxes and sidebars, alongside the stories of teachers and children. This will allow you to easily locate and sift out the detailed skills that will go into your expanding inclusion teacher's toolbox. By featuring detailed tips and strategies this way, we hope to avoid interrupting the main narrative. But this also makes it easier to use the different aspects of the book in whatever way works best for you.

Starting in chapter 5, we present one specific template for organizing your plans for children. Facsimiles of this document, which focuses on strengths and interests, questions, goals, strategies, and progress, will appear in the middle section, as the teachers in the stories choose and adjust their goals and strategies. We wanted to include this for readers who benefit from clear, detailed models. You can adapt this template directly from the way it appears in the book. But we do not want to intimidate readers who may not have the time or resources to generate specific documents or whose working style doesn't benefit from them. Inclusion stresses that everyone's learning style is different, and that goes for adults too. This is why we focus on the basics.

With our two children's stories concluded, part 3, The Wider View, looks behind the scenes to focus in more detail on what makes a relationship-based inclusion program possible.

Each chapter in part 3 explores in greater detail a different aspect of the foundation needed to make inclusion work for everyone in a relationship-based classroom. Chapter 9 digs deeper into basic elements of an inclusive community for children. What kind of classroom can teachers create to encourage children who will become invested in each other's growth and learning? How can teachers create a mutually supportive classroom through their expectations, routines, curriculum, and interactions with children? Chapter 10 offers ideas for collaboration among teachers, providers, and administrators. What kind of training and development does a staff member need in order to support children and parents? What kind of ongoing support do teachers need? Chapters 11 and 12 look at parents' experiences of inclusion and how to create an inclusive parent community. How can we understand and support parents when their children are challenging? And how can we create a parent community that supports individualized approaches and individual children, even when those children take extra energy or disrupt the class? Finally, chapter 13 wraps up the book with a look at how inclusion can affect the whole field of education, as well as each teacher's individual developmental journey. Additional specific tools and techniques are included in the appendixes.

We do not try to sweep the challenges of inclusion under the rug. We know from our own experience and our work with other teachers that supporting children with special needs is one of the most complicated tasks we face in education today. We address specific pitfalls or sticking points throughout the book. We pay particular attention to how to achieve the basic balance of inclusion: honoring and fostering each child's unique style and strengths, on the one hand, and offering timely support or even intervention, on the other.

The children portrayed in part 2, Danny and Michelle, are composites of many children we have worked with over the years. But their challenges and the ways the teachers work to support them are authentic and very common to inclusion programs. We have successfully applied the approaches in the book to children with all kinds of challenges or disabilities—physical, cognitive, and relational. We did not try to specifically address every kind of special need. We tried to create two profiles that would illustrate how to recognize and support children's challenges. The teachers in these stories are also hybrids of many teachers we have worked with over the years. We tried to portray them as real human beings with the full range of feelings and responses that teachers experience as they take on challenges. We compressed the timeline of the *Engage-Reflect-Plan* process in order to fit it into the narrative range of one program year. In real life, the process, especially as it pertains to outside assessments, might take longer, depending on the pace and nature of the family/teacher relationship as outlined in chapter 11. Likewise, all the children, teachers, and family members referenced in the book are fictional amalgams or have had their names changed unless otherwise noted.

We also addressed the thorny issue of using the "he" or "she" pronoun in a way that would most accurately reflect real experience. We balanced "he" and "she" more or less evenly when referring to children. When talking about teachers, however, we leaned more often toward "she." It is true that one of the authors is a man who, along with the rest of The Little School staff, advocates strongly for men to see early childhood education as one of the most exciting and important career paths on earth. But that does not alter the fact that early childhood education is a field that grows and thrives largely from the contributions of women, and we want to reflect that.

We use the term *teacher* throughout the book to refer to all child care professionals and the term *program* or *school* to refer to all early childhood settings in order to acknowledge the hard work and high quality of early childhood education across the spectrum. In some cases, we refer to specific settings. We often use the term *children with challenges* to refer both to children with identified special needs and those who are experiencing any kind of challenge that calls for special response or plans from teachers.

We Did It; So Can You

As you read, you will no doubt notice that the teachers in the fictional program we write about enjoy many resources. Nevertheless, this fictional preschool reflects our actual program—The Little School, a part-time program where teachers have time away from children to meet and plan. We also enjoy low teacher-to-child ratios, teams of teachers working together, and very committed parents. You may be inclined to wonder, like many of the teachers we work with around the county, how you can adapt the practices from this kind of program into your world.

We include some discussion throughout the book about how practitioners in different circumstances can use specific tools. But we portray a high standard on purpose. Part of the benefit of inclusion is that it both requires and inspires you to set the bar higher. We want you to see what an inclusion program looks like when it has grown over time with effective support. Keep in mind, however, that this fictional program, no matter how rich in resources it may be, is based on a real program. We did it. So can you.

Our commitment to inclusion inspired us to create this kind of program. It wasn't always this way. Part of our message is that inclusion leads individual programs and the field of early childhood education toward more effective priorities. Our commitment inspires us to find ways to develop our programs and build networks of support that allow us to serve children the way we feel they deserve. It can also help you connect with resources and supporters in the community who share your commitment and can help your program grow and thrive.

But you needn't have these resources now to use the ideas in this book. A key discovery in our own journey as teachers is that the *stance* you bring to your work—your outlook, your mood, your determination to succeed against difficult odds—is one of the most powerful teaching tools you have. So aside from techniques and practices, one of the most important things we hope you will gain from this book is enthusiasm. All innovations and progress began with someone who was not only determined to solve a problem but also excited and intrigued. Learning more about inclusion will help you feel more confident and optimistic about working with children's challenges. But finding a way to feel more confident and optimistic will also open the door for you to learn more from your own strengths and talents and from local collaborators and additional resources. We hope you will enjoy the adventure, as you read this book and throughout your life as a practitioner.

Acknowledgments

As first-time authors, we owe a very high debt to a very large number of people. There isn't enough space to thank everyone in enough detail for his or her support and contributions. We hope that each of the following people holds in their hearts the importance of their work.

First and foremost, we wish to thank the current and past staff of The Little School. This is a book about the *school's* approach to inclusion. We three authors have taken on the role of recording and sharing the approach. But given the title and focus of the book, it should come as no surprise that the perspectives, practices, and ideas contained herein were developed and nurtured through *relationships* in a loving and creative community over twenty-five years. We are blessed at The Little School to have worked with some of the most dedicated and insightful teachers we've ever known. A few key contributors—cofounder Tim Treadway, Lisa Treadway, Sarita Escobar, Dawn-Monique Del Bonis Elkin, Jetta Jacobson, and Trina Matthews—have, through their long-term partnership and personal expertise, played especially important roles in the school's inclusion practice.

We also thank the children, parents, and families at The Little School. As we three authors grow as teachers and as people, we broaden and deepen our understanding of how relationships guide the quality of education. We are thrilled and grateful to have worked with such loving, devoted parents and, above all, such inspiring children. We have tried to show how crucial their contributions to our practice have been. There is no way to adequately acknowledge them here.

In the actual creation of this book, there are, again, more people to thank than space allows:

Susan Etlinger, Barbara Henderson, Barbara Kalmanson, Megan London, Lee MacKinnon, Daniel Meier, Alice Nakahata, Jiryu Thongnamsap, Molly Treadway, Leon Wanerman, and Serena Wieder shared their personal stories and insights with us on everything from classroom practice to writing and publishing.

Victoria Augustus, Steve and Christine Bent, Rhoda Chew, Margaret Coles and Haruwn Wesley, Jetta Jacobson, Sotweed Schneble, John and Ellen

Shields, Mica Saldivar, and Lisa Treadway graciously allowed us to use their personal stories in the text.

Lia Thomas contributed hours to research and citation support from long before the first draft. Michael John McCourt helped track down key source materials.

John De Souza, Lisa Giannone, Kathryn Maleeny, and Lisa Treadway took the photographs and devoted days worth of effort (and patience) to getting them right.

Alice Nakahata, Megan London, David Worton, Melodie Younce, and Fiona Zecca read early drafts of the book and offered indispensable feedback and advice. We are deeply indebted to them for showing us the way to the final draft.

The Little School Board of Directors, composed entirely of parents, provided multiple layers of support. They approved the use of the school's name, stories, and images from the classroom without hesitation and arranged material support for the project. They have also showed exceptional enthusiasm and confidence for the project from the start.

David Heath and Kyra Ostendorf at Redleaf Press have been our tireless champions from before the beginning of the project. They have guided us through the process from the proposal stage onward, and, with good cheer and understanding, fielded all the confusion, anxiety, and uncertainty that we threw their way. Carla Valadez also answered endless queries about research and citations. Jim Handrigan provided guidance on photos and graphics. Our editor, Jeanne Engelmann, shepherded us with clear-headedness and skill through the process of turning an unwieldy and ambitious first draft into the book you are now holding.

Our special thanks go to Dr. Barbara Kalmanson for writing the foreword. Dr. Kalmanson, Gwen Wong, and Janet Green Babb also have provided years of generous and insightful consultation to our inclusion program.

And for reasons that she alone understands, our special thanks to former Little School administrator Ellen Baker.

Finally, our families, to whom this book is dedicated, endured our distraction, absence, and stress with unwavering acceptance. Their love and partnership gave us the inspiration, courage, and, most of all, protected time and space to take on what without them would have been an impossible task.

To each of these people, and countless others whom we could not mention by name, our most sincere thanks.

Part 1

The Foundation of Relationship-Based Inclusion

Why Inclusion?

"I have a child in my group who dumps everything onto the floor."

"One little boy in our class doesn't talk. He just plays with the same toy bus in the corner."

"Chelsea disrupts the routines. She yells and runs off during group time."

"I don't know how to support a child who uses a walker. I don't know how to respond to the other children's questions about her or to the questions of the other parents."

"I don't know what this child needs."

Teachers in every kind of early childhood program—family child care, infant-toddler centers, preschools, and elementary schools—encounter children similar to those mentioned above and find themselves asking the same questions. Certain children seem to need support and responses we aren't sure we know how to provide. Some children may have a particularly hard time picking activities and sticking with them. Others may be aggressive or withdrawn in their connections with their peers. Some may have special physical needs. Still others have difficulty managing transitions or routines. As teachers, we like to feel that we "know" children and have the skills to help them thrive in group settings. But there are always some children, or some things about all children, that we feel we don't "know"—or at least we aren't sure what we can do to support them.

There's No Blueprint

We—the three authors of this book—are not specialists, nor are we special education teachers. We are, respectively, the director, program director, and lead teacher in a traditional, part-time nursery school. We, along with the rest of our staff, became interested in taking an active approach to adopting an inclusion model, mostly because we wanted to be able to make our program work for a few specific children at a time. At first, we felt ill-equipped and nervous about the idea.

There is one moment in our evolution as an inclusion program that we like to share with teachers who are feeling unsure themselves about their skills with children's challenges. About fifteen years ago, a therapist whose child had attended our school recommended that we admit one of her clients, a three-year-old boy with autism. She was confident that our approach to understanding and supporting each child as an individual could work for him. A graduate psychology student was providing in-home support for the boy's family and could come to class with him.

This therapist, the graduate support teacher, and the teachers in our program who would be working with this child sat down before he began our program to make a plan. We asked for some specific instructions on how to work with children with autism in a preschool classroom. After an awkward silence, our colleagues from the world of therapy admitted that they had been counting on us to figure it out.

Our first reaction to this was panic—*there's no blueprint!* But since we trusted our colleagues' trust in us, we decided to give it a try. We would just do what we knew how to do and see what happened. It didn't turn out to be easy or magical, and we certainly didn't cure our young client of autism. But he had a more successful experience in our program than we would have imagined at the start. And so that initial realization—there's no one correct blueprint—turned out to be very important. It gave us the freedom to learn that regular teachers and care providers can use their basic skills to learn how to serve children with challenges.

It is important here to make clear that inclusion can mean many different things to many different people. Since inclusion began as an extension of the early intervention movement in special education, it has grown in many different directions. It is also important to acknowledge that different children and families have had different levels of success in inclusion programs. Some children really do need specialized settings. And many researchers and educators who helped develop inclusion programs have rightly pointed out that teachers must learn enough basic skills to do it right (Odom 2000).

Unlike many of the people in the field before us, we did not start out as a special education program. We are part of the wave of inclusion that started at the other end of the spectrum—regular early childhood educators trying to keep learning enough to serve one child at a time. As such, we won't try to describe the one and only correct model of inclusion or to take in all the ideas and practices in the field. What we can offer to you (and, we hope, to the field of early childhood education in general) is a *practitioner-based* approach to inclusion that we developed in our classrooms. We were lucky to have support and training along the way. We share this book with you because what we do has worked for almost all the children we have known, not because we developed it in a university setting or proved it with research studies. And that is exactly why we think it can work for you.

As our confidence with inclusion grew, we began to share some of our experiences with fellow teachers—informally at first, then later in workshops and conferences. What we discovered was that teachers all over the country are asking the same questions as we are, and, whether they know it or not, are moving toward the inclusion model themselves.

Teachers share a lot of their questions, challenges, frustrations, and anxieties with us:

- They don't know what techniques to use with children with unique profiles.
- They feel they don't have enough time, space, or staff to take care of everyone.
- They have different viewpoints from families, pediatricians, or even their own coteachers and administrators.

As teachers make honest and vigorous efforts to support all the children in their care, these challenges become natural and universal. Teachers often feel powerless and overwhelmed in their basic, everyday practice. Adding children with special needs into the mix can intensify these feelings.

How Inclusion Has Evolved

A generation or two ago, teachers may not have encountered some of these children. It is easy to forget in today's world that preschool education or group child care was not commonplace even thirty years ago (National Center for Education Statistics 2007). Children with differences significant enough to make routines, socializing, or curriculum very challenging probably didn't participate. Others were simply thought of as difficult. In the elementary schools, children who had identified special needs were segregated into special education programs. Many of us who came of age more than a decade or so ago can well remember that separate population of children who attended class in portable classrooms located at the far end of the play yard and who interacted mostly with their teachers during recess and lunchtime. Still others were confined to residential care.

Three things have changed since then:

- The number of children in preschool programs has exploded. Changes in our economic structure and the roles of families have made early childhood education a fundamental element of our society.
- We have learned volumes about child development. Our understanding of children's unique learning styles, the relationship between children's strengths and their challenges, and the universal dynamics of early development have radically altered our concept and our expectations of childhood. Our abilities and approach to identifying and assessing young children's challenges has evolved many lifetimes in just a generation. The number of preschool children who are either assessed with specific developmental challenges or whose challenges lead teachers and families to seek additional support has climbed dramatically.

- Finally, as a result of this rapidly changing climate, the education community has begun to turn away from the practice of educating children with special needs in separate programs. We have begun to recognize that strengths and challenges for all children exist on a more continuous spectrum than we once believed. The worlds of general education and special education have begun to move toward each other.

Even the federal government acknowledged this change in its Individuals with Disabilities Education Act (IDEA) legislation of the 1990s. A new model of education has grown from the idea that a far greater number of, if not all, children, regardless of strengths and challenges, will benefit from being educated together in the same program. Since this approach is based on making a successful community for everyone, it has been called *inclusion*.

A Brief History of Inclusion

As late as the mid-1970s, there were no federal laws or guidelines for providing children with disabilities access to free public education. One out of five disabled children received no public education (U.S. Office of Special Education Programs 2000). In 1975, Congress enacted the Education for All Handicapped Children Act (EHA) as a standard, rather than a law. The EHA was the first step in guaranteeing educational access for all, but it focused on separate special education services for children with disabilities.

The 1990s saw a large-scale rethinking of the need for access and equality for the disabled. The Americans with Disabilities Act (ADA), along with key legal challenges by individuals, prompted congress to rewrite the EHA as the Individuals with Disabilities Education Act (IDEA) in 1990. It was significantly revised as the Individuals with Disabilities Education Improvement Act (IDEIA) in 2004.

Perhaps the most significant change from EHA to IDEA was the principle of the *least restrictive environment*. The act states,

> To the maximum extent appropriate, children with disabilities, including children in public or private institutions or other care facilities, are educated with children who are not disabled, and special classes, separate schooling, or other removal of children with disabilities from the regular educational environment occurs only when the nature or severity of the disability of a child is such that education in regular classes with the use of supplementary aids and services cannot be achieved satisfactorily (U.S. Congress 2004, 118 Stat. 2677).

IDEA also created provisions for children between birth and three years with diagnosed disabilities to receive early intervention through their local school districts and mandated that children with disabilities receive either an Individualized Family Service Plan (IFSP) during these years or an Individualized Education Program (IEP) during school-age years.

Inclusion as an educational movement began to develop during the same period. Many special educators in the late 1960s realized that children with challenges benefited greatly from early intervention. Shortly after, pioneers in the field of special education began setting up pilot programs to test the effects of placing toddlers and preschool-age children with differences in classrooms with "typically" developing children. While these programs were often viewed as successes, they were different from inclusive preschool programs today: as many pioneers acknowledge, they pulled special education practices for elementary school students downward to preschoolers, and the programs were created for therapeutic research (Bricker 2000). It was only later, as the IDEA-era movement toward "mainstreaming" took off, that inclusion moved into the world of existing early childhood programs, and teachers began to develop practices tailored to accommodating preschoolers of all strengths and challenges.

Families, educators, administrators, and legislators have carried on a lively debate since the dawn of inclusion on whether children with disabilities should never, always, or sometimes share curriculum and classrooms with their typically developing peers. The issue has been addressed from the perspectives of moral responsibility, educational effectiveness, and, especially as public schools face growing budget challenges, financial efficiency.

In early childhood education, inclusion became a focus of great interest as the number of children under five years of age identified with special needs began to climb in the 1990s. Without the safety net of public schools to guarantee access for all children, early childhood educators faced the difficult choice of accommodating children with challenges or leaving their families with little or no alternative. In this light, early childhood educators have felt the moral pull toward inclusion strongly.

While differing viewpoints are far from resolved, inclusion has been accepted as an important educational philosophy and practice. A joint position statement by the Division for Early Childhood and NAEYC states

> Early childhood inclusion embodies the values, policies, and practices that support the right of every infant and young child and his or her family, regardless of ability, to participate in a broad range of activities and contexts as full members of families, communities, and society. The desired results of inclusive experiences for children with and without disabilities and their families include a sense of belonging and membership, positive social relationships and friendships, and development and learning to reach their full potential. (Division for Early Childhood and the National Association for the Education of Young Children 2009, 2)

What Is Inclusion?

At its heart, inclusion is a very simple concept: educate children with and without disabilities together, in the same programs. Underneath that surface, however, lie some very powerful, and perhaps more complicated, ideas:

- All children have strengths and challenges.
- The definitions of *typical* and *atypical* are important in some ways, but they are also artificial in some ways.
- All children and families deserve to be part of the same community.
- We are all part of an interdependent community.

For us, the ideas above suggest that *all* programs are inclusion programs.

Many early childhood programs feel uneasy about including children with special needs. But it is becoming clearer each year that we really have no choice. It is estimated that up to 17 percent of children in the United States have developmental disabilities (Boyle, Decoufle and Yeargin-Allsopp 1994). They may qualify for services through their local school district's early intervention programs or through other provider networks. They may someday have an IEP or IFSP, which defines specific developmental, behavioral, or educational goals to address specific challenges. Individualized Education Programs are discussed in more detail on page 46 of chapter 4. Many more children have subtler challenges that will not result in a formal assessment or a plan for therapeutic intervention but that still can make for a hard fit with the classroom or group setting.

If mainstream early childhood programs cannot serve children with challenges, what will? Even if a therapeutic program were the right fit for all these children—and we argue in this book that it is not—the number of children with challenges far exceeds space in special settings. This leads us to the conclusion that inspired us to write this book: if all programs are inclusion programs, then all teachers are inclusion teachers.

Why Inclusion?

Why would we *want* to make our programs inclusive if we didn't have to? One of the most profound things we have learned about inclusion is that it is not just a response to challenges. Inclusion, at its best, is a model that enriches every aspect of a program, from the experience of the child, to the skills of the teacher, to the harmony and diversity of the school community. Not only are there multiple benefits to inclusion, but there are also many reasons why we want our programs to be inclusion programs.

Children Benefit from Inclusion

Inclusive programs are not based just on the belief that children with challenges should be part of a mainstream program. Inclusive programs operate on the belief that all children have strengths and challenges and are fundamentally the same kind of people. As we begin to look at all children through this lens—helping them use their strengths to address their own challenges—we begin to see all children in a more fully defined way. This allows us to support all children more effectively. The children themselves are able to see their similarities and differences more clearly and see themselves as linked to all their peers rather than as members of separate populations. In this way, inclusion plays an important role in our efforts to teach mutual acceptance and create multicultural learning communities. And as you will discover throughout this book, strategies and ideas that help one child very often benefit entire groups of children.

Teachers Benefit from Inclusion

Successful inclusion leads teachers not just to new skills and knowledge but also to new ways of looking at children in general. It trains teachers to think of the basic building blocks of identity—how minds and bodies work, and how each person engages with the world. It builds a teacher's ability to see connections among the children in her care and common threads within a classroom community. Inclusion also provides teachers with tools for building self-knowledge and ways for using one's own strengths and style to better understand and serve children. As we discuss in detail later in the book, inclusion leads teachers to a strength-based view of children. The benefits of this perspective are huge.

On a broader level, inclusion trains teachers to view challenges as opportunities. Children who inspire us to try harder, learn more, or use our skills in creative ways make us better teachers. A breakthrough with one child will equip us to better support all children throughout our careers. Progress that we achieve through struggle is the most satisfying kind of progress. For all these reasons, a commitment to inclusion fosters a creative, problem-solving approach to teaching and offers a model of teaching as a lifetime adventure of personal growth.

Families Benefit from Inclusion

Effective inclusion practices require deep and authentic partnership between teachers and families. Teachers must learn to extend their respectful, strength-based view of children to families as well. As a family's expertise about their own child is respected and incorporated into plans for other children, families learn about their own strengths and are inspired to see themselves as capable and competent. They are also drawn into an environment in which they can learn about how children grow and learn and what kinds of perspectives and tools can make them more effective and happy families.

The dedication to collaboration in an inclusive program builds bonds between teachers and all families and among all families. This inspires families to support their community, to commit to caring for each other, and to share their strengths and resources. It also presents a model to bring challenges out in the open and address them in a creative spirit of problem solving.

All Communities Benefit from Inclusion

The old model of regular and special education implied that challenging behavior could disqualify a child from membership in a class or school. It set up a two-tiered society of children who could succeed under "normal" circumstances and children who needed to be segregated. The old model fostered division and judgment and placed the responsibility for school and social success on the child. Children who can succeed in "typical" programs never get to know their peers with unique needs and profiles. They view them with increasing suspicion. The current concern in educational circles over bullying is tied to this view of some children as entitled and others as burdens. It is also tied to the opposite view, which sees some children as victims and others as villains.

An inclusive model turns the lens around. Schools, families, and communities take the responsibility for a child's success. Challenges are viewed as sources of connection rather than division. The program, to at least some extent, adapts to the individual and the specific group, rather than the other way around. When a child struggles, the adults search for ways that foster success rather than for reasons why the child fails.

In this model, inclusion suggests a community where everyone is committed to supporting each other. Challenges and struggle become catalysts for improving the community together, rather than barriers that need to be removed from the community. The community becomes a place for sharing the difficult sides of life openly, a place for cooperative problem solving. The world is no longer divided into typical and atypical, winners and losers, bullies and victims. Think of what future generations of children can accomplish in a community in which they learn about all kinds of people in detail and build insight, confidence, and skill for supporting each other. Simply put, in an inclusive setting, all kinds of children can befriend each other.

• • •

We find that many teachers have already discovered these benefits themselves and that those who haven't can readily agree to them. But next, they often ask, how do you become an inclusion teacher? How do you develop a toolbox of techniques to serve children with autism, or Down syndrome, or cerebral palsy? How can you transform your physical space to accommodate special needs? How can you find the time in an already overloaded profession to gain specialized, therapeutic expertise?

Our answer to these questions is the reason for this book and its main topic: *the skills and viewpoints necessary to successfully include all children come from basic best preschool practices.* You already possess the foundation for becoming an inclusion teacher or for developing an inclusion program. A *relationship-based* approach—one in which teachers know all their students as individuals and are dedicated to finding unique ways for individuals to thrive in their programs—is the beginning of successful inclusion. For these reasons, we also strongly believe that early childhood programs, in which children have the time and space to create their own learning and in which teachers can help them learn to use their strengths, are the most effective settings for inclusion.

To be sure, there is a lot to learn. In this book, we suggest some key perspectives on child development that may be new to you and that may inspire you to do some reading and learning. We show you specific teaching tools and practices that will stretch your perspective or your approach. We offer ways to help you adjust your priorities or your teaching style to most effectively support all the children in your care. We hope you will be pleasantly surprised, as we have been in our inclusion journey, to learn that the new or different aspects of inclusion make up a smaller part of the picture than the basic skills and strengths all teachers have. Inclusion is much more a matter of applying your skills in new ways than it is a new set of skills.

• • •

In this chapter, you learned how all programs have been faced with the challenge of inclusion. You also saw how inclusion is, far from just a necessity, a means of enhancing and broadening program quality. You learned how inclusion benefits children, teachers, families, and communities. You reflected on why teachers would want to embrace inclusion and learn to think of themselves as inclusion teachers. In the next chapter, you will examine the roots and basics of relationship-based education, the platform upon which all teachers can learn the tools of successful inclusion.

Principles of Relationship-Based Inclusion

Think for a moment about a child who just adored you and whom you adored. Maybe it was a child who loved to sit in your lap and read books or a child who brought you pictures she had joyfully created at home. You knew and appreciated and loved this child so much, and you knew that she was secure and happy that her teacher loved her so much. At drop-off or pickup time, you just couldn't wait to see her mother or father to share some gem of an experience and express to her parents what an amazing child you thought she was. And her parents, who, like most parents these days, didn't have too many people in their lives who knew and loved their child so well or even saw her nearly as often as they did, would just shine with joy over these little passing connections. In return, they would share their own gems of experiences and insight with you. They would tell you, every now and then, when they had the chance, what a huge difference it made to have another adult in their lives who knew and loved their child as they did.

Because caregiving, nurturing, and family support are such a large part of early childhood education, relationships have always been at its core. Relationships are, after all, one of the main things that make early childhood education different from academic instruction. So, in many ways, all early childhood education—family child care, preschool, center-based care, after-school programs—is relationship based. Relationship-based education, as an organized idea and practice, isn't all that different. In some ways, it just means following the natural priorities of our field.

Pioneers of Relationship-Based Education

Although relationship-based education has only appeared as a specific idea in journals and at conferences over the last ten years, many of the threads of the approach have been building for over a century, from the minds and spirits of some of the most important thinkers in the field of education.

John Dewey, who pioneered many of the elements of constructivism in his lab school at the University of Chicago in the 1890s, was an early relationship advocate. His school was based on the idea that people learn best when they work together on meaningful tasks. Dewey and his colleagues were among the first to introduce the idea of teachers working with groups of children over long periods of time, to focus on the growing relationships in the school as the foundation for learning. Dewey strongly believed that education must be cooperative and interdependent to be effective (Dewey 1916).

Lev Vygotsky, a Russian educational researcher who built upon Jean Piaget's theories of cognitive development in the late 1920s, argued that learning is a fundamentally interpersonal process. He recognized that children look to the people around them to learn patterns of behavior and to make sense of their own experience. Vygotsky saw all humans connected over time and space in an ongoing relationship, affecting each other in small and large ways (Vygotsky 1978).

John Bowlby and Mary Ainsworth gave us the main ideas of attachment theory in the 1950s and 1960s. They believed that a secure emotional attachment to important adults is necessary for a child's growth and exploration. They taught that with a secure base of emotional support from families and teachers, a child learns to independently engage with the world. When adults provide a balance of structure and freedom, a child learns to comfortably manage his inner state and outward behavior (Bowlby 1982).

Urie Bronfenbrenner was one of many developmental psychologists in the 1960s and 1970s who focused on a child's development within many connected layers or networks of relationships—family, school, community, and society. He contributed the key idea that understanding a child's context is crucial to understanding a child (Bronfenbrenner 1979).

Loris Malaguzzi and the educators who developed the Italian education practices of Reggio Emilia from the 1940s through the present day put many of these threads together into a holistic approach to early childhood education. This Italian approach began with a government commitment to children's services as a universal right. So it is no surprise that the educational philosophy flows from and focuses on the relationships and the connection between children, teachers, parents, and the surrounding community. Individual people and relationships guide a fluid approach to curriculum and even the arrangement and use of the physical environment (Malaguzzi 1998).

Although American educators have paid most attention to the curriculum materials and projects of Reggio Emilia, its integrated view of relationships as the guiding force in all aspects of early childhood education has proved very influential as well. It is particularly interesting to consider the Reggio focus on integration of community services and the idea of school as a place that serves all children in a community. This helps to make clear the basic connection between relationship-based education and inclusion.

Psychologists **Stanley Greenspan and Serena Wieder**, working from the field of therapeutic services for children with special needs, created the Developmental-Individual-Difference, Relationship-Based (DIR) model. The DIR model sees teaching as a process of fostering children's ability to relate and regulate through play. Teachers are primarily interested in establishing a give-and-take, play-based relationship with children in order to foster their abilities to connect and communicate with others in ever more reciprocal and self-aware ways (Greenspan and Wieder 1998, 2006). Their focus on a child's temperament and sensory integration profile as the foundations for social, emotional, physical, and cognitive development has been so useful to our inclusion work that we will return to it at length in the next chapter and throughout this book.

Over the past decade, brain research based on electronic imaging of brain activity has confirmed many of the ideas of these pioneers: children's minds develop based on their observation of relationships around them and of patterns of behavior; the mind is programmed to recognize and reproduce patterns of behavior; and children use others around them as mirrors, not just of behavior but feeling and affect (Perry and Szalavitz 2007; Siegel 1999). Brain research has shown us very dramatically that the relationships in a child's life are the most important and effective factors in how learning takes place.

These theorists and researchers offer much for us to think about. Clearly, the type and quality of relationships have a strong influence on what children gain from a classroom experience. What kinds of relationships between teachers and children, and among children themselves, support the positive growth and development of *all* children, regardless of ability? Throughout this book, we discuss many strategies that support a relationship-based inclusive classroom. Nevertheless, individual strategies can be a lot like the individual ingredients of a recipe—you have some flour, sugar, eggs, and lemon, and you know that they can make something delicious, but you need a recipe to pull it all together. Similarly, a set of overarching principles about relationship-based inclusion can help you connect and understand all of the strategies, ideas, and practices that follow in this book.

Principles of Relationship-Based Inclusive Education

The set of principles that follow are intended to guide you, not only through this book, but also through your attempt to implement relationship-based inclusion in your classroom. Here are our thirteen principles of relationship-based education:

1. We are more same than different.
2. Our differences make us who we are.
3. A child cannot be known separate from her context.
4. Individualizing is essential.
5. Individual support creates community strength.
6. Sometimes an individual bends to the needs of a community. Sometimes a community bends to the needs of an individual.
7. Bodies matter.

8. Brains matter.

9. Emotions matter.

10. Relationships matter.

11. Play is the key.

12. Work from a strength model for children, families, teachers, and programs.

13. A reflective teacher committed to openness and active learning can be an excellent inclusion teacher—with a little help from the community.

We describe these principles in terms of their impact on children in classrooms. But they have implications for human relationships between people of any age. As a matter of fact, the first principle helps explain that there is not one set of behaviors, values, and practices that are good to teach children and another set that applies to the real world of adults. The same kinds of relationships that help children grow and thrive also support adults in the very same ways. Throughout the book, we will explore what these principles have to say for children and for the adults who influence them.

Let's explore each of these principles more fully.

We Are More Same Than Different

Human beings are each completely unique, yet at the same time very similar to each other. Our universal needs and desires vary some from culture to culture, but all of us drive toward mastery, gain satisfaction from social contact and play, and thrive when offered acknowledgment, respect, and opportunities for learning.

This is the reason that children, including children with special needs, learn best in the context of meaningful relationships. A teacher who understands these basic human needs can see past the disability to the child who is eager to play. A teacher who finds ways to navigate obstacles created by labels or genetics finds a child eager for meaningful interaction.

While techniques and strategies are useful, the guiding light of this principle shows that, to best meet the needs of children in your care, you should

- Be human.

- Connect.

- Play.

- Clear the child's path of as many obstacles as you can.

Whatever the unique strengths, challenges, or developmental profile of any child you work with, remember that he is longing for play, mastery, social contact, and opportunities to learn. And so are you.

Our Differences Make Us Who We Are

There is another universal truth about humans. Every one of us has strengths, and every one of us has challenges. No one is perfect. Each of us has much to offer.

To help clear obstacles from a child's path, you must know the details of her particular challenges. To meet her need for appreciation and respect, you must know the details of her particular strengths. And to provide the right opportunities for learning and mastery, you must know each child well. Knowing a child well involves knowing her strengths, challenges, preferences, interests, developmental and sensory profile, experiences, family, culture, and community.

This is not something you do only for children with special needs. To teach and support *all* children, you must know this much about every child, and your knowledge must affect how you support her in the classroom.

When you know this information, the richness of each child, what he has to offer, and what he needs from you as a teacher, becomes clear. In the context of this richness, it becomes clear that every child has special needs and that every child has strengths upon which to draw.

A Child Cannot Be Known Separate from Her Context

A child cannot be understood outside of her context. We know this as early childhood educators, and yet frequently we forget to examine our own program as a potential source of a child's difficulties. And we forget to reach beyond our own cultural lens to understand the beliefs and practices of other cultures, family systems, and communities. To enact this principle, you must listen, learn, and remain open to new experiences and information.

You must be as interested in questions as in answers. For example,

- If a child has difficulties in a program with ten transitions a day but no difficulty in a program with four, what does that tell you?

- What if a child can be aggressive in the unstructured part of your day, when fifty children share the same space and teachers shout to be heard, but the same child is never aggressive in a group of twenty children and calm teachers? Is the child creating a problem for the program, or is the program creating a problem for the child?

- If you think that a child needs to learn to stand up for herself, and you find out that the family has religious beliefs about turning away from conflict, does that change your goals for the child?

- If you think that a child needs an assessment because of her lack of initiative and self-help skills, and you find out that the child has always been dressed, bathed, and hand-fed, does that change your opinion?

Individualizing Is Essential

Individualizing is not merely an idea but a strategy and a practice. If an early childhood teacher meets the individual needs of each of the children, then it is a small leap to individualize to the child with special needs. Thus, an inclusive classroom is born.

The idea that individualizing is essential arises out of the first three principles. Individual differences and the contexts children live in have an impact on their learning. The ways that acknowledgment and learning opportunities are offered to children must be individualized to reflect their unique profiles.

If we ask teachers to individualize children's opportunities to learn in all developmental domains, including the social, emotional, and sensory realms, we are asking a lot of teachers and of their lesson plans. But learning does not occur simply through planned, direct instruction. It also occurs in the context of relationships. Many important individual needs are met through the teacher's individual relationship with each child. These individual needs or opportunities can also be met through the children's relationships with each other. Relationship-based education makes it easier to individualize to the whole child. Relationship-based inclusion goes further to meet the individual needs of teachers and parents as well.

Individualizing may sound complicated, but it is often very simple. For example, if the painting activity is intended for fingers and hands, make sure to have an option for the children with tactile sensitivity who would prefer using paintbrushes. If the painting activity is intended for brushes, leave room for those who need to explore more with their bodies.

Some children with special needs benefit from having a song that signals each transition. For other children with special needs, a picture board with a photograph showing each part of the day is helpful.

Is it any surprise that many "typical" children also benefit from the song or the picture board during transitions? This example illustrates the most practical and obvious benefit of reaching out to meet the needs of individual children in a group: because of the commonalities among humans, what benefits one child often benefits many children.

Individualizing also benefits many children over time. A teacher who learns the value of music as a wonderful learning channel has added an important tool to her toolbox. A teacher who provides support to visual learners as well

A child in this class had real difficulty regulating. The yoga exercises the children learned were a great help to him. So was this simple activity of "passing the squeeze around the circle." The other children gained useful calming tools as well. When they demonstrated what they had learned for their parents, parents were surprised that their children could gain these kinds of skills and self-knowledge. Everyone learned from these simple efforts to support a child's challenges.

as to auditory learners will reach a wider range of children. Through supporting children's challenges, we become better teachers.

The benefits of offering children individualized support abound. If each
child gets his needs met, then everyone will relax and be ready to learn. The
classroom culture will be one of patience, flexibility, and support. At a very
early age, all of the children will learn that everyone has strengths and everyone has challenges. The children will become the cocreators of a positive social
and emotional atmosphere.

There is a Chinese character for double happiness. The character evokes
happiness multiplying for all. By committing to a classroom in which everyone's individual needs are met, each individual gets what she needs and the
entire class gets a boost in its social, emotional, and cognitive development.
Everyone benefits through the experience, and the benefits last for years.

Sometimes an Individual Bends to the Needs of a Community. Sometimes a Community Bends to the Needs of an Individual.

It is circle time, the fourth week of school. Just as circle time begins, Bobby
tells everyone that he has lost his special rock. He asks everyone to look for it
right now! It has taken the teachers three weeks to notice that Bobby always
has some good reason why everyone should pay attention to him just as
circle time begins. They now decide to start helping Bobby learn how to get
his needs met in satisfying ways that work well within a community. This
goal includes helping him learn how to join circle time when everyone else
does. A teacher goes over and quietly says, "We'll all look for your special
rock at cleanup time. Now it is time to sit down."

It is circle time, the twelfth week of school. Just as circle time begins, Sasha
tells everyone that she has lost her special rock. She asks everyone to look
for it right now! This is the most language Sasha has ever spoken in school.
Until now, she has quietly cooperated with all of the teachers and children,
doing whatever anyone asks. She has not formed a special relationship with
a teacher or a child. The teachers decide to take this opportunity to let Sasha
know that she is an important member of the community. "Wait, everybody.
Before we sit for circle time, let's all search the room for Sasha's rock! It is a
special one that she brought from home."

Often in our society, we have asked people with disabilities to conform to
artificial standards—to fit in—instead of seeing what we can all gain through
universal access. In an early childhood setting, we want everything to be as
accessible and sensitive as possible. And yet we become oddly attached to our
routines and schedules, our environment and daily practices. Enacting this
principle means examining each situation and asking yourself if it is a case
where the community can bend to the individual or if the individual needs
to bend to the group. Everyone, regardless of need, must sometimes bend to

the needs of the wider class community. And everyone, regardless of ability, deserves to have the community bend toward him sometimes.

Often the default response in a classroom is to ask students to bend to the community. In an inclusive classroom, the question of who should do the bending has a different answer each moment. The inclusive teacher remembers to ask the question "Who should bend this time?" Simply by regularly asking the question, you will more frequently find times when it feels reasonable and easy for the community to bend to the individual.

The rest of the community may be ready to sit up straight on the bench and listen to the teacher, but sometimes someone is just not up for it. Why not give him a cozier seat so that he, too, can pay attention?

Bodies Matter

As early childhood educators, what do we know about young children and their bodies? We know that the bodies of young children provide a vital channel for learning. We know that young children express a great deal through their bodies (sometimes too much when they are angry). We know that the bodies of young children need to move.

And yet, talking and listening are still the main modes of communication and teaching in our classrooms. What if we used what we know about the body as a foundation to support children's academic, social, and emotional learning? What if responding to the needs of a child's body became the magic key to ensuring that a child was ready to learn, play, and interact?

- What if, for example, children did meaningful movement when trying to learn a concept (such as the life cycle of a plant)? Might that enhance their learning?

- What if children were never asked to sit longer than a few minutes without being asked to move some part of their body? Might they be better able to attend between movements?

- What if a child who hits his friends or knocks things down when he gets overstimulated got to have some vigorous physical activity before classroom playtime? Might he be calmer during playtime?

Throughout the book, we share additional ideas that can help you move toward a deeper understanding of the role bodies play in the classroom. We have also offered many photographs of children moving their bodies. Some of the ways they move may seem dangerous, or inappropriate, or silly to you. If you feel that way, we want you to ask yourself a second time—is it really (dangerous or inappropriate or silly)? Of course, safety is paramount. You need to use your best judgment in the moment. We hope the physical images of children in this book stretch your sense of how much children should be moving in the classroom. Adults are often trying to get out of their heads and into their bodies. Let's celebrate how much young children actually *are* in their bodies!

Brains Matter

Bodies, relationships, emotions, and brains are all connected. The wiring of an individual brain creates how that individual experiences emotions, relationships, and learning. If you know more about how an individual's brain works, you can better meet the needs of that particular individual. Keeping in mind what you know about brain development will also support the learning of all of the children. The theory of sensory integration and the DIR model come from an understanding of how the brain, emotions, relationships, and bodies work together.

In some sense, bodies, emotions, and brains are so interwoven that it is impossible to separate out the workings of each. Whenever we refer to the sensory system and how experience or information is processed by children, we are talking about processes in the brain. Here is a story of how all of these elements might work together:

> Every day, six of the children at a time went into the bathroom to wash their hands. Every day, during this part of the routine, Maira would start shouting. When the teachers learned that her brain had difficulty processing unexpected touch, they understood that the children jostling each other in the bathroom was too much for Maira. The teachers saw that her defensive fight-or-flight response was not a willful act to get attention and disrupt the group. They decided to send her into the bathroom with just one other teacher and child whom she felt comfortable with. They also helped Maira and her peers understand that some people were still learning to feel comfortable with touch they didn't expect. They helped Maira find successful ways to make contact and decrease her sensitivity while increasing the understanding of differences among her classmates.

Emotions Matter

We all know now that emotions play a critical role in how intelligence develops. And even if research wasn't there to tell us so, we know that how someone feels about himself plays a critical role not only in school but in life success.

Emotional intelligence is the ability to identify and manage one's own emotions and to identify and respond to the emotions of others. Emotional intelligence has been identified as a key tool for success (Goleman 1997). As we travel throughout the country, teachers everywhere want to talk about how to help the many children they encounter who seem to have great difficulty learning to manage their own emotions. The current emphasis on emotional intelligence, positive self-concept, and child-centered approaches shows how eager the field of early childhood is to pay attention to the critical role emotions and emotional development play in learning.

Throughout the book, we look more closely at the link between children's brains, sensory systems, and emotional responses. We discuss how to respond to emotions in the classroom to support children's social and cognitive skills. We explore how teachers can use their own emotions and affect as successful teaching tools. And we look at the importance of emotions in working with adults. This knowledge about emotions can help our work with all children, especially our children with special needs.

Relationships Matter

Julian was unable to connect with peers. He chose areas of the classroom that were quiet and unpopulated. Occasionally, he would observe his peers at play but did not try to engage directly. When his teacher Regina would join him on the floor with whatever activity he initiated, he would light up and talk to her about what he was doing. She often wrote down what he said and shared his words with the group at meeting time so the other children would begin to get to know him. She also made sure to show Julian all of the fun things his classmates were doing. Soon he sought her out and enjoyed sitting on her lap. Eventually he began to join in playing wherever Regina was in the classroom. Regina used her ability to forge strong relationships with of all the children as a way to help them get to know one another and feel safe together. She used herself as a literal bridge for Julian to learn how to play with his peers.

Relationships support learning in all developmental domains. Miriam M. Witmer, a professor of education, has thought deeply about the role of relationships in the educational process. Citing research, Witmer demonstates that learning *only* occurs when students actively engage in the learning process and that students actively engage when what is presented is meaningful (Caine and Caine 1994). Witmer further points out that students often find an experience meaningful when it satisfies emotional needs (Glasser 1998). Relationships in the classroom affect student achievement because cognition and emotion are interconnected (Caine and Caine 1994). Witmer concludes that

> developing and fostering teacher-student relationships should be considered an integral part of daily lesson planning (Witmer 2005, 224).

We agree. In fact, we would say that relationships should be at the foundation of an educational curriculum—hence the term *relationship-based inclusion*.

Play Is the Key

Experts in the field of early childhood education have thought a lot about play, and there are differing points of view. Results-based policies and standards may not fully support a play-based approach. But if there is anything that most early childhood teachers know, it is that play is a key to learning.

This idea about the relationship of play and learning is a significant contribution that early childhood educators can make to the field of special education. For many good reasons, the field of special education focuses on specific, measurable behaviors. It may include playful means to reach those objectives. But as early childhood educators know, the value of play is that it is child-initiated and self-chosen. In this book, we explore why play is exactly what the children with special needs in your classroom should be doing—and how you can help.

Work from a Strength Model for Children, Families, Teachers, and Programs

There is no question that working on our challenges is an important part of the learning process. But focusing solely on challenges can be discouraging for students. If a teaching approach instead uses a child's strengths as the foundation for learning, this fosters joy, motivation, enthusiasm, and optimism. Fostering these traits leads to better learning outcomes. Focusing on the strengths of adults (such as their teaching or parenting strengths) leads to better outcomes among adults as well. If we lead with people's strengths, they respond in positive ways.

Below are examples of how teachers in a strength-based class might speak to children:

- "Donna, can you remember where we end our reading in the story today? You have such a good memory."

- "Antonio, I know you don't want to come to circle time. But we are trying to figure out something difficult. You have such good ideas. We need you."

- "Ari, you couldn't throw the ball in the basket, but you kept trying! I know if you keep practicing like that, you will be able to do it one day."

- "An-Li, you are still learning to keep children safe. I am helping you to remember. I know that one day you won't need my help anymore. You will be able to do it all by yourself."

A Reflective Teacher Committed to Openness and Active Learning Can Be an Excellent Inclusion Teacher —with a Little Help from the Community

Early childhood educators are motivated to help children learn. Early childhood educators also know about child development and how to translate what they know into their work in the classroom. We believe that because of these particular skills and dispositions, early childhood educators make excellent inclusion teachers.

You might ask how this can be true if an early childhood educator doesn't have specialized knowledge about each disability. What if she doesn't know all of the right techniques to use? What if she doesn't know how reasonable her expectations are for a child with a special need? Yes, early childhood educators need to learn some new skills and information. But some educators without a special education degree feel as if they are not qualified to teach children with special needs.

This concern is similar to that of new parents, who also don't feel qualified. "How will I ever bathe this baby, diaper her, dress her, feed and carry her without hurting or injuring her?" the new parent asks. And indeed, sometimes infants are put into water that's a little too warm or diapered in a way that pinches. But they grow and thrive anyway, because the strong, loving relationship with their parents fortifies them and allows their resilience to flourish.

Using the principles above, early childhood educators can form an affirming and supportive relationship with each child in just the way that child needs. They can create classroom communities where, in fact, *everyone* gets what they need and everyone supports each other, including the teachers and families.

And if they make a few mistakes along the way, that is okay. After all, teachers are human too.

• • •

In this chapter, we introduced the model of relationship-based education. We reviewed how brain research and educational theorists and researchers have contributed to an understanding of relationship-based education. Thirteen principles that serve to guide relationship-based education were introduced. Early childhood educators can use these principles and the best practices they already know to become excellent inclusion teachers.

In the next chapter, we look at sensory integration theory and DIR, tools that add important ideas to the early childhood educator's inclusion toolbox. These two approaches give educators a new way to look at and understand *all* children.

Chapter 3

Sensory Integration Theory and the Developmental-Individual Difference-Relationship-Based (DIR) Model

One year I worked with a child who loved to pretend but constantly got into trouble with his friends for getting too close or getting too rough. The faster he moved, the more disorganized he became—to the point where he didn't seem to be able to take in our words anymore. Another child walked around carrying train engines held tight in each fist. He didn't want anyone to touch him, and he did not engage much with peers or materials. He always wore the same soft sweatpants and faded turtleneck shirt. When he was upset, he would cry and cry. It was very difficult for us to soothe him. Luckily both of these children's families brought them to a local developmental pediatrician who recognized they both had problems managing their sensory environment. She sent them both to an occupational therapist to help them with what she called *sensory integration difficulties*. The occupational therapist recommended I read a book called *The Out-of-Sync Child* by Carol Kranowitz (1998). That was how I learned about sensory integration. At the same time, I started learning about Developmental-Individual Difference-Relationship-Based Model. Boy, did all of this new information make a huge difference in the way I look at and responded to challenging behaviors that come up with ALL children!

—Cassandra Britton
Early Childhood Educator

Because preschool teachers know so much about how to help children move up the developmental ladder, they are wonderfully equipped to teach children with special needs. It is mostly a matter of learning how to use the tools they already have. As teachers at The Little School, we have learned two additional tools that have been so tremendously helpful in our work with children that we want to share them with you. One of these tools is a theory called Sensory Integration Theory. The other is an approach known as the

Developmental-Individual Difference-Relationship-Based Model, called DIR for short. Learning about these additional tools enabled us to make the best use of the tools we already had.

You don't need to become experts in either of these tools before you put them to good use. We actually learned about them as we learned about one child at a time. We'd get a little information from a workshop or a specialist, and then we'd see how it applied to a child we were working with. *Then* we'd look at other children and see how it applied to them. Pretty soon, we were using these tools to look at ourselves, our parents, our friends, and every new child who came into our school.

In this chapter, we offer a basic introduction to these ideas. It should be enough to allow your own observations to kick in. There are also many resources that offer more information about both tools. Actually, sensory integration and how it relates to overall regulation (emotional coping as well as doing basic things like toileting, eating, and sleeping) is becoming a common topic in early childhood education. You may already know a lot about it. We hope that soon the DIR approach becomes a more common part of the conversation as well.

A Basic Description of Sensory Integration

We all know about the five senses: sight (visual), sound (auditory), smell (olfactory), taste (gustatory), and touch (tactile). A. Jean Ayres (1979), the woman who came up with Sensory Integration Theory, was very interested in the senses she considered autopilot, or unconscious. She understood that the human body processes incoming sensory information in ways that help keep people organized, focused, and well regulated. Ayres expanded the thinking about one of the old standards—touch. She saw the sense of touch in a broader way, beyond what people actively feel with just their fingers. Instead, she described the unconscious sense of touch as it relates to the entire skin and how people process everything that the skin comes in contact with. Another unconscious sense she helped us understand is the vestibular sense, or the sense of balance and movement. While the sense of balance and movement may not sound so important, it has a big impact on the rest of the sensory system and how people experience everyday life. A final important, unconscious sense is the proprioceptive sense, the internal sense of how the muscles, ligaments, and joints are working together as people move their bodies. These last two senses may not be as easy to understand as the first five, but they are easy to observe and to address in children.

We all know children who just seem to need a lot of physical contact with the world. They wham into play structures, bam into their friends, knock you over with their hugging enthusiasm, and fling themselves into the middle of the circle at circle time. These are children who need more proprioceptive input, or information from muscles, ligaments, and joints, to understand what is going on with their bodies. If you incorporate heavy lifting during playtime, tight squeeze hugs from teachers, a heavy blanket or sandbag on their knees at circle time, you might have calmer children.

How about the child who never seems to stay still? She is constantly wiggling in her chair, hates to stay seated at snacktime or group time, and never seems to choose activities you set out on tabletops. This child keeps wiggling because she can't seem to get enough vestibular information to her brain to have a clear sense of where her body is. She needs lots of input from movement, but running around might seem to get her even more disorganized. That's because the proprioceptive sense works with the vestibular sense. She needs more proprioceptive input, coupled with vestibular action, to help her know where her body is in space. She needs all that heavy lifting, pushing, pulling, hanging, tight squeezes, and lap weights too.

As a matter of fact, proprioceptive input is helpful to *everyone* to remain focused, organized, and attentive. But our wiggly girl also needs more movement. Maybe spinning from a suspended disc or a turn in a swing will be helpful to her. And since wiggling in her chair is inappropriate, give her a bumpy cushion or therapy ball for her seat. On these seats, she can wiggle to wake up and pay attention, instead of get in trouble.

In school, we learned that we take in information about the world through the five senses, and that was it. One additional simple piece of information opens up a world of new understanding and possibilities. Each of us has an individualized way of taking in information from each sense. A sense can be highly responsive or dulled. And it can be everything in between. If a person has highly sensitive hearing, he will most likely be able to hear aspects of music most of us cannot. He might also find a noisy roomful of people (such as a classroom) a very uncomfortable experience. Suppose someone's visual sense is dull. She will visually take in less information and might frequently miss important visual cues. Go through each of the senses and imagine what it might mean to have an overly sensitive, just right, and under-sensitive (or dulled) sense.

How would a child's experience of taking in the world through his particular sensory profile affect his ideas about himself and the rest of the world? If he has a smooth sensory profile, things might come easily to him. He might feel pretty competent. With a different, "bumpier" sensory profile, the world might be a confusing place where nothing comes easily. This child might have a sense of himself as stupid and incompetent, even if he never hears this from anyone else. People's sensory profiles have a major impact on how they experience the world, learning, their school life, and themselves.

Thinking about children through a sensory lens not only provides great insight into their emotional, social, cognitive, and motor selves, but it also gives you ideas about how you can influence these aspects of the child's development in fundamental ways. And that is what makes it such a powerful tool.

How would the sound-sensitive boy we described previously react to an everyday, noisy experience like the classroom? He might whine a lot out of discomfort. He might lose his focus and move around quickly, the way you might when you are at an overly crowded, noisy party. He might sing loudly to himself or otherwise try to drown out the noise. He might seem fussy and unhappy. And the girl with under-sensitive vision might miss social cues. She might not respond appropriately to the body and facial messages of her peers and teacher. She might be the one who never seems to know what is going on and constantly asks the teacher to repeat instructions. The other children use their visual sense to complete the picture of what the teacher tells them. She cannot. The other children think she's clueless, and privately, the teacher does too.

If the teacher, and even the children, understood that one child was overly sensitive to sound and the other had a hard time picking up visual cues, they might have more sympathy for them. Armed with this insight about sensory profiles, you might have more sympathy for your challenging children too. More importantly, you will feel empowered to work with and understand each child. Children who seem to be challenging or less socially adjusted will be transformed into children with specific sensory profiles whom you can help.

The Integration of the Senses

The body does not just take in information. Information, or input, comes into the body through a sense. In the tactile sense, for example, the information gets sent to the brain through the skin. It is integrated with other input from other senses. The brain and body decide how to react. That is sometimes called the *output*. A child touches the hot stove. The brain registers heat and pain, decides to move away, plans how to make the motor system work to take that action, and sends a message to the appropriate muscles, ligaments, and joints. Just as each of us has an individualized profile for each of the senses, each of us also has an individualized profile for every step of the process described above, from input to processing the information to motor planning to action. Challenges can occur at any point. As with all of the topics we are discussing, the challenges may rise to a level where they are identified as a special need. Or they may simply become part of what makes up a child's unique profile of strengths and challenges.

Motor Planning

When sensory information comes to the brain, the brain decides what it wants to do. Figuring out how to make the body enact that plan is called *motor planning*. Because people express what they know, think, feel, and want through their bodies, how well the motor planning system works is very important.

Planning how to move, or motor planning, is not exactly the same as coordination, although they certainly are related. A child with weak motor planning skills might have poor coordination. She might also have difficulty forming words because she can't get the muscles of her mouth and tongue to do what she wants. She might have trouble following directions because she can't figure out how to get her body from point A to point B. She might seem clumsy or slow or very passive. Like the proprioceptive or vestibular sense, motor planning may be hard to understand in the abstract, but it becomes clear when you look at children through the lens of their motor planning. If you observe, you can see that children with challenges in motor planning have a hard time using their bodies effectively to accomplish what they want.

Regulation and Arousal

To be ready to learn, the body and mind must be calm enough internally and externally, physically and emotionally, to take in, process, and act upon information. How people control and manage their bodies on an unconscious level is called *self-regulation*. Regulation influences how easily or chaotically someone sleeps, eats, toilets, responds to emotions, and stays alert.

In order to be ready to learn, the body and mind must be at just the right level of alertness for the task at hand. Some tasks, like a lecture, require a person to be relaxed and quiet but alert. A test requires a person to be even more alert. Running an obstacle course requires alertness, readiness to act, and high energy. To go to sleep, the mind and body must be calm, relaxed, and ready to let go of thought and action.

Each of these describes different states of arousal that are influenced by our individual ability to regulate the arousal level. Some people move smoothly from one arousal state to the next and have a great deal of control over their state of arousal. For others, this is not true. Once they are aroused and stimulated, it is very hard to get their bodies and minds to calm down. Or they may often feel sluggish, and it may be hard to get the attention system aroused enough to easily take on the everyday challenges in a classroom.

Regulatory system and arousal levels can be affected by external stimuli, such as noise, or internal stimuli, such as hunger. What impact do internal stimuli, such as anger, fear, hunger, and sleepiness, have? What about the impact of external stimuli, such as noise, a busy visual environment, touch, and a chaotic social situation? For your students having difficulty, you need to answer these questions to help them to be ready to learn. These are also essential questions if you want to help your children develop positive social skills and the inner resilience to overcome obstacles.

Just as with the sensory system, each of us has a unique regulatory and arousal system. And it is very much linked to the sensory and motor planning profile. To understand systems helps us to understand the others.

Bringing It All Together

To sum up what we discussed above:

1. Each of the senses presents a unique profile.
2. The way the senses integrate presents a unique profile.
3. Motor planning, arousal, and regulatory systems interact in unique ways with the sensory profile.

All of these systems might react differently in different situations and at different times. You are probably asking yourself how looking at children through this complicated lens could ever be useful. But the proof is in the pudding. When you start to try to understand children by examining their sensory, regulatory, arousal, and motor planning profiles, these topics will come alive. You will have many aha! moments. Your understanding about the child will fall into place. And you will start to have ideas about what you can do to help the child.

The children will also be able to make sense of these seemingly complicated intellectual ideas. Individual sensory profiles, motor planning, arousal, and regulatory systems leave people somewhere on a continuum between feeling very comfortable some of the time to feeling very uncomfortable all of the time. Their profiles also allow people to move through the world and accomplish what they want on a continuum from very efficiently and effectively to very inefficiently and ineffectively. One thing children know very well is their own internal experience of the world. They may not be able to put it into words, but they know if they are uncomfortable or if they can't easily do what they want. When you start to give them information or tools about their sensory system or regulatory system, you will be surprised at how positively they respond.

From this brief introduction, we encourage you to play with what you have learned about the sensory system. See if a sensory lens helps you understand people you know or children you work with. Think about your own sensory profile. Are you under-sensitive in any sensory realm? Overly sensitive? As with any other learning, sensory integration theory will be more useful to you as you integrate your knowledge with real life experiences.

Let's play with your new sensory lens right now! Look at the photos below of these children. What observations would you make? Can you use some of the sensory language you've learned in your observations? What questions might you ask yourself about these children's sensory preferences to guide future observations?

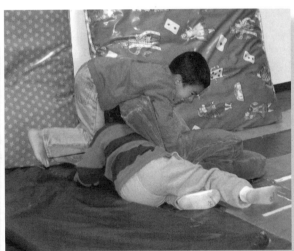

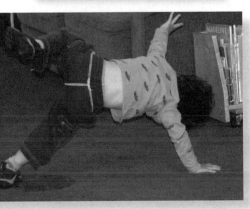

The DIR Model

Many years ago, a group of psychologists became interested in how infants and young children use relationships to learn through emotional (or affective) channels in the brain. Because some children with special needs do not have easy access to these channels, Dr. Stanley Greenspan and Dr. Serena Wieder, key members of the group, developed and shared a therapeutic intervention for working with children called the Developmental-Individual Difference-Relationship-Based model, or DIR model.

The DIR approach assumes that, when you are working with a child, your work must be based on three things:

1. Start with the child's current level of development with the goal of moving the child through each of the next important developmental levels.

2. Take full notice of the child's individual sensory, arousal, regulatory, and motor planning profile, based on the notion that a child can learn better when these aspects are understood and addressed.

3. Look at the skills and styles of the people in closest relationship to the child, the ones who will be attempting the therapy.

In the most basic application of the DIR approach, the parents are the therapists. The DIR model works through emotionally based learning. Parental relationships—the closest relationships a child has—are the most likely to influence emotionally based learning. For emotionally based learning to be effective in an educational setting, the teachers need to build strong, positive relationships with children.

Greenspan and Wieder (1998) identify six developmental levels or milestones that a child reaches through emotional experiences. They call these *functional emotional milestones* and have identified the ages that a child typically would reach each one.

- Milestone 1: Self-Regulation and Interest in the World (ages 0–3 months)
- Milestone 2: Shared Attention and Pleasure in Relationships (ages 4–5 months)
- Milestone 3: Two-Way Communication (ages 6–9 months)
- Milestone 4: Complex Communication (ages 10–14 months)
- Milestone 5: Emotional Ideas (ages 19–30 months)
- Milestone 6: Emotional Thinking (ages 31–42 months)

We will refer to these milestones throughout the book and will borrow Greenspan and Wieder's terminology when doing so. These developmental milestones are integral to the DIR approach.

The DIR model takes a child at whatever milestone he has achieved, regardless of his age, and helps him move up the ladder of development, using these milestones as a guide. At The Little School, we have also found these milestones a useful reference in the small moments we have with children in our classrooms. When a problem arises, we might wonder to ourselves what milestone the child is functioning at in that moment. Thinking in this way can guide our response. To help you learn the milestones, we have specified the age at which a typical child masters each milestone. Keep in mind that a child with challenges might reach these milestones at a different age than the stated one.

Milestone 1: Self-Regulation and Interest in the World (0–3 months)

Because humans learn through experience, in order to learn, a child must take an interest in the world. He must also be internally calm enough to be able to take in information. In their book *The Child with Special Needs*, Greenspan and Wieder describe this stage in infants:

> After nine months in darkness, a baby is born. Suddenly he is plunged into a world of light and sound, movement and touch, taste and smell. A sensory extravaganza! All this information is exciting and stimulating to the baby, but at the same time he has to learn not to be overwhelmed. His very first challenge is to take in this sensory panorama while regulating his response and remaining calm.
>
> Gradually, he finds things that focus his interests and at the same time can be used to calm himself—Mother's face, Father's voice, the soft texture of a blanket next to his skin. Little by little the infant learns to balance growing awareness of sensations with the ability to remain calm. This pair of skills is the most basic building block of emotional, social, and intellectual health. Without it we can't learn, we can't develop relationships with others, we can't survive in our highly stimulating world (1998, 72).

Milestone 2: Shared Attention and Pleasure in Relationships (4–5 months)

In order to learn through a relationship, a child must be able to take pleasure in sharing a relationship and have the ability to pay attention to a shared experience with someone. When infants gaze into our eyes, they are sharing an experience with us. That shared experience is wonderfully confirmed when they smile in response to our smile!

Milestone 3: Two-Way Communication (6–9 months)

We communicate not just with language but with facial expression and body language. When you smile at an infant, you open a circle of communication.

When the infant smiles back, she closes it, or completes one full circle. When you cover your eyes with your hands, you have opened another circle. As the infant waits before your covered eyes, she wiggles in anticipation. When you uncover your eyes and she squeals in delight, she has closed the circle. When the child says "more," she opens yet another circle of communication. You close it by playing peekaboo again. Two-way communication allows learning to occur through relationships.

Milestone 4: Complex Communication (10–14 months)

As the number of circles of communication a child opens and closes increases, so does the complexity of the communication. What happens as the peekaboo episode continues? Maybe the child gets overwhelmed and cries, communicating that she wants the adult to stop. The adult does indeed switch the game. Or maybe the adult tires first and says, "No more," and the child whimpers, expressing disappointment. From a simple shared smile, the circles have come fast and furiously to include anticipatory excitement, shared pleasure, requests for continuation, requests for an end, and disappointment on someone's side. The numbers of the circles and their complexity have increased.

Without necessarily saying a word, the child at this stage can express a whole range of emotions and desires. With this wide-ranging expression, her individual personality becomes more obvious. She also is able to interpret other people's gestures and communication. She begins to perceive the feelings of others.

Milestone 5: Emotional Ideas (19–30 months)

You can see how emotional ideas, wishes, and preferences and a greater sense of self can develop from the complex circles of communication described above. A child experiences a sense of wanting something to continue. Then she experiences a sense of wanting something to stop. She also experiences what it feels like for someone to have a desire different from or opposed to her own.

Representational play is a main arena for young children to explore emotional ideas, wishes, feelings, and intentions. Greenspan and Wieder write about how children begin to have emotional ideas:

> The child's ability to form ideas develops first in play. The child uses toys to weave stories, and through these stories he experiments with the range of intentions and wishes that he feels. Baby dolls are fed by Mommy dolls. People inside a house are threatened by giant bears. Cars crash into other cars (1998, 82–83).

In this kind of play, things become symbols. A paper towel roll becomes a bottle. A tissue becomes a baby's blanket.

The child also starts to use more words at this stage. The child learns that words, too, are symbols. The child can use the word *no* to symbolize everything from "I don't want to" to "I don't want *you* to" to "I am grumpy." Greenspan and Wieder explain the significance:

> Each symbol is an idea, an abstraction of the concrete thing, activity, or emotion with which the child is concerned. As he experiments more and more with pretend play and words, he becomes increasingly fluent in the world of ideas (1998, 83).

Play can seem very simple but be laden with emotional ideas and meaning for the child. When the adult joins the child's play, how much more meaningful the play becomes to the child.

Milestone 6: Emotional Thinking (31–42 months)

To understand milestone 6, it is useful to review the first five milestones:

1. First, a child gets calm enough to pay attention.
2. Next, the child can share attention and pleasure with someone else.
3. The two communicate.
4. Communication becomes more complex. The child begins to express a wider range of feelings and desires and to interpret the feelings and desires of others through their communication.
5. The child begins to express wishes, feelings, and ideas through play and words. The child is now using symbols.

So feeling has led to the use of symbols and a greater sense of self. In this final milestone, the use of symbols and a greater sense of self lead the child even further, to emotional thinking but also to concepts and logic that we traditionally understand as cognitive development.

Again, the main arena for this development is representational play. But now, instead of small little snippets of play unconnected to each other, the child starts bridging ideas together so that the play is more complex and interesting and makes more sense. Here's Greenspan and Wieder again:

Whereas in stage 5 a child might dress up a doll, then, seeing a crayon, scribble, then, seeing a drum, pretend to be a drummer, a child at the stage of emotional thinking connects the pieces together. For example, she might have the drummer play for the dressed-up little girl and use the crayon to make invitations for the performance (1998, 86).

This coherence in play also reflects a more coherent internal sense of self. Now the child can identify a feeling and even link it to the cause: "I'm mad because you took my cookie." And perhaps she can begin to see that *you* might be mad if she took *your* cookie too. The child can now truly begin to problem solve, both through words and actions.

There are now logical bridges between ideas, perceptions, and emotions. Because everything is linked, concepts like space and time begin to make sense in that personal way children have of experiencing what "five more minutes" and "far away" mean. Soon, she will be ready to learn about time and geography in less personal terms. Her personal experiences of "five more minutes" and "far away" will allow her to give meaning to the more formal, abstract concepts she learns later on in school. She will make meaning of *all* abstract learning through the emotional and symbolic thinking she brings to it. That is why it is so important for future learning, as well as for future relationships, that a child go through these six developmental milestones. Most children achieve these quite easily in early childhood. Some children with special needs do not.

Tools DIR Offers to Relationship-Based Inclusive Preschool Teachers

At The Little School, we did not learn the functional emotional milestones until many years after we borrowed concepts from DIR to use in the classroom. In fact, we did not even know that we were borrowing concepts from DIR! It was Dr. Barbara Kalmanson, a psychologist who advised the staff at The Little School, who first introduced us to the DIR approach without applying a label to it. Kalmanson was one of the psychologists who worked with Greenspan and Wieder to develop the DIR approach. Every time Dr. Kalmanson would visit to observe a child, she would praise what we were doing with the child (making us feel successful) and then make one comment or suggestion. We didn't know it then, but these single comments or suggestions contained the important kernels of the DIR approach.

When we, the authors, first decided we wanted to talk about some of the concepts and methods of DIR in this book, it was very daunting. Like sensory integration theory, DIR is a complex model, and it is hard to do it justice in a short and simple introduction. So we decided to share it with you the way Dr. Kalmanson shared it with us.

We can't offer you praise for all of the things you are doing right, but we can offer some of the kernels of the DIR approach that we have found very useful in our work with children. We hope that by presenting some specific ideas one by one, we can offer you some valuable new tools in your work with children without overwhelming you with too much information.

Follow the Child's Lead

In the DIR therapeutic intervention, regular, consistent time with a child should be spent in "floortime" (Greenspan and Wieder 2006). Floortime means playing with the child, building on whatever the child does or shows interest in.

If you follow a child's lead, you guarantee that whatever you and the child do together has meaning for that child. Following the lead supports the child's capacity to take initiative, which enables the child to develop original ideas and thoughts. Play and action that have meaning build the child's sense of self and the child's cognitive structures, ideas, thinking skills, and ability to symbolize—the work of the sixth milestone. Following a child's lead also makes learning a pleasurable, positive experience and leads to greater confidence in the learner.

In many respects, the purpose of floortime mirrors the purpose behind emergent curriculum. But unlike the general approach of emergent curriculum, this tool of *following the child's lead* is specifically intended to be used *in play* as a way to work with individual children in your classroom, especially children who are having a challenging time. This kind of lead-following play can occur between one teacher and a child for two minutes, five minutes, twenty minutes, or frequently throughout the day. It can happen between one child and one teacher, or other children can participate.

When using this tool to further a child's learning, you playfully join in with whatever the child is doing at that moment. Once you've got several circles of communication going, you may be able to add a new element or twist to the play without leaving behind what the child found so pleasurable. The child is rolling a car back and forth. You roll another car alongside. Then maybe you crash into the child's car. What happens next? It depends on what the child does. The lead keeps returning back to the child. By following the child's lead, you learn more about the child. You build the relationship. You bolster the child's confidence. Importantly, you also build on the child's emotional ideas and symbols.

Two-Way Communication

Following the child's lead and two-way communication are valuable tools to keep in mind when working with children who are very shy, with children starting the program who don't speak English, with children on the autism spectrum, or with any children who have social-emotional challenges.

The basic idea of two-way communication is that you want to get communication going (with those circles opening and closing) any way you can. Remember, not all communication is verbal. Facial expressions and gestures are communication. If you hold out a toy to a child and he accepts, you have communicated. When you ask him if he wants to swing, he puts his head down, and you say, "It looks like you don't want to," you have communicated. The more these kinds of communications happen, the more comfortable and confident the child will become. The more confident he becomes about his communication, the more he will *want* to communicate. Soon, he may even initiate the communication.

This new way of thinking will open up avenues for more children to feel successful in their communication with you. It will be especially valuable in your work with children with autism. Remember the example above of the child who is rolling a car back and forth, and you crash your car into his? If he pulls his car back, and then rolls it forward to crash into yours again, he is closing a circle of communication. It is just as if he answered, "I'm fine," to your, "How are you?" Recognizing actions, facial expressions, and body language will allow you more communication with children who are difficult to communicate with and, just as the children feel more successful, so will you.

Affect—for the Child and the Teacher

As preschool teachers, we all know when we've captured a group of children. Their eyes are bright, their faces alert, their bodies are eager. They can't wait for what happens next, and they can't hold back their comments. Because some children on the autism spectrum are nonverbal, some practitioners in DIR have come up with a term to identify how you know when you've gotten this match between what the child wants to learn and what you are doing— "gleam in the eye" (Greenspan and Wieder 1998, 125). This gleam in the eye

The following series of photos underlines the elements that support play with peers for children challenged in their play and relational skills: 1) a teacher who uses high affect to captivate children, 2) symbolic play with high, motivating interest (like the shark play in the following photos), 3) a teacher guiding the play and guiding the children towards interaction. All three elements are present in this series of photos.

The teacher has certainly captured the attention of the child in the boat with her frightened expression.

Now she directs the child's attention to the other child, the shark.

It worked! The child in the boat is now looking at his shark peer.

Uh-oh—he has lost his focus on the shark and has turned back to the teacher. With her fearful expression and steady gaze on the shark, she subtly redirects his attention back to the shark.

Once again, it is successful.

As the child loses attention, the teacher uses high affect again to try to draw him in.

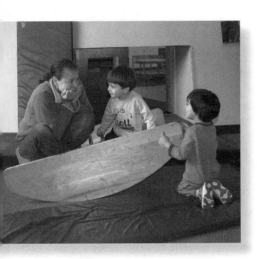

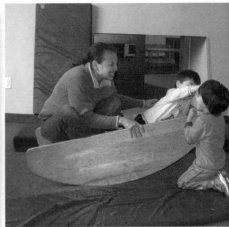

Her fearful expression draws the attention of both children. The shark starts to talk.

The shark's conversation has refocused the boy in the boat toward him.

The shark has been vanquished!

The photos above are very useful to see how a teacher might work with a child with play or relational challenges. We do want to note that both of the children in these photos actually have very strong social and play skills. Neither child has any goals in these areas. In that sense, the photos illustrate that these teaching skills are useful for work with all children, whether or not the children have challenges.

is what you are going for with children who can't otherwise let you know that they like what you are doing.

Sometimes the right material, activity, or topic produces the gleam in the eye. Another strategy that is successful in capturing children is your own affect. Sometimes the affect that grabs children is your own joy and enthusiasm. Sometimes it is acting scared or sad or confused or angry or mean or embarrassed or shy or tricky or frustrated. Young children are grabbed by displays of emotions. Successful clowns use this knowledge to great success.

How do you convey all of these emotions? By your voice, facial expression, and body language. For children who have trouble reading social cues, the more exaggerated (while still authentic), the better. Even when you are trying to engage one individual child, don't be surprised if this tool grabs a whole crowd. Young children find the display of affect irresistible. Displays of high affect work really well when setting limits too!

When children themselves are expressing a lot of affect or emotion, they are involved and invested in what is happening. Use those times as teachable moments, as long as the children are behaving safely. Some of the best opportunities for social learning for hard-to-engage children on the autism spectrum, for instance, come at times when the child is frustrated. If a teacher jumps in too quickly, the social opportunity might be lost. A child gets frustrated because someone's car is in the way, and he howls out his frustration to the other child, opening a loud circle of communication. You help the other child understand this communication and this second child stubbornly says, "I want to play here too," closing the circle. The boy with autism pushes his car at the other car (opening another circle) and the other child pushes back with his car (closing it). These two children have completed two circles of communication almost without your involvement.

Drawing Children into the Play of a Child with Challenges

When there is a child with special needs amid typically developing children, there is a tendency to want to help the child with special needs increase her play skills by bringing her into the play of the other children. This approach often fails. Instead, as much as you can, bring the other children into the play of the child with special needs.

It is often hard for a child with special needs to follow the tempo and manage the stimulation of the play of a group of children. If you bring the children into the play of the child with challenges, she has much more motivation to stick with the play. And because self-chosen play has meaning to the child involved, she has a head start in making a connection to the meaning of the play. The experience of having children join her choice of play will scaffold her ability to play with children.

For this strategy to work, the child's self-chosen activity has to appeal to others. For our boy who loves cars, a complex roadway could draw him and other children together. If you have a girl obsessed with colored balls, a marble runway for the balls will attract others. The largest draw will always be the teacher's involvement and enthusiasm for the play. By making the play of the child with challenges interesting through your own enthusiasm and interaction in the play, you will draw other children over to the play. You can then provide the bridge for further interactions among the children.

Flexible Expectations Allow for the Individual Creation of Meaning

We caught one of the best examples of the value of flexible expectations in *Relationships: The Key to Teaching and Learning in the Early Years,* a teacher training DVD we created (Little School 2004). The DVD shows actual classroom vignettes. In one vignette, a child wandered away from the two-year-old class's circle time. The teachers let her wander and then enticed her back in. Then they would let her wander off some more. One day, as she was wandering, the class started singing "The Wheels on the Bus." She went over to the block shelf, got the yellow school bus off the shelf, and brought it back to the circle. She got it! She was connected to what the class was singing. Eventually, she started bringing the school bus over whenever she wanted everyone to sing "The Wheels on the Bus," and you can bet they did!

If the teachers in this classroom had been more concerned with rules, routines, and expectations—"Minnie, sit back down! It's circle time!"—they never would have allowed her to show that she was making bridges betweens words, ideas, and symbols. She might never have been part of circle time, and the teachers would never have known that she wanted to be a part of it. A relationship-based, inclusive teacher cares more about helping her students make meaning out of their experiences than about rules, routines, and expectations. When this approach is consistent and made clear to the children, they won't mind when the rules are bent for another child. They know that when it is important, the rules will be bent for them too.

Bodies Matter

Both DIR and sensory integration theory tell us that in order to learn, children need to be calm and regulated. Take that one step further—in order to learn, children need to be internally comfortable. How do we make bodies comfortable? Our information about the sensory system provides guidance. Some children need quiet cuddling; some children need to spin; some children need deep pressure; and some need action. Children learn better if you give their bodies what they need before you ask them to learn. And the more intense the needs of their bodies, the more they might need individual sensory time before taking on the most demanding learning challenges of the classroom.

Repeated experience of a needed sensory diet might also strengthen a child's sensory system and ability to regulate. Requiring attention to sensory needs at one point doesn't mean a child will need the same kind of sensory input for the rest of his life. Giving a child his needed sensory input helps the child in the moment *and* strengthens his ability to learn more independently down the road. The DIR model incorporates sensory work, floortime, and semistructured problem solving (Greenspan and Wieder 2006). The model emphasizes the link between learning and the body.

Including sensory activities for the whole group is easy. You do it already with action songs, movement activities, and physical games. Your activities will become more specifically tailored as you think and learn more about sensory integration. When you become very skilled, you will be able to incorporate a specific child's sensory needs into the physical activities of the whole class.

. . .

In this chapter, you have learned about two valuable tools of the relationship-based inclusive teacher—sensory integration theory and the DIR approach. Sensory integration theory inspires us to understand how each child takes in information through a variety of senses, integrates the information from all of the senses, and decides what to do about it. A child's sensory profile influences how she experiences the world and how she sees herself as a learner and a friend. The motor planning system—the system that plans how the body will move itself to get what it wants—also has a big impact. The arousal and regulatory systems are equally influential on someone's ability to be a good student and friend.

The DIR model helps you understand how learning occurs through the emotional experiences children have as they engage with others in relationships. It provides six functional emotional milestones that help you understand the developmental ladder children must climb for this learning to occur. The milestones help you understand the crucial role of play in this emotional learning. Some of the kernels of DIR show you how to help children play better:

- Follow the child's lead.
- Use the child or the teacher's affect.
- Draw children into the play of a child with special needs.

The DIR model reminds you of the importance of helping children open and close circles of communication and how gestures, facial expressions, and howls of frustration can all be considered communication. It also reminds you to be flexible with rules and routines if doing so will allow children to make more meaning out of their experiences. Finally, both the sensory integration theory and DIR model underline the importance of paying attention to the role of the body in learning environments.

Now that you have two important tools to help you better understand and work with individual children in the classrooms, you need a method to direct your understanding and work when a child has challenges. The *Engage-Reflect-Plan* cycle discussed in the next chapter provides that method.

A Way to Begin: The Engage-Reflect-Plan Cycle

In my career as a teacher, I felt at times that my classroom was operating in a crisis management frenzy. I often found myself overwhelmed by the needs of a few individual children. These children seemed to take up the majority of my time and energy, and the rest of the group was left to struggle on its own. When I could find the time to talk to my coteachers about the children in the class, we usually got hung up discussing what was hard. When I first started working in a school that used the *Engage-Reflect-Plan* approach, it seemed daunting, like a lot of work and a lot of thinking and talking. In a fast-paced and constantly changing classroom, there just didn't seem to be the kind of time or space for that detailed kind of process. All of the thinking and talking just seemed like too much of a good thing.

But over time—and not much time—I began to find that much of what I was already doing, what came naturally to me as a teacher, were actually steps along the way to this more organized and satisfying way of working with the children and families. The reflecting and planning became easier as I learned to take pressure off myself to always have things go perfectly. I liked feeling as if I knew what would help individual children and the class as a whole. I have let go of the guilt I used to feel when I simply sat down and played with children. Now I know that when I am exploring the children's world, I am learning about and meeting their needs. I find that when I am truly enjoying myself playing with the children, as opposed to constantly managing them, the whole group seems more relaxed. The kids come together and seem to be working along with me in making the environment more . . . manageable! Being able to enjoy the moments that are fun puts me in a better place to explore not only how to have more fun but also how to make the moments that aren't as fun a little easier.

—**Megan London**
Teacher

We have already shared principles of relationship-based inclusion as a foundation to make sense of your work with children. The principles provide a framework to help understand specific situations and to help analyze and make decisions about policies and practices.

It is equally important to have a foundation that guides the daily work of individualizing to the children in your care. Individualizing to several different children while teaching the entire group is a challenging task. How do you begin? How do you know where to start or when you are finished? How do you know what to do?

The relationship-based inclusive principles fit nicely into a cycle of action and behaviors on the teacher's part that we summarize as *Engage-Reflect-Plan*. This cycle can guide your work with all children, from the moment you meet them until they leave your classroom. It also suggests guidelines for how to partner with families to discover more about their children and how to best meet their children's needs in the classroom.

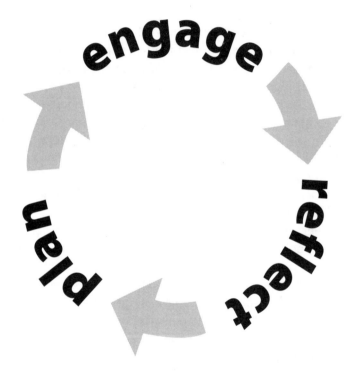

The primary *Engage-Reflect-Plan* cycle: Beginning with engaging, the three phases follow in a cycle of steps that leads back to the start and continues indefinitely.

All children in your care benefit when you engage with them, reflect on them, and plan for their needs. But if children are thriving, they might not need you to organize your reflections and plan for how you engage with them. A teacher would not typically use the more formal version of the *Engage-Reflect-Plan* approach described in this chapter and book with every child in a classroom. It is intended to be used when children need more organized help and support to succeed in a classroom. Most children with identified special needs could benefit from a teacher's use of the *Engage-Reflect-Plan* approach. But it is also useful when a child is not thriving or is really challenging, and you don't know why.

Engage

The first part of the cycle, *engage*, describes the active part of the teacher's relationship with the child in the classroom. You first engage to let the child know that you accept her on her own terms. This same kind of engagement should occur with families. As teachers reflect acceptance, genuine interest, and pleasure in getting to know the child and family, the groundwork for trust is laid. You must plan and care for the real relationships between teacher and child as thoughtfully as for any other part of the program. The same is true for the adult relationships. Family-teacher partnership and collaboration are not just added elements to the classroom curriculum. They are at the center of classroom curriculum.

Engaging means more than just establishing trust. Engaging with children means playing with children. It means playing with children in all sorts of ways, but most particularly, it means following the children's lead in play. To follow a child's lead, you not only let the child choose the kind of play, you let her set the tone, themes, and course of the play. In one sense, you become the ideal playmate, following willingly and enthusiastically wherever the child takes you (as long as it is safe). Simply by following the child's lead in play, you convey to the child how interested you are in her, how much you respect her ideas and skills, and how much you value your time together.

As you play, you closely observe and listen to and learn about the child. By listening and observing, you will be able to attune to the child's strengths and interests. You will also be more likely to gain insight into her challenges as you see them through her eyes. You will learn about the child's likes and dislikes, preferences, and relationships in school and out of school. You will learn what is important to the child and what is getting in her way. This kind of information gathering supports all of the principles and is the key to creating an individualized plan. A teacher must have the right balance of observing, listening, and learning, as well as of doing, acting, and telling. You need to take in as much as you put out. This is necessary to truly know children, and the teacher's modeling of give-and-take in relationships also helps the children develop these capacities.

Reflect

By engaging, you learn so much about a child. You will also have learned by watching the child interact with others in the classroom and with the materials, activities, and routines of the day. Conversations with the child's family will provide still more information. You may have also observed the child interact with his parents or other family members. And there may be additional information on written forms the family or others have submitted. If a child is already working with a specialist, hearing the specialist's impressions and questions about a child will also be valuable at this stage. Once you have gathered all of these observations about the child from a variety of sources, it is time to organize what has been learned.

What does all of this information tell you? Does it begin to create a picture of the child's sensory profile? Does it help you understand the child's developmental profile? Does it suggest how to build on the child's strengths? Can you now describe any challenges the child has in your setting that get in the way of his thriving there? Does the information raise any questions for you? Are there similarities or differences between your observations and the family's descriptions? Do you want to talk more with the child's family at this point to reflect together on what you have learned?

Reflection is really about organizing what you know about a child. It allows you to get to know him better. It allows you to see if there are ways that you can support him in the environment to learn more, to play deeply, to relate happily, to thrive. Reflection shows you what you know, but it also shows you what you don't know. Your questions about the child are as important as your answers. Once you have organized your reflections about the child, you can plan for the best way to individualize to him in your classroom.

How do you reflect? There is no one right way. Partly, you are mentally reflecting and organizing information about the child all the time. "Uh-oh, he has a hard time with transitions. Better give him a warning next time." We would like to suggest taking reflection as many steps further as your program will support. There are a wide variety of ways to reflect about children, just as there are a wide variety of ways to give and receive information about them with their families. Whatever method you use, we suggest that you place importance on this step of reflection. You will be surprised by how much you know, how much reflection will help you further engage with the child, and how it will lead directly to planning what other steps you want to take to support this child in your program.

Plan

Planning will begin to happen as you reflect on what you know about the child. Even in the example above, where the teacher noticed the child had difficulty with transitions, a plan immediately followed the observation: "Better give him a warning next time."

A *plan* can be as simple as the notes you jot down on the floor and as elaborate as a meeting between teachers, families, director, and specialists to come up with what accommodations and supports the child needs in school. Such an accommodation plan is known in the public schools as an Individualized Education Program or an IEP (see box on page 47).

Planning accommodations and supports for children may sound intimidating, but here's the truth: if you have taken time to reflect based on observations gathered through your authentic engagement with the child and family, planning can be the easy part. And the more you do it, the more ideas you will have to draw upon in your plan for any particular child. Remember, accommodations or support are nothing more than answers to these questions: How can this child be most comfortable in my classroom? How can this child learn in my classroom? How can this child be happy in my classroom?

If a child comes into your program with identified special needs, he may have an IEP or an Individualized Family Service Plan (IFSP) in place. If he becomes identified while in your program, he may be assessed and receive an IEP or IFSP. Here is a simple introduction to these documents.

An IEP is

- Federally mandated by the Individuals with Disabilities Education Act (IDEA).

- Required for any child over three who the school district has determined has special needs after an assessment process.

- Looking at a child across all developmental domains.

- A description of how the child learns, how the child demonstrates learning, and what teachers and service providers will do to help the child learn most effectively.

- A document with specific goals for the child.

- Developed by professionals and families.

- Reviewed and updated yearly.

An IFSP is

- Federally mandated under IDEA for any child through the age of two (and in most states until the child is three) who has been determined to have special needs by the designated regional agency.

- Similar in its basic purpose and components to an IEP but is an interagency plan for children and their families, not a plan specifically related to schooling.

- A plan that includes more services to support the family or therapy conducted in the home.

- Generally replaced by an IEP by the time the child is three years old or when a review determines that the child is no longer eligible for services outlined in the IFSP.

In part 2 of this book, you will examine examples of teachers engaging with children, reflecting, and then coming up with plans. Although we've provided lots of ideas about specific supports and accommodations, we haven't tried to offer an exhaustive list. You already know more than we could fit in one book. Try this: think of as many children you have taught as you can. Remember especially the shy ones, the aggressive ones, and the ones who drove you crazy. Make a list of the different techniques you tried to help them. We think you will be surprised by how long your list is. And if you haven't taught any children yet, no worries. We suspect figuring out how to help individual children in your class will be one of your favorite parts of teaching.

A plan should include goals for the child. Again, a goal might be as simple as "Sammy will have an easier time transitioning from one time of day to another." The plan might include some goals for the teacher. "I want to remember to speak softly when I approach Maria." Don't forget to think about how the ideas in the plan will actually get implemented—who will do what when.

Have you included families in your plan? For simple challenges and plans, doing so isn't necessary, but when you are helping a child tackle larger challenges, remember that families are your partners. They can ensure the success of a plan in many different ways. You will only know what is realistic for families by engaging with them, which brings us to a very important aspect of the *Engage-Reflect-Plan*: families should be part of planning.

A Never-Ending Cycle

In order to know what kinds of help families can provide, what makes sense to them, and what they think will be effective, you have to sit down and talk things over with them as part of your reflection. In this sense, the reflection and planning stage often occur somewhat simultaneously. As you talk and plan with them, you get to know them better. The engagement deepens. And what do you do with your plan? You take it back to the floor and try it out with the child the next day. As you try things out, you get a response from the child. If you've come up with the right kinds of supports, the response will be positive, and you and she will be having a pretty good time together. And once again, the engagement deepens. Whatever stage of the cycle you are in, the other stages are present in some form. And one stage always leads you on to the next and then back to the beginning. You engage, reflect, plan, and then re-engage, reflect, and plan some more. You don't have to spend too much time thinking about it. In the beautiful way cycles work, once you get the hang of it, it all happens naturally.

• • •

In this chapter, we introduced the *Engage-Reflect-Plan* cycle, a method that guides you in meeting the individual needs of children who require a higher level of support in the classroom. When you engage, you build a relationship with such children and learn about them. When you reflect, you look at what you have learned about each child in an organized way. When you plan, you come up with goals for the child, strategies for how to help him meet those goals, and a plan for how to implement the strategies.

In part 2, we will show what this might actually look like in an early childhood classroom. We meet two teachers, Angie and Mike, as they meet a new group of children. We follow their efforts to meet the needs of Danny and Michelle, two children in their class. We examine in great detail how to implement the *Engage-Reflect-Plan* cycle with children and families by exploring the story of Angie, Mike, Danny, and Michelle.

Part 2

Including All Children: Engage-Reflect-Plan

Chapter 5

Engage: The First Step Is Understanding

It is 9 a.m. on a sunny day in early September. Angie and Mike, the teachers in the three-year-old class, have been busy for the last few days, performing countless tasks to get ready for the start of school. After all the grown-up work, they are excited to be back in their comfort zone—playing with children in the classroom.

But they are also nervous; these are new children and families. The teachers know how important it is to help them all—children and parents alike—have a positive and comfortable first impression of school. This is the beginning of the children's whole lives in a setting outside the home.

Being good teachers, they take a deep breath and try not to pay too much attention to their nerves, however inevitable those may be. They know that besides doing and saying the right things and helping to create a happy, comfortable environment, a big part of their job is to get to know these children and families, starting right now, on day one.

The first child bounds right into the room, her face lit up with a smile. She doesn't spend much time returning the teachers' greeting or following her father's suggestion to "say hi to your new teacher." She just goes right to the art area and begins pulling stickers off the waxed sheet and plastering them all over her arms. She squeals in delight. Angie, after having introduced herself to the girl's father and exchanged some information, sits down across from her at the art table. In no time they are talking and laughing together. Angie makes a note to herself, just in her head: *Likes to start at the art table. Connects happily with teachers once she finds what she likes to do.*

Another child stops in his tracks at the door, does an about-face, and buries his head in his mother's legs.

"What's wrong?" she asks. "You were so excited about coming to school! Say hello to your teacher."

"It's okay," Mike replies. He gets down on his knees a few feet away from the child, who is still hiding behind his mother, and speaks softly to both of them. "Lots of children feel a little shy their first time at school. You can take as much time as you need. When you feel ready to come in, you'll see some stickers at the art table, some playdough, some train tracks . . ."

At the mention of trains, the boy's head pops out from behind his mother. He peers past the teacher into the room.

"Train tracks!" his mother says. "How did your teachers know you love trains?" The boy disappears into his hiding place again.

"Tell you what," says Mike, "I'll put a few train tracks and trains right here where you can see them, and you can play with them right here." Mike goes to the block corner to raid the Brio bin. As he turns around to take a few pieces back to the doorway, he nearly trips over the boy, who has crept in behind him. The boy begins to dig hungrily through the box of tracks.

Help this child feel okay about needing warm-up time, Mike thinks to himself. *Loves trains.*

Soon the room is full of children and their parents or caregivers. Some lead their parents around by the hand to explore each corner of the room. Others have left their families behind to paint at the easel. Still others camp out on their parents' laps, just watching and taking it all in. A few get into tugging matches with peers on their first day. Others are cutting a very wide path around their peers. Those families who can take the time stay for a lot or all of the first day. Others say their first good-byes—some with no noticeable reaction, others with tears.

A bright-eyed girl with pixie-length blonde hair enters with her mother. She drifts past the teachers without making eye contact and heads towards the dramatic play area. Her mother calls after her.

"Michelle, say hi to your teachers," she says. Her mother smiles and rolls her eyes a little. "I'm Catherine. That's Michelle. She doesn't talk a lot."

"That's okay," Mike replies. "I'm glad to see she likes the classroom."

"Oh, she loves to play," Catherine replies. "She can play by herself for hours at a time."

Mike follows as Catherine joins Michelle and gets down low at her side. Michelle looks at each toy on the play food shelf. Her lips move constantly. Mike tries to hear if Michelle is talking or singing, but she keeps such a quiet tone, that it's hard to tell. Michelle wanders next to the playdough table, with Catherine again staying close by. Catherine also speaks softly.

"Oh, look," Catherine says, "little letter molds." Michelle examines each one and lays them side by side in a tidy, alphabetized row. Mike notices that Michelle looks toward and reaches out to her mother a few times, but she doesn't make eye contact or speak to her. When another child sits down at the table, Michelle calmly but promptly gets up and moves on.

Plays well by herself. Long attention span, likes letters, and knows the alphabet, Mike thinks to himself. *Needs time and space to connect with new people.* Both Angie and Mike take care to make only gentle, quiet overtures to Michelle during the first morning. But Michelle does not respond. The teachers readily accept Catherine's suggestion that she stay for all of the first morning.

The teachers' heads are swimming by now—so many names, so many things to notice and remember, so many things to say and do right. And new children are still arriving! One of the last to wander in, a few paces behind his mother, is Danny.

Danny neither bounds into the room nor locks up and clings to his mother's legs. He tiptoes in slowly but with purpose, high up on his toes, grinning from ear to ear. His sandy hair is pushed in a heavy fringe over his ear. When he sees a teacher, his smile grows even wider, and he throws an arm over his eyes.

"Danny," his mother says quietly, "this is teacher Angie. Remember we read about her in your letter from school?"

"He's been so excited to come," she says. She holds out her hand. "I'm Martha," she says. They exchange a few words as Danny makes his way to the block corner. He stops when he sees two other boys building tracks next to each other and watches them intently. After a few minutes, he moves to the manipulative table and begins putting Duplos together. His hands work quickly. In no time, he has made a stack of rectangular blocks with perpendicular arms.

"Lymakween!" he exclaims, holding his creation up to his mother and Angie.

"You made Lightning McQueen!" his mother exclaims. "He's very hard to understand," she says quietly to Angie.

"But he knows a lot about movies," Angie replies.

"His brother is eight," Martha explains.

Angie's mind is buzzing. She wants to note as many of Danny's many already visible strengths as possible, and some questions: *likes building with blocks, interested in fantasy themes, observes peers, connects with adults, interested in both materials and people.*

• • •

This is, of course, a fairly clean and simple snapshot of an inclusive classroom. Anyone who has worked with young children, even in settings where only one or two new families are starting at once, knows that the real picture is much more complicated. But even this slightly flattened picture gives us many examples of how teachers can begin the process of *Engage-Reflect-Plan* from the moment they meet new children.

Engage: Connect, Observe, and Play

Let's start with a closer look at what we mean by *engage*. The teachers know that each child's success, and the success of the program, relies on their knowing each child in detail. A trusting, comfortable, and respectful relationship between each child and her teachers is the foundation for both relationship-based programs and inclusion. Teachers cannot achieve this just by offering the right materials or routines. They must also devote time and attention to *playing together* with children and *taking in*. They must learn how a child likes to be approached, what kind of greeting and connection is most comfortable, how the child goes about exploring the world, where she likes to go in the classroom, and what she likes to do.

By observing each child closely and incorporating their observations into an individual kind of relating, the teachers offer the benefits of relationship-based inclusion to all the children in their program. Angie noticed that Danny blocked his eyes when he entered the room but also that he looked curious and

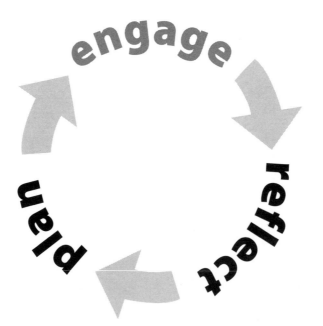

The *Engage-Reflect-Plan* cycle from the Engage stage: As you engage, you reflect and plan.

excited. She used these observations to find a balance between holding back, so as not to overwhelm him, and making a friendly overture nonetheless. Mike noticed that Michelle used gestures to connect with her mother but not eye contact. He used observation of a child's relationship with her mother to learn how he might relate to the child. Take note here of how even just the *engage* piece of the *Engage-Reflect-Plan* cycle is a cycle unto itself. The observing leads to the relating, which facilitates more observing, and so on.

The Engage subcycle: Engaging requires an ongoing cycle of observing and relating.

Let's examine this episode more closely to pull out some guidelines that connect back to the ideas we presented in chapters 2, 3, and 4. Some of these themes focus on understanding a child's sensory integration profile. Others put the functional emotional milestones and the floortime perspectives from the DIR model into action:

- Individualizing is essential.
- Think sensory.
- Focus on communication.
- Focus on a child's strengths and preferences.

The nap is just pretend, but the connection gained through the play between the children and teacher is real.

Individualizing Is Essential

As you can see from the story above, teachers have a classroom plan, program philosophy, and routines and expectations that are consistent. Predictability and order are necessary to establish trust and comfort. Nevertheless, teachers use their observation-based knowledge of each child to help him find an individual way to connect with and enter into the order of the environment. They *individualize* their program, and in doing so they send a message to the child that his unique profile is healthy and competent and can fit into an organized community. On day one, this happened in small ways. Mike offered to bring train tracks to the door for a shy child. Angie and Mike accepted Catherine's suggestion that she stay for the first session. These were little changes to the order of the program that allowed the children to feel comfortable and safe.

But individualizing, as we saw, is also a matter of tailoring how you respond and relate to individual children. With each child who entered the room, Angie and Mike made quick choices about how close to approach, how much talking to do, how excited and boisterous to be or how quiet and gentle. Individualizing means that as teachers get to know a child, they reflect what they see in each child back to him in a respectful way, assuring the child that he is known and accepted. The teachers then help that child find an individual way to begin to explore.

Think Sensory

Angie and Mike noticed what kind of activities their new children preferred, how much language they used, and what their social style seemed like on first impression. But as relationship-based inclusion teachers, they are also looking for information about the children's basic sensory style. They look at what kinds of physical experience or exploration they seem to crave—climbing, hugging, putting things together, putting paint on their hands—and what kinds they seem to avoid. Michelle showed a strong preference for uncrowded areas or defined places, like her own chair. When a child came near, she moved away. These cues suggested that she was somewhat spatially defensive. They are looking for clues about how children use their senses—their eyes, ears, and their sense of touch—to explore. When Danny entered a new room, he seemed to feel a little overwhelmed and shut down the input to his eyes.

The teachers are also looking for information about what kind of vestibular and proprioceptive input children seek or avoid. Danny buried himself deeply in his mother's shoulder at first and returned to her throughout the morning, crashing into her for strong, tight hugs. This gives a hint that he was a child who sought out a lot of tactile and proprioceptive input. As is often the case, Danny had shown a high need for some kinds of input—deep touch and pressure. But he had also demonstrated a sensitivity for other kinds—visual input. So the teachers are looking not only at individual pieces of sensory information but also at how the children integrate the different pieces and how the pieces begin to add up to a sensory profile.

Finally, the teachers are looking for each child's pattern of arousal and regulation. Some children, like the little boy with the trains, go into reverse at the classroom door but get up to third gear in short order, as he did when he found a favorite kind of toy. Others, like Michelle, seem to drift through the morning in second gear. Nothing about the surrounding environment revved her up or slowed her down.

Remember the first and most basic functional emotional milestone from DIR that we discussed in chapter 3, self-regulation and interest in the world (Greenspan and Wieder 1998). If children have ongoing difficulty mastering this one, they will have a hard time moving on. Paying attention to a child's pattern of arousal and regulation, along with his emerging sensory and motor profile, gives teachers the most broadly useful information they can get.

Focus on Communication

The third functional emotional milestone of DIR, two-way communication, is an everyday concern of all preschool teachers. As we establish relationships with new children, we use communication—through language, gesture, and affect—and we foster communication. Angie and Mike were mindful about using two-way communication to bond with each child. They used observation and playfulness, and they individualized. But they also noticed some significant elements about Danny's and Michelle's communication styles that might become important. Danny had a lot of vocabulary and had begun to grapple with symbolic themes. He built something out of Duplos, gave it the identity of a character from a movie, and named it. But his verbal articulation was very young, and he had a hard time making his ideas known to others. Angie and Mike took note right away that an active, busy boy with lots of ideas would need support getting those ideas across.

Michelle posed a larger set of communication questions. She not only did not communicate verbally, although she had language, but she did not seem to close those nonverbal circles of communication, such as eye contact, shared attention, and affect. She didn't light up when her gaze caught those of her teachers, nor did she look anxious about new adults.

Each functional emotional milestone is built on the preceding milestones. So when we notice children who lack two-way communication, the functional emotional milestones give us a structure to work backward. Has this child mastered the first milestone—self-regulation and interest in the world? What about milestone 2—shared attention and pleasure in relationships? This process is important because it suggests that although we focus on communication, we may need to work on much simpler themes with some children in order to promote it. In general, it is useful to know when you must help a child get to point A before you can work on point B or even point P.

As teachers work to build connections, there are many ways to communicate to a child that you understand. When this child missed her mother, she cared for the baby doll as a way of coping with her sadness. The teacher responded, not directly to the separation sadness, but in the child's chosen mode of symbolic play by pretending to call the baby doll's mom. You can almost see the connection and trust between this teacher and child growing as they play.

Focus on a Child's Strengths and Preferences

Children are often at their least competent and confident in a new setting. It is easy for a teacher to see a child's challenges looming large, for indeed that is how it often feels from the child's and parent's perspective—*my child will only cling to my legs; she was so excited, and now she's fragile and crying; this child is a handful; he's pretty nonverbal for his age.* But skilled teachers know that a child needs time to bring all her strengths and preferences into a care setting. Furthermore, they know that it is crucial to look at the whole picture from the start and begin to identify the positives: what does this child like to do and what are her strengths? Cultivating true respect and appreciation for what a child likes to do and does most easily will help her become comfortable and competent in this setting. It will foster the child's process of bringing all the sides of her personality and her most confident self to the world outside the family. It is the process of seeing a child's personality as a set of opportunities and gifts rather than as challenges and management tasks.

Danny showed many clear strengths and preferences on day one.

Danny

1) Took great joy in connecting with new adults

2) Well-developed fine motor skills (Duplos)

3) Good organizational capacity to construct something from an idea

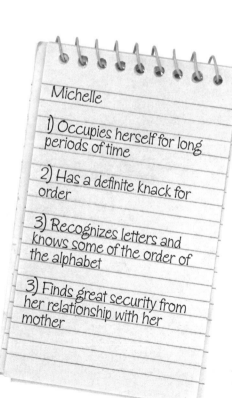

Michelle

1) Occupies herself for long periods of time

2) Has a definite knack for order

3) Recognizes letters and knows some of the order of the alphabet

3) Finds great security from her relationship with her mother

Michelle was a little harder to see from the perspective of strengths. But by taking time to observe, Mike was able to recognize a few.

This is not spin control, and it doesn't mean teachers don't think about possible challenges early on. Especially with Michelle, the teachers found themselves focusing on several perplexing questions. But focusing on strengths and preferences allows teachers and children to partner in a way that will add up to good management by helping motivate a child to engage and shine.

These, then, are the building blocks of the first part of the *Engage-Reflect-Plan* cycle—*engage*. Here, even on the first day, the teachers are both learning about and supporting children through a combination of observing and interacting:

- They make a point of starting the engagement process with both children and their parents.
- They use the knowledge of each child's parent to begin to know each child quickly and fully.
- They take care to set up a two-way partnership.

The vignette about Michelle and Danny's first day illustrates how the core concept of *engage* relies upon the principles of relationship-based education discussed in chapter 2:

- Take honest, authentic interest in each person in your program.
- Leave time and space to take in as well as put out.
- Devote careful attention to talking, working, and playing together in order to build positive, individualized relationships.

The episode also shows how teachers focus on each child's unique strengths and preferences, make note of questions, but also use patience where their questions are concerned.

. . .

In getting to know a child, there will be many quiet moments to engage and to get to know

. . . who likes to be read to

. . . who likes to hug

. . . and who likes to be tickled.

As teachers and children engage, it is a good time to learn a child's sensory preferences and see

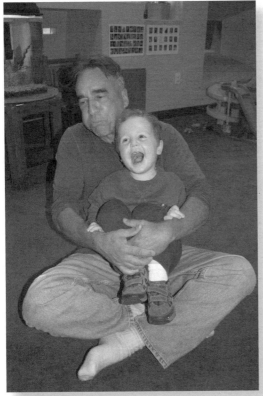

… who likes to be squeezed

… who likes to be tipped

… and who likes to fly!

· · ·

What about children who set off alarm bells, even on first impression? When you observe each child closely, questions about some children will come up even as you focus on strengths. How do you fit these questions into the process of building a trusting, honest, yet positive relationship with children and their families?

Let's return to Danny and Michelle. We will follow the experience of children whose profiles led to bigger questions and see how teachers with a relationship-based inclusion perspective might try to support their unique needs.

· · ·

Danny continued to enter the room with a mixture of joy and shyness. He developed a trusting relationship with Angie and Mike and liked to cuddle with them and read books. He also liked to talk about snippets from his favorite movies, although, as his mother had pointed out, his pronunciation seemed much younger than his skill with concepts or his vocabulary. He was very hard to understand.

Danny also continued to spend lots of time on his own. He preferred the block corner and the manipulative table, and he continued to exercise his skills by putting things together. As he had on the first day of school, Danny showed high interest in his peers. Even as he worked intently with Duplos or unit blocks, he watched children nearby with a steady gaze.

A pattern began to develop—when Danny was away from teachers, he would work on his own quietly and with purpose, watching his peers. After a few minutes, he seemed to switch into another gear. He would jump up and begin windmilling his arms around, dumping all his work onto the floor. Other times he would lunge at his peers, pushing them over or pressing his head against their chests. At still other times, he would begin to yell snippets of dialogue from movies. "That's just great!" he would shout, or "Destroy the humans!" Although he was very interested in movies—he even had a favorite classroom car he called Lightning McQueen—he had a hard time getting involved in pretend play. He would show his cars to other children and initiate building a road or driving cars together. But after a moment or two, he would hurl his cars through the air or head-butt someone and dump everything on the floor. He seemed preoccupied with fantasy themes of danger. He also liked to shout out "I'm the winner!"

Angie and Mike found that they were dropping what they were doing half a dozen times each morning to intervene. When they did, Danny would bury his face in their shoulders. He seemed almost incapable of hearing any of the verbal limits they would try to set at these times. Sometimes he would begin to cry. Every now and then he would, on his own, turn to a child he had hurt and say, "Sorry." Angie and Mike noticed that Danny made a point of staying near his teachers after these episodes. He was becoming more and more physical with them as well, drawing them into deep cuddling, hugging, or wrestling.

After a few minutes, Danny would move away from them, back to one of his favorite spots. Then, it seemed, the cycle would start all over again. Although he loved to come to school and loved his teachers, his attempts to play and connect with peers left him in constant trouble. And it was all too clear that he felt bad about negative responses from peers and teachers. Angie and Mike couldn't help noticing that Danny was very dependent upon them. He wanted to be close to them much of the day. They were also necessarily spending a lot of time with Danny. But much of it was spent setting limits after he had done something wrong. They worried that Danny was connecting challenging behavior with getting attention from them.

• • •

Many children in your care spark questions in your mind. They may not have language; they may work on their own with the same puzzles every day and not engage with peers or teachers; they may have physical challenges. But it is important to note that even when you have questions or concerns, the more you can focus on engaging the child early on, the more you will be able to reflect and plan. If the child enjoys school and generally seems able to participate, teachers can give him more time to make sense of group settings. They can continue to build their relationship with his family and learn about the child from them, noting observations and questions and giving honest details to the family along the way.

For many children, the engage process can be unhurried. Ideally, the first months of a child's experience can be devoted to relaxing and relationship building with both children and families. Of course, with all children, the *Engage-Reflect-Plan* cycle occurs on some level from the start.

• • •

Angie and Mike were not sure yet if Danny needed more support or just more time. He was certainly struggling in some ways. And he was one of those children who single-handedly added volumes to the teachers' workload and the stimulation and tension level in the room. But they had worked with many children who had experienced rocky starts to school like Danny's but who had settled down. And Danny loved coming to school.

Michelle, on the other hand, became despondent when her mother first left her. She cried so long and so hard that other children who had said their good-byes calmly began to cry as well. Still others became noticeably anxious in other ways. They began to run, yell, or dump toys on the floor. Even the teachers were on edge.

Angie and Mike were used to children crying at early separations. But they were usually able to win the children's trust and help them find ways to become comfortable. With Michelle, they had not been able to establish a connection before Catherine left her. Now, she refused their contact or comfort. She would squirm and cry even louder if they tried to pick her up or pat her back. And she took no notice of their reassuring words. She did not respond to any of their approaches—reading books about separation, singing songs about mommies coming back, touring the classroom to find something familiar or enticing that might help. She continually moved away from the teachers. She sat by the door and wailed. The only word that Angie and Mike could make out through her crying was "mommy."

Some children's challenges make it much harder to transition into or enjoy a program and do not allow the luxury of time and patience before plans must be made. Michelle was clearly one such child. How do teachers maintain their observational, strength-based, relationship-building approach when a child struggles right from the start? How can teachers make the most of the engagement process if they feel they must reflect and plan within the first few weeks? Here are a few guidelines that can keep the Engage thread active even when teachers have to hit the ground running:

- Identify and note challenges.
- Identify details of a child's sensory profile.
- Try some things before you know what's going on.

Identify and Note Challenges

The teachers make a point of focusing on and leading with a child's strengths. But they also turn their close observation skills toward a child's challenges—what does she avoid, what comes least naturally to her, where is she least comfortably engaged in the program? Remember, also, that DIR's functional emotional milestones give you a framework for placing challenges in a sequence of development.

Teachers can't help but notice that all children's strengths and challenges are bound together in a cycle. Michelle had a great capacity to engage and stay focused in her own internal world of play. She had a loving relationship with her mother and accepted her mother's guidance with ease and skill. But these strengths were the very things that also made it difficult for her to bond with teachers and peers and to accept them as substitutes for her mother. Early in their relationship with a child, the teachers don't hurry to respond to or help a child master these challenges, although, as we will see below, they will keep an eye out for opportunities. But at this stage, it is most important to compile observations and insights into each child.

Identify Details of a Child's Sensory Profile

On the first day of school, the teachers made casual observations about each child's sensory preferences. Now, in order to respond to a child's specific struggle, they look deeper.

As you read in chapter 3, beneath a child's preferences and choices—their likes and dislikes, their style of exploring—is a unique combination of sensitivity and curiosity that guides everything else (Ayres 1979). Each child is working hard to take in and make sense of all the physical, sensory, cognitive, and emotional sensations of being alive. Some find certain elements—noise, light, being close to others, tactile sensations, to name just a few—harder or easier to take, more or less naturally comfortable. Getting to know a child's constitution and temperament—her package of sensory, motor, and physical preferences and needs—is vital to knowing her physical, social, emotional, and cognitive styles. Knowing how sensory, motor, and physical experience can help the child feel more calm, receptive, organized, or safe over time is the broadest and most effective teaching plan you can make.

So in Michelle's case, the teachers tried to make sense of some elements of her sensory profile that they felt might help provide her with some support. They noted that she seemed to avoid touch, at least in the new setting of the classroom. They saw that she explored space with her body and took in a great deal of information with her eyes. But they also saw that she did not look to people's expressions or affect. Using the DIR functional emotional milestones as a guide, they began to ask how her apparent challenges with milestone 2—shared attention and pleasure in relationships—might be contributing to her emotional challenges around separation. She seemed to want her own space and moved away when people came close, although she had not reacted that way to her mother. They also saw that Michelle focused on music, made many musical noises of her own, and seemed sensitive to noise.

● ● ●

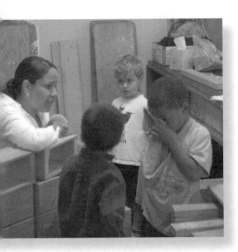

As teachers engage with children in play or sit back and observe, they learn more and more about children's strengths, challenges, preferences, interests, and sensory styles. What information might you, as the teacher, gain from these children at play? What questions might you ask yourself about them?

Try Some Things before You Know What's Going On

This may seem to belong to the plan part of the cycle more than the engagement phase. Angie and Mike take care not to try to figure out Michelle or Danny. They use observations to note what can be clearly seen and known, and they keep track of questions about how the children engage with the world and how best to support them. They share some of these observations and questions with parents and wait to raise others until they feel doing so will be most effective. But they also know that as teachers, they can use their basic play partnering and mentoring skills as part of the relationship-building process.

This is why we call the first phase of the inclusion cycle *engage* rather than simply *observe*. In order to know and understand children as we build relationships, we have to work and play with them. We focus on gathering information, but we can't do it effectively just by sitting back and watching. As we've indicated before, the *Engage-Reflect-Plan* process is a cycle—each step feeds into the other in a never-ending circle. But each step is also a smaller cycle unto itself. Engaging requires a loop of taking in and putting out. Later in their work with Danny and Michelle, Angie and Mike will organize a more detailed plan of action. But as they focus on understanding their early responses to their program, they know that for each child, they have to try something now.

• • •

In Michelle's case, Angie and Mike felt they needed to do something significant right away. Michelle would not be able to even begin the relationship-building process until she could get comfortable with separation, the school setting, and the teachers. Because they were relationship-based teachers and Michelle resisted forming relationships, Angie and Mike realized they would need help from the one person with whom Michelle clearly did relate: her mother.

Angie and Mike needed to let Michelle's family know they were feeling stumped and needed some help to make their daughter's separation process a success. They needed to make it clear that Michelle's process was different from that of most children her age, who usually let their caregivers comfort them after this much time together. And the teachers had to let Michelle's family know the other children were feeling stressed by Michelle's crying. So Angie and Mike asked Michelle's parents to sit down with them to help them understand Michelle better and make a plan to support her transition into school.

Angie and Mike made a very clear decision not to lead off the conversation by telling Michelle's parents that they thought something was wrong with their daughter. Their biggest goal, besides coming up with a plan, was to build a real, trusting relationship with Michelle's parents. They focused on earnestly seeking information and advice. They asked Catherine and Scott, Michelle's father, to describe Michelle at home.

"She's very imaginative," Catherine began. "She loves to dress up like a princess. She loves to dance."

"She has an incredible memory," Scott added. "If she hears a song once, or does a puzzle, she never forgets."

The teachers brought Catherine and Scott up to date on Michelle's constant crying and her rejection of their support. By now, Michelle had cried through four straight sessions.

"Usually children Michelle's age let us help them by now," Mike added.

"Michelle has always been very sensitive to loud sounds," Catherine responded, "but lately she's become really agitated. She covers her ears a lot and cries whenever there's a loud sound, like if I turn on the vacuum cleaner."

"She starts crying as soon as the car gets within a few blocks of the building," Scott added. "She can be very stubborn. She does best when she knows what to expect. New things can really throw her."

After the meeting ended, Angie and Mike tried to sort through all they had learned. Michelle liked to dress up and pretend. She had an excellent memory and was especially interested in music. It could be difficult for her parents to get and keep Michelle's attention. She had a good strong will, but with it came a high need for predictability and control in order to relax and engage. She was much more playful and interactive at home. As the teachers had noticed, Michelle was very sensitive to sounds. They wondered if the sounds of the classroom were hard for her to manage. They also wondered if the sound of her own crying was creating a cycle of discomfort for her, as it was for everyone else in the classroom.

Angie and Mike decided to take a step outside the box. They asked Catherine to come back into the classroom to support Michelle while the teachers worked on building a relationship with her. This was an unusual plan. The teachers had spent the last few weeks helping the children get used to seeing their parents leave. Mike in particular worried that this plan might give Michelle the idea that her mother would stay with her forever. Would this move her backward instead of forward in her separation process? Angie pointed out the strain on the class and the difficulty they were having in moving beyond separation. Michelle's upset was proving contagious.

Despite the unknowns, everyone agreed to try this new plan for a week and evaluate its effects. Catherine made the necessary arrangements to free up time to accompany her daughter to class. She also brought in some of Michelle's favorite music CDs. Angie and Mike put some of her favorite storybooks in the book corner. Many of these were special favorites of Michelle's classmates as well. The teachers were excited. If the plan accomplished nothing else, it had inspired a very positive parent-teacher partnership.

Some clear questions were emerging that Angie, Mike, and Michelle's parents highlighted together. How could Michelle's auditory sensitivities work in a group care setting? Why did she avoid her peers? Other questions lurked, but those seemed enough to contemplate for now. Everyone agreed to watch Michelle's progress and revisit these questions later.

Over the course of the week, Michelle's behavior changed dramatically. She stopped crying completely. Initially, Catherine stayed close while Michelle returned to her active exploration of the classroom. This allowed the teachers to observe Catherine's expertise. She spoke to Michelle in a very soft, calming voice and supported her at transition times by singing some details of what was happening next. She helped Michelle settle into table activities by getting her comfortable on a chair and then pushing it all the way up to the table so Michelle was very snug and stable in her seat. At group times, she held Michelle on her lap, allowing her to move away when she got restless but keeping her near the action.

After a day or two, Catherine began to pull back, and Michelle began to explore more on her own. Angie and Mike provided a comfortable adult chair for Catherine, and she began to bring a book to read quietly by herself. The teachers began to take turns moving in and working with Michelle, just as they had seen Catherine do. Occasionally Michelle would look over to see that her mother was close by, but then she would return to her own activities. When teachers sang to her, she lit up and was far more responsive during transitions. As she began to bond with the teachers, she was more accepting of their support when they led her through the schedule of the day.

Now that they could share experience with Michelle, the teachers soon began to learn more about her. They noticed she had a tendency to move from activity to activity rather quickly and still avoided areas where other children were playing. She did not seem comfortable sitting still for any length of time unless pushed tight up to the table or sitting on a lap. But she seemed delighted to be at school.

At times she would catch quick glimpses of peers, and she was now quite relaxed with teachers if they joined in her self-initiated activities. Michelle learned the teachers' names and began to make simple requests of them. She stayed close by the action at large-group music time and was happy to sit and eat snack when teachers remembered to push her seat in close to the table. The teachers started singing more—all the transitions were announced with song. Interestingly enough, all the children became more responsive.

The other children were noticing how much happier Michelle was. They said things like "Look, Michelle's not crying anymore!" They were interested in this new classmate who seemed more ready to join the group. Seeing her relax clearly helped them to relax. The teachers, students, Michelle, and Catherine (still in the corner with her book) were all feeling more relaxed and excited by the changes.

After five class sessions, the teachers and Michelle's parents decided that Catherine would stay one more day and would then try to stage a separation. They considered breaking the day into two parts when Catherine first left the classroom, so they could reunite during yard time if Michelle became overwhelmed again. Everyone decided to play that by ear. Catherine would make sure to be available in the building during yard time, and the teachers could call her in if things began to get unmanageable. Everyone knew that Michelle might cry, but with a positive impression of school in place, they accepted that possibility as healthy.

The decision yielded success. Michelle did miss her mother and showed some distress. But it was much more minor and short-lived than before. And she let the teachers comfort her. When something upset her, she reached up and allowed them to rock and talk to her in the soothing, melodic tone of voice they had learned from Catherine. The other children became invested in getting tissues for Michelle when she cried and celebrating when she became calm and stayed with the group. There was a palpable feeling of empowerment for all.

Angie and Mike still had questions regarding Michelle's auditory sensitivity, communication style, social engagement abilities, and emotional readiness to separate from her parents. They knew they would need to return to them soon, but for now they agreed to take things a step at a time and gather more information while building relationships in the classroom with all the children. But they did take a moment to come up with some simple goals and strategies (note how these goals incorporate the sequence of functional emotional milestones):

Goal:
   Michelle will say good-bye to her parents and get comfort from the teachers daily. When she needs to cry, she will see the teachers as her helpers and work through her upset in a reasonable amount of time.
Strategies:
   1) Make a small photo album with pictures of Michelle's whole family so she can look at it for comfort. Make a similar album for all the children.
   2) Post a picture schedule of the day, ending with a picture of the children reuniting with their parents—this will also be helpful to all the children.
   3) Teachers will sing to Michelle frequently. They will get down to her level and use a very soothing voice to calm her.

Goal:
   Michelle will begin to see school as a place she wants to be! Her anxiety about coming to school will decrease. She will begin to feel more comfortable around her peers.
Strategies:
   1) Teachers will help peers understand that Michelle's ears hurt when things get too loud.
   2) Teachers will give peers helper roles in getting a tissue or helping to sing a soothing song when Michelle is upset.
   3) Teachers will encourage simple social interactions when peers are close—for example, children will be encouraged to pass their own snack around the table to one another. Michelle will be encouraged to ask for what she wants and offer food to children sitting next to her.

Danny did not require such immediate and detailed planning. But Angie and Mike still felt they needed to try a few things to help him succeed in their class. First, one of them would make a point of greeting Danny at the door and giving him a big hug. This would help them make sure to get off to a positive start together. That would be a big improvement over connecting with Danny for the first time when he was in trouble. It also would give him some of the strong physical contact he seemed to crave. Second, as long as a teacher was greeting him, why not help steer him to the manipulative table and play with him for a few minutes? This would help Danny get and stay organized around his favorite activity, give him the companionship that he sought out, and also help teachers support him if other children came over and wanted to play. It might also give the teachers a chance to prevent and redirect aggression before, rather than after, the fact. Finally, they decided, they would remove Danny from play if he did act aggressively toward other children, but they would give him a quick, one-sentence verbal limit and focus the bulk of their attention on helping him calm his body down.

. . .

While these strategies or plans for Michelle or Danny might qualify as therapeutic intervention, the teachers are not even thinking along those lines. These are just universal responses that inclusive, relationship-based teachers make for each child. If Michelle or Danny's challenges grow larger over time, these early interactions will leave them well prepared to provide further support.

The main point is that the teachers haven't rushed to diagnose the children, and they haven't raised questions about development too early. Nevertheless, they haven't been idle in supporting the children's strengths, preferences, and challenges from the start. They don't need to know everything before they try something.

Working with Parents—Building Trust, Communicating Honestly

Michelle had presented Angie and Mike with an unusual need to collaborate closely with her family in the first weeks of school. The results had been both satisfying and effective. Angie and Mike knew that they needed to communicate clearly, honestly, and regularly with Danny's parents as well. They recognized that they were still in the relationship-building process with both Danny and his parents and that they did not have enough information to address Danny's entire profile. But as they did with all their families, they made sure to give Danny's parents a few details about Danny's personality and activities, both what he enjoyed and what was hard for him every day at drop-off or pickup time. When they could, they communicated through e-mails. And as Danny began to struggle, they made a point of framing the issue clearly, being honest with their reportage, and sticking to facts and questions for now, rather than trying to explain what was going on.

They also made a point of learning more from Danny's parents about what Danny did and how he acted in other settings. Because doing so required time, they took the lead in setting up systems to communicate more often than they did with some other families: they talked on the phone and e-mailed back and forth once a week.

In late September, Danny's mother had pulled Mike aside at pickup time. "I know you've been telling me about his hitting. But I just saw it for the first time. He grabbed that little boy over there for no reason and just clobbered him on the top of the head. I'm really concerned. I feel awful for that poor little boy. Do you think I should call his mother?"

Mike noticed that Danny had his face buried in his mother's shoulder. "Let's talk on the phone when you get home. We can think that part through together, and then maybe we can make a time to sit down and have a thorough talk."

"Okay," Martha replied, looking down at the ground and pursing her lips. It was hard for Mike to tell if she liked the idea.

"But," Martha said, looking up, "when he hits like that, do you tell him it's not okay and have him apologize? I've just never seen him act like that and I . . . I don't want my child to be a bully." Her eyes were clouding up with tears.

Mike was torn. Which angle to address first—Danny's behavior? His status with the group? The teachers' response and the safety of the classroom? Danny's mother's obvious distress? Mike knew that Danny was well aware of his challenges, and he was reluctant to discuss much in Danny's presence.

Mike decided to comfort Martha first. This was similar to how he supported children when they were having strong feelings. "It's very hard to see your child hit another," he said. "I know how you feel. Let me just assure you for now that we're supervising closely, and we've found a few ways to work with Danny that seem to help. And when he forgets to keep his classmates safe, we definitely stop the action and take care of everyone. Let me make a suggestion. Take Danny home and get him down for his nap. Then call me. We can talk as much as you want without interruptions, and we can do it today."

"Okay," Martha said. "Yes, I'd like to talk in confidence."

During the follow-up conversation, Mike suggested that Danny's parents and teachers sit down together for a meeting. At that meeting, Danny's father told the teachers, "He gets mad at his older brother and hauls off on him once in a while. But he's not wound up and aggressive all the time at home. He loves to play with all of us, and he usually is just fine. He does like to wrestle with me and his brother, but he never hits unless he's really mad. Lots of times he just loves to build with Duplos or blocks or color from a coloring book. He's a very happy, calm child at home. Our main concern is how hard he is to understand."

"When I'm with him," Danny's mother added, "I don't let him get away with anything. If he gets too hyper or if he hits his brother, he gets a time-out. I know you do a good job of letting kids do their own thing and helping them learn to solve problems, but Danny needs to know he can't get away with hitting his friends."

Angie and Mike came away from this meeting with several important insights. First, they learned that Danny was calmer and more organized in the home setting than at school. Second, they realized that Danny's parents were aware that the parent and teacher perspectives differed in some significant ways for their child. And most of all, they realized it was time to organize their knowledge about Danny and prepare to make a more detailed plan.

. . .

In this chapter, you have read how relationship-based inclusion teachers begin to engage with children and parents from the very start of their partnership. You explored the importance of both playing with and observing children. You learned how teachers focus on children's strengths, preferences, and sensory profiles to get to know them from the ground up. And you saw how even in the earliest stages of engaging, teachers must begin to note questions and challenges and sometimes even jump right into planning. In the next chapter, you will explore how continued challenges in children inspire teachers to create more organized and detailed plans and put them into action.

Chapter 6

Reflect-Plan: Putting Understanding into Action

Classroom life settled down considerably after her mother began dropping Michelle off again. By mid-November, Michelle occasionally had good-bye tears. But they were fairly short-lived and managed with a soothing back rub or a hug, accompanied by gentle, musical, comforting words from her teachers. The teachers began to see more of the child her parents knew at home. She sang and talked to herself as she shimmied in and out of dress-up clothes. She stacked plates in the house corner and sometimes put pretend food on them. She enjoyed climbing and sliding on the classroom climbing structure. She piled letter shapes into a play purse and laid them out on a blanket. Sometimes she would allow a teacher and even another child to join her. But she always wandered off after a few minutes, and she still did not make eye contact or communicate verbally.

The teachers celebrated her successful separation process and beginnings of peer contact. Despite the improvement, they continued to notice other challenges they wanted to understand better. Whenever they could, they took a moment in the classroom to write down some anecdotes and questions about her behavior.

Angie's and Mike's first attempts at helping Danny get organized in the classroom and control his aggression had also shown some signs of success. With a teacher's support, Danny could work for a few minutes at a time on building, and he even had some calm, positive play experiences with peers. He still showed great interest in playing with friends and often shared toys on his own. He had begun to seek out two or three boys who shared his interest in cars and movies. They sometimes even had short conversations about block building. But Danny was still dumping toys and pushing, head-butting, or hitting children at least once a day. And when teachers did not provide one-on-one support, Danny was becoming more overstimulated and less organized. He yelled and wiggled his way through group times and snacktime. He ran around the room, pulling books off the shelf, while the teachers tried to help children put on their coats to go outside. In fact, Danny had begun running around the room a lot. He seemed to be preoccupied with racing around the same circuit between the tables, holding his arms out and hitting other children or knocking things off the shelf as he passed by. He had also discovered the play pots and pans in the house corner, which he banged together as he moved in a circle through the room.

Angie and Mike were feeling pressured. They were committed first and foremost to providing a physically and emotionally safe classroom. Danny seemed to challenge their abilities to provide this, despite some good thinking and responding. They felt stressed about this on the inside—Danny disrupted their confidence about being good teachers. But they were also beginning to feel pressure from the outside: other children, and their parents, were understandably becoming wary about Danny.

Mary, the mother of one of Danny's regular playmates, approached Angie at pickup time one day. "I need to talk to you about something," she said, sounding strained and urgent. "Luke has been coming home every day with a story of something Danny did to him at school. He says Danny pushes him or throws blocks at him. And I just saw Danny hit him over the head with a plastic shovel. That kid is out of control!"

Angie wanted to defend Danny and Luke and Danny's budding friendship. But she knew she had to first address Mary's concern so that Mary felt respected and acknowledged.

"It is true that Luke has been on the receiving end of some unpleasant incidents. We are very aware of it. We've had several talks with the director about what to do about it. The most important thing to us is that every child feels safe. I know Danny's parents feel terrible about his aggression and want it to stop as much as you do. The thing is, Danny doesn't strike out in anger. It seems to happen when he is having fun with Luke and just gets so excited. His body gets out of control. He really cares about Luke. And Luke is really drawn to Danny. But that doesn't mean Luke should have to deal with being physically hurt."

"Well, I'm glad to hear you think it is a problem too. I don't know if he gets excited or what, but whatever the reason, I want him to stop hitting my son. If Luke likes him, I don't want to tell him to stay away from him, but I will if this doesn't change. If you're working on it, I feel better. But if it goes on, well, maybe I'll talk to the director."

"Thanks, Mary. I appreciate that," Angie replied. "And who knows?—the boys may end up being good friends. I've seen many a three-year-old friendship start from a bumpier beginning than this."

• • •

Sometimes children who really enjoy each other have the most conflict. Cooperating with another person is complicated, and friendship is even more complicated. The teacher can provide a safe container until children learn how to calm themselves and gain problem-solving skills.

· · ·

As we discussed in the previous chapter, Angie and Mike realized that they had to put together some sort of action plan quickly to support both Michelle and Danny in the first weeks of school. They were able to respond even while getting to know them. But at this point in the year, they used their experience and insight to recognize that it was time to set up a more thorough plan that would draw from clear, specific goals and strategies and help Danny and Michelle meet them. And they knew that the first step in the process would be to organize and consider what they had learned so far.

Reflect—Organizing Knowledge

Teachers learn to do a lot of reflecting while they engage with children. Reflection is one of the thousands of things, along with bathroom trips, curriculum ideas, food allergies, timely communication, and schedules that you must keep in mind at the same time. Somehow, you are able to gather observations, knowledge, and insight while juggling everything else. Researcher

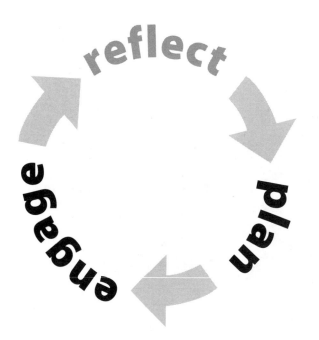

The *Engage-Reflect-Plan* cycle from the Reflect stage: As you reflect, you begin to plan and continue to engage with children.

Donald Schön (1983, 49), in his influential book *The Reflective Practitioner*, calls this "reflection in action," a kind of knowing that happens even though you sometimes don't notice it.

But there comes a time with many children in your care when you need to flesh out and organize your observations, knowledge, and questions. Perhaps it happens when you plan parent-teacher conferences, complete required ratings scales for each child, or prepare a child to move to a new school in a new town. For many children like Michelle and Danny, teachers feel the need to reflect in-depth to better address challenges. Reflecting acts as the bridge between engaging and planning—building a relationship and getting to know each child as an individual and then coming up with goals and strategies for support. A good plan of action requires careful reflection in order to work.

For people who work in the public sector or other settings in which some kind of written documentation of children's progress is required, reflection can work to support your mandatory record keeping. In the state of California, for example, teachers in state programs are now required to complete a developmental ratings profile for each child every six months. The ratings profile is supposed to be backed up with documentation. The kind of documentation teachers collect and organize to complete the ratings profile is exactly the same kind of information you would use to organize your reflections:

- Naturalistic anecdotes—things you noticed and wrote down while the child was playing or quotes from the child.

- Observation notes—specific notes you made during a planned observation time.

- Drawings the child made.

- Photos of the child's work or the child engaged in an activity.

- Videos of the child engaged in play or activities.

Once you use the information you gathered about the child during your period of engaging to help you fill out the required ratings profile, you can then use the ratings profile as a piece of the information to help you reflect on the child. Ratings scales rarely offer a complete picture of a child, but they certainly help you organize some of what you know about her. And these ratings profiles or other required assessments or information you are required to complete will also be useful when you come to the planning stage of *Engage-Reflect-Plan.*

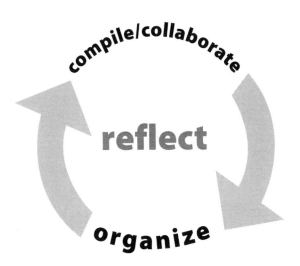

The Reflect subcycle: Reflecting requires an ongoing cycle of compiling/collaborating and organizing information and observations.

Finding ways to reflect is the first step toward an effective process for supporting challenging children. There are as many different methods and routines for reflecting and planning as there are teachers and programs. What are most important are to begin to think about reflection, in whatever form works for you, as a skill and a process, and then to practice reflecting. You may be able to use a computer to create virtual files that can be easily updated. You may prefer to put all your sticky notes and scratch paper into an actual paper file. You may be a person who can keep files in your head. But one way or another, it is crucial to make sure you process individual observations and knowledge as you go deeper into your work with a child. You will want to be able to have your carefully tended portrait of her at your fingertips to make the most of your process. And as you assemble this bigger picture, you can return to some of the basic principles of inclusion to guide your process:

- Focus on strengths.
- Think through questions in detail.
- Focus on what you can observe.
- Bodies matter! Focus on sensory and motor style.

Taking the time to reflect helps you organize your knowledge about a child and deepens your ability to individualize.

Focus on Strengths

When we think about children with challenges, it is natural to focus on the challenges. But as you read in chapter 5, effective planning draws on a child's strengths. Strengths and challenges are closely linked, and any good plan will use a child's strengths to help him work on challenges. But more importantly, focusing on a child's strengths will help you see beyond the struggles of the classroom and use a balanced image of the child to help him feel better. Teachers must always be ready to take the lead in creating a positive attitude and picture of a challenging child.

Think through Questions in Detail

Rather than just focusing on the most obviously challenging behavior, try to express your concerns or frustrations about a challenging child as a set of questions:

- What is this child trying to do?
- What seems to get in the way?
- When does this child seem happiest or most successful?
- When does the child struggle the most?

Teachers often have hunches about a child's challenges: *he just wants to get out of routines; he doesn't want to have to share; no one has ever said no to him; he's aggressive because he doesn't understand other children's intentions.* Oftentimes, there is more than a grain of truth in these hunches. But if you drift into assumptions or explanations, you miss the chance to reflect and learn. So it is very effective to learn to ask questions in a way that promotes further observation, exploration, and learning.

Focus on What You Can Observe

The habit of focusing on real, concrete observations is an important part of using questions instead of making assumptions. If we build lots of small images of a child's actual style and behavior into a big portrait, we learn more than if we speculate about a child's challenges or intentions. For instance, Angie jotted down these observations on a sticky note during class one morning:

> Danny walks on his toes until he reaches the sensory table. Puts his hands up, waves them over the water, then puts them down. Peers into the water for five seconds. Goes up on toes again, turns around, walks toward book corner. Stops and peers at two children looking at a book together. Says something quietly to himself and turns around.

It only took two minutes. But these notes were more useful than if she had thought to herself: *Danny wanders around most of the day trying to figure out what to do. He goes to places like the sensory table, then gets spooked by the sight of water. He can't figure out what to do with the water or the toys. He watches kids but doesn't want to make friends. He prefers to talk to himself.*

Bodies Matter! Focus on Sensory and Motor Style

The sensory integration lens is particularly important as you reflect. It is one very effective way to use observable facts to gain better understanding. As we have discussed, children's challenges are often rooted in the basics of what makes them over- or undersensitive, what kinds of input are easy or hard for them, what they strongly prefer, and what they avoid. How does a child respond to noise? How does he use his eyes? How does he like to move? What kinds of touch are comfortable? What kinds are uncomfortable? Does his engine run high? Does it run low? What kinds of physical experiences make him more comfortable, or receptive, or organized? What kinds of experiences have the opposite effect?

As you are beginning to observe in the narrative about Danny and Michelle, the many overlapping sights, sounds, textures, and experiences of an early childhood program are often extra hard for children with challenges. By paying close attention to how an individual child responds to the specific elements of your program, you will make the most of the reflection process.

When you capture this kind of detailed information about individual children, you begin to build an archive that can be useful to you both now and later. When children with similar strengths and challenges enter your program over the years, you can return to the knowledge, goals, and plans that worked in the past. In this way, each minute you can find to reflect on a child will serve as an investment in more efficient and effective practice later on.

One last point about reflection: there is a very fine line between using observations to understand the underlying causes of a child's challenges and making a lay diagnosis. Teachers can observe, but they should not and cannot diagnose. Teachers can use their concrete knowledge of a child to figure out if his sensitivity to being touched is one reason for his wariness with other children. But they cannot use the same information to determine that he has sensory integration dysfunction. They can deduce that a child's absence of language is playing a part in his difficulty with routines and expectations. But they cannot define the problem as an auditory processing disorder. Teachers can be relatively certain that a child's strong preference for playing with letters and numbers all day has something to do with his challenges with understanding social or emotional cues. But they can't know if a child has Asperger's syndrome. It can be very useful to look for underlying causes in your attempts to support children. But even your understanding of causes must be rooted in what you can see and what you know as a teacher. And your process of compiling knowledge and making sense of it should alert you to when you have reached the limits of your expertise and may benefit from outside support.

• • •

Angie and Mike kept building up their observations and questions about Michelle as she became more comfortable in the classroom. After a few weeks, they had many observations to review:

Michelle holds on to Catherine at good-bye time. Catherine says a clear good-bye and tells M. she will pick her up in the playground later. M. lets go and watches her mother leave. Then she runs to the door and calls out for Momma. They look at a brag book of family pictures together and M. points and names each of her family members.

Michelle does not stay in any area if it becomes busy with motion or sound from peers.

Michelle has been walking around reciting colors and letters. When we try to break in and ask her a question, she turns away and continues with her self-talking.

M. does not like to sit down and stay at circle time. She stands at the outskirts of the group, watching. She is not disruptive and seems interested in what we are doing.

Today M. sat down with the group at snacktime and named aloud all the family members who appear on her place mat.

Transitions in general are bumpy for M. A teacher needs to give her an individual warning and help her stay with the program. Sometimes she gets upset and cries as we physically help her to move along.

The teachers organized these snippets they had captured into a few categories of things they now knew about her:

Auditory sensitivities: Michelle still seems sensitive to noise from peers. She avoids noisy play spaces and is hard to reach in the often noisy outdoor play yard.

Avoidance of peers: Michelle is spending a lot of time in motion and seems to avoid places where peers congregate. She does not offer or receive much eye contact in general.

She accepts comfort and touch from the teachers but generally tends to avoid other children.

Communication style: Michelle labels objects and answers yes or no questions about things she wants or is very interested in. But she is not answering "wh" questions or asking any of her own. She does not put words together into phrases very often. She loves to have things sung to her. She does not initiate conversation with teachers or peers. Most of her talking is directed to herself.

Social style: Michelle does not offer or take in eye contact for more than a few seconds at a time. Her longest interactions are based on her own initiative around things she wants to do.

Attention: Michelle tends to do a lot of flitting around in the classroom. She stays longest when playing alone in quiet areas, engaged in self-chosen activities, when positioned at table, or when activities are structured, predictable, and repetitious.

Making a Plan

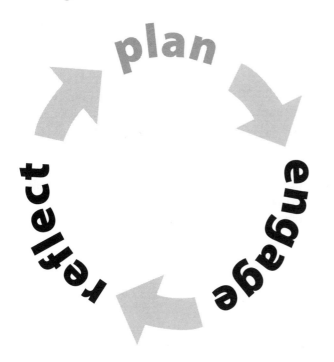

The *Engage-Reflect-Plan* cycle from the Plan stage: When you make plans, you implement them by engaging with children. You then reflect upon how your plans are working and return to the planning stage.

Reflecting involves developing a way of recording your observations and knowledge about an individual child that can be updated and revised throughout a child's time in your care. To turn these observations into a plan for more systematic support, the next step is to draw upon your organized insights and knowledge to create specific goals for the child and classroom strategies or practices to help him meet those goals. An effective plan is built on

- Strengths
- Goals
- Strategies
- Progress

Each of these elements plays a key role in offering support. Angie and Mike had already noted many strengths and questions for Danny and Michelle. They had jumped ahead to some goals for Michelle when they set up their plan to support Michelle's separation. These informal notes could now be incorporated into the first draft of their full plan. Now they were ready to think of goals and strategies.

Defining Appropriate Goals

When you first begin to observe and work with a child, the goals you set up may be vague or very detailed. They may not even be goals that you would expect a child to meet in a specific way. They might be more like the flip side of a child's strengths—things that don't come as naturally to him, or activities or experiences that he avoids. For Michelle, becoming comfortable with separation was clearly the first goal. The teachers didn't have a plan yet. It was simply obvious that they needed to get started on that kind of support right away. We saw in chapter 5 how Angie and Mike turned their main goal into smaller, more specific objectives.

When you decide to make a plan, the first step is to use your observations and reflections to choose goals that are developmentally and temperamentally appropriate and that meet the child's own individual needs. You must then weigh them carefully to choose the most important ones.

Of course, as with all the steps in this process, you won't get a perfect recipe at the start. It is always necessary to revisit and adjust a plan as it evolves. (We have more to say about monitoring and updating in the next chapter.) But at the same time, you do want to choose goals that will flow naturally into strategies.

• • •

The Plan sub-cycle: Planning requires an ongoing cycle of goals and strategies informing each other.

Angie and Mike sat down together to write up their first draft of a Strengths, Goals, Strategies, and Progress (SGSP) document for Danny. They began by formalizing the strengths and questions they had noted so far. Next, they came up with two goals:

Strengths and Interests:

Able to focus on activities and organizes long enough to create something.

Good receptive language skills.

Very connected with children. Has good relational capacity.

Can be very affectionate.

He is very appealing to a wide spectrum of kids in the classroom—potential leadership skills.

Likes dramatic themes from movies and understands lots of pretend concepts.

Questions/Challenges:

Aggression—pushing, hitting, head-butting.

Throwing & dumping, crashing.

Runs in a circuit around room frequently.

Becomes disorganized and overstimulated easily—almost always over-stimulated and often aggressive when he comes in contact with others.

Likes heavy touch, weight?

Pervasive reliance on teachers' bodies for holding, crashing, pushing.

Requires close supervision.

High need to seek out sensory input—contact from others.

Defensive or sensitive or overstimulated to some sensory input.

Very hard-to-understand speech. Reluctant to use language with peers.

Goals:

Danny will increase his ability to maintain a comfortable level of arousal and organization in the classroom. He will choose 3-5 activities during open choice and stick with them through 3-5 steps. He will learn to choose a new activity when he finishes with a previous activity.

Danny will continue to form positive relationships with peers. He will increase his ability to play and to play with friends for five minutes at a time. He will replace physical aggression with words.

This list did not cover everything that the teachers felt was challenging for Danny or that they would have liked to support. It consisted of the two main goals that they felt should make up the first part of the process. Part of the key to making appropriate goals is to think of them as cumulative. That is, children must master the most basic goals first before they can make progress on more detailed, mature, or complex goals. Recall the ideas behind the DIR functional emotional milestones—each milestone is built on the ones beneath it (Greenspan and Wieder 1998). A child who has not mastered milestone 1, self-regulation, may not be ready to benefit from goals around milestone 3, two-way communication. Goals should focus on helping children master the simplest, most fundamental developmental milestones.

The functional emotional milestones can seem a little overwhelming at first. But we have found that like Piaget's cumulative stages of cognitive development (1971), they offer a template for understanding individual children's needs that becomes easier to understand as you use it.

Notice that each goal is stated very broadly at first. One goal addresses the big question of arousal and organization. The other goal addresses the issue of positive relationships with peers. After the main theme, each goal has more detailed objectives that lay out exactly what Danny will be able to do to show improvement for the basic goal. This approach, modeled in part after school district Individualized Education Programs (IEPs) and Individualized Family Service Plans (IFSPs), makes for an effective flow from general to specific. It is important to know what the big goals are but also how they might translate into specific improvements in capacities and behavior. This process also helps teachers turn broad goals into specific teaching strategies, which we will look at next.

Building strengths, challenges, and questions into goals for a child can be done in any number of ways. You need not devote a great deal of time to writing up anything formal. You must learn to adapt the basic idea to your style of learning and thinking and to the structure of your work environment. Remember, individualizing applies to teachers and programs as well as to children and families. Since Angie and Mike had hit the ground running with Michelle, their thinking was farther along when they decided to make a comprehensive plan. So when they wrote the first draft of an SGSP for Michelle, they already had a lot of their plan in place:

Strengths and Interests:

Excellent memory for letters, numbers, colors, and music.

Very connected with family.

Strong will.

Loves to climb, slide, run, and dance.

Good with puzzles.

Likes play that is very organized and predictable, i.e., putting on and taking off dress-up clothes.

Preferences:

Drawn to letters at playdough, manipulative or art tables (less so in books or stories).

More responsive when things are sung to her.

Prefers to play one-on-one with teachers, avoids peers unless things are very structured and/or predictable.

Does not respond well to someone speaking a lot of words at once to her.

Stays longest at tabletop activities when her body is very clearly anchored.

Challenges:

Michelle does not stay with social interactions very long in general.

M. avoids peers unless the activity is structured and predictable. She often leaves play areas when peers join her.

M.'s language development is very tied to getting her needs met, labeling things, and answering simple yes and no questions. She is not yet speaking in phrases, initiating interactive conversations, asking or answering "wh" questions.

M. tends to wander and move from activity to activity unless she gets help to physically settle her body.

Michelle is sensitive to sound.

Questions:

What is making back-and-forth social interaction difficult for Michelle?

What makes Michelle avoid peer contact?

Do we have an accurate picture of Michelle's language development? Is her language development where it should be? Is she having trouble understanding what is being said to her?

Goals:

Michelle will engage in more back-and-forth interactions that last longer with teachers and peers.

Michelle will learn the names of her classmates and feel more comfortable interacting with them in general.

Michelle will improve her ability to take in what is said to her and respond with more complex language. She will learn to ask and answer "wh" questions.

Michelle will move through the classroom routines more smoothly in general.

The idea of adults articulating goals for children is complicated. In play-based preschool models, we hold in very high esteem the idea of the child as the agent of her own development. If we let children explore, child development theories suggest, they will find their own goals and strategies to grow. Many people argue that what children need most from adults is time and space to develop their own inner lives and personalities. The idea of adults determining what a child should work on and how a child should work on it can feel like a departure from these important values. Teachers, administrators, and parents in early childhood programs often wonder why they should dissect and analyze children and decide what children should work on, rather than just love and respect them and give them time and space.

It is true that teachers take on a great responsibility when we decide on goals for children. You have to be very careful not to impose your values, agenda, or especially assumptions. But in our experience, identifying goals and strategies and helping children to meet them can be a way of honoring and promoting their independence, uniqueness, and initiative. Goals and strategies can help children feel more competent and fulfilled, but more important, they can help children meet their own desires and initiatives and feel recognized and respected by the adults in their lives. We make plans for the children in our care, *and* we give them time and space to construct their own worlds. This is but one of the many cycles that must link together, rather than work in opposition, in both basic best early childhood education practices and inclusion.

A careful process of reflection is the key to making goals that respond to children's authentic needs. Appropriate and effective goals come from teachers' detailed and respectful collection of anecdotes and questions about individual children. Insights from and collaboration with families is key in the process as well. When teachers take care to develop a detailed, rich picture of a child, one that places equal emphasis on a child's strengths and challenges, the goals they envision for the child come from the unique needs of that child herself and consistently address what the child herself is trying to achieve.

Developing Strategies—Using Strengths to Address Goals

Danny's teachers felt confident that they had chosen the two most basic and important goals for the start of their support plan. Now they had to look deeper into their observations and knowledge to come up with strategies for helping Danny move toward them. Just as their detailed goals had come directly out of their observations, the strategies could come directly out of goals. For example, for goal number one . . .

Danny will increase his ability to maintain a comfortable level of arousal and organization in the classroom. He will choose 3–5 activities during open choice, and stick with them through 3–5 steps. He will learn to choose a new activity when he finishes with a previous activity.

... the teachers came up with these strategies:

Strategies:

Teachers will work with parents to develop a sensory diet of activities to help Danny achieve a more comfortable level of arousal and organization over time.

Teachers will use facilitated large-motor and dramatic play to provide Danny with opportunities to explore his interest in crashing, hugging, squeezing, and other forms of deep contact.

Teachers will experiment with heavy lifting, swinging, hanging from monkey bars.

One teacher will help organize an activity around his motor preferences one time per day.

Teachers will create a choice chart of activities.

One teacher will try to greet Danny each morning with a big hug and go straight into making a choice from the chart. Danny will pick the tile from the chart that matches the activity he wants to do and put it on the space labeled "I choose . . ."

One teacher will accompany him to his choice and help him break the activity down into steps and stick with the activity through 3-5 steps.

When Danny appears finished, a teacher will help him move the activity tile into the envelope marked DONE and choose another. One teacher per day will follow this process through at least two choices.

Teachers will develop the futon in the book corner as a calming corner for Danny to learn to take a break.

Teachers will help Danny pick out some favorite books and toys to stock the corner. Teachers will help Danny recognize when his engine can use breaks in the calming corner and when his engine feels ready for more play.

Teachers will model the idea of breaks in general and possibly help him and one or two friends take breaks outside the classroom to do gross-motor or focused activities together.

• • •

· · ·

Mary Sue Williams and Sherry Shellenberger's *How Does Your Engine Run? A Leader's Guide to the Alert Program for Self-Regulation* (1996) describes a program in which children are taught to think of themselves as cars with engines. Sometimes those engines can be running too fast, making it hard to control. Other times they can be sluggish and slow. At their best, the engines run "just right," giving children the right amount of momentum to focus their attention on what they want to do.

The program suggests activities the authors call *engine changers,* which support regulation (or getting the engine "just right" for the job). As part of the program, children learn about their own sensory profiles. The program is designed for children who are functionally eight years or above, but many early childhood professionals (including the teachers at The Little School) are adapting the program for preschoolers. Teachers are encouraged to model self-reflection about their own engine and engine changers in order to introduce the concepts. Next, teachers point out to children what seems to help the them feel "just right" as they go about the different parts of their day. The authors caution against primarily pointing out engines that are running too fast or too slow. This negative approach impedes the children's ability to incorporate the metaphor in a useful way.

These strategies flowed from goals and observations. More important, they used Danny's strengths and preferences to help him work toward goals. Although we have discussed this earlier, we mention it again precisely because it is not always obvious. Goals often revolve around helping a child do more of what he avoids or dislikes or otherwise expanding his tolerance or interest in activities or relationships. So it is natural to want to convince a child to take a break from activities he may repeat or to just try something new and learn to feel comfortable with it. And in a carefully designed support plan, these threads play an important role.

It is important to remember that children choose things for reasons. Even when you want them to broaden their experiences or grow, you must start with the things they *can* do or *choose* to do. Then you help them build outward from that strong center. Danny's teachers combined several useful observations: he liked to hug and crash, he frequently took breaks, and he trusted the teachers as supports. They used these to think about how to make it possible for him to begin to stretch his ability to interact with people a little.

Take note of a few other characteristics of the strategies. First, the teachers made a point of being specific. How many teachers will do what for how long and for how many times? Again, your first attempt at these specifics may not be perfect. You have to try strategies in the classroom to see how well they will work. But it is important to think of as many details as possible so that

A calming corner and/or a calming box are two great classroom regulation tools. A child can take a calming box to any quiet place in the classroom or playground. A calming corner can be as simple as a cushion in a corner. A half curtain to cut down the stimulation is a nice added touch. In this calming box, the teacher has included (clockwise from the top): a book to look at, an unlit candle to blow out, pipe cleaner and beads for beading, a textured ball to squeeze, a balloon to blow (or try to), a suggestion to get a teacher or friend to rub your back, markers and paper for drawing, and an elastic fabric for stretching. By having a variety of options, children learn what in particular helps calm them down.

you can remember and carry out plans amid the countless other priorities and duties you must remember when you are with children. Thinking of specifics also helps you assess how to adjust a plan, since you can easily revise numbers. Second, they are thinking from the sensory perspective for both children. The goals focus on the simplest milestones for both children—self-regulating and relating. These are the basic capacities described in the DIR milestones. The strategies focus on sensory and motor experiences that will help Danny achieve the basic needs and become more able to move on to emotional, social, and cognitive progress.

It is just as important that Danny's teachers have created a strategy that can be achieved within a typical early childhood education classroom. Only one teacher will make a point of doing some focused work with Danny for a few minutes each day. If the opportunity arises to work with him for a longer stretch of time or to work with him three or four times in a single day, all the better. But in the planning stage, you want to take care not to overwhelm yourself with ambitious or cumbersome strategies. Just as children need to break down tasks into achievable steps, you must break down support plans into achievable steps. A steady string of small successes can add up to great progress, but a large and complicated first step can stall the whole process. Finally, notice how Angie and Mike have folded some of their earlier, less formal plans for Danny into this more organized system. For both Danny and his teachers, this will provide a smooth transition into the plan and take advantage of what has already worked.

This child has chosen a small music box from his classroom's calming box. Next he chooses an unlit candle. The pretend activity of blowing the candle out encourages him to take deep breaths—one of the best regulating tools we have at our disposal.

Family Child Care Note

You might want to notice that this plan could easily be adapted to a home environment:

- Deep pressure can come from something as simple as a bear hug.
- Heavy lifting can be accomplished by the real work children love, such as carrying full laundry baskets or other items, moving chairs or tables or easels, carrying toys inside and out.
- Hanging a bar across a doorway just a few inches above child height allows a safe stretching experience.
- The choice chart can be as simple as pictures of activities drawn on construction paper and a stick-figure drawing of a child to put on the activity of choice.
- A calming corner can be any space that is clear and that is only used for calm times:

    - A cushion against the wall and one below it on the floor.
    - An area behind a chair near a wall.
    - A corner with a piece of furniture near to make a half nook.

- A refrigerator box reinforced with duct tape. Ours has lasted for years.
- To make it special, you can hang up a pretty piece of fabric; a box with magazine pictures of nature, a feather, and a candle to pretend to blow out; some picture books or a photo book from times together; a piece of soft fabric to hold or drape; a lavender eye pillow.

In our experience, using detailed observations to define appropriate goals and drawing strength-based strategies from those goals are the keys to successful support. In addition, you should think about the whole group and try to embed individual goals into group play.

Think about the Whole Group

A plan for an individual child is a kind of web woven from threads of observation, insight, and goals.

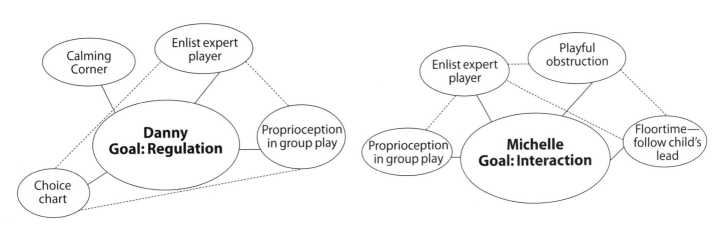

A web of strategies around a goal for Danny. The dashed lines show how strategies can be linked.

A web of strategies around a goal for Michelle. The dashed lines show how strategies can be linked.

Each plan for each child then becomes a thread in an even larger web of strengths, goals, and strategies for the entire group. At first, this can seem overwhelming. You do not want one child's challenges to have a negative impact on the group or the classroom environment. In the same vein, you do not want your focused attention on one child to leave other children underserved. When you have plans for several children, as is common with inclusion, you must figure out how to juggle all these plans at the same time.

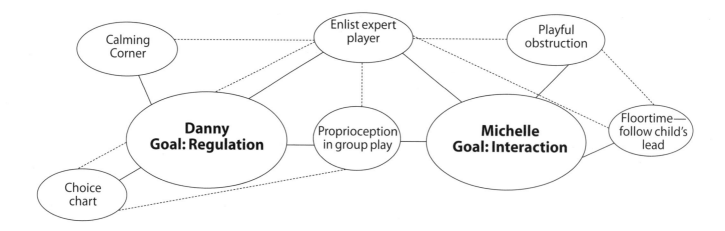

Common strategies can be merged to further goals for different children. Note how enlisting an expert player and using proprioception in group play can work at the same time for both children.

Keep in mind that what is good for one child is often good for the entire group. Goals for individual children often overlap. *Individual support creates community strength.* Many children in Angie's and Mike's class needed to take breaks in a calming corner, just like Danny. The quiet, singsong voice that captured Michelle's attention soothed and captured the attention of the entire group at transition times. In chapter 2, you read how important it is for the individual to bend to the community and vice versa. Part of what makes inclusion work so well is that the community and the individuals meet in the middle, and everyone benefits. Rather than pull teachers and children in different directions, goals for individual children can help bring a group together and support everyone's growth.

Here, a child's need to work on balance turns into activities that everyone can enjoy and benefit from.

Embed Individual Goals into Group Play

Classrooms are effective places for children with challenges to grow because they offer groups of peers a playful environment. As children have fun together, they can inspire each other to stretch their skills and preferences in ways that don't often work in therapeutic, one-on-one settings. This is one reason we stress that inclusion relies on a playful approach. This means that teachers should foster a curious, playful outlook. But more important, it means that whenever possible strategies should be placed in play curricula. While many children with special needs encounter obstacles to being playful, and some seem to need therapeutic intervention before they can know how to play, intervention must be playful and focused on play.

There are two reasons for this:

1. Children, even those who are struggling, respond to a positive, playful proposition more than to a businesslike workload of therapy. Play addresses goals without highlighting a child's differences to herself or her peers. A playful attitude is therapeutic.

2. Playful intervention for one child can attract many others, create chances for children to make connections, and benefit all children. Most of the goals and strategies that teachers choose for one child can help almost all the children in their care.

This is the core of inclusion education: *we are more alike than different*, even in the kind of support we need. Here are two examples that show how you can balance combining goals and strategies for two or more children and embedding individual goals into group play at the same time.

• • • •

Maddie, another child in Danny's class, had some physical motor delays. She had seen a physical therapist when she did not begin to walk at one year. She kept her arms up high in a guarded position and cried out often when children approached her. Like Danny, she seemed to have challenges settling into activities and playing comfortably with peers. But where Danny seemed to jump right into play and then become overloaded, Maddie huddled in corners and kept everyone at bay.

The teachers had developed some strategies for Maddie with help from her parents and physical therapist:

- Help her unlock her pelvis with leg stretching exercises.
- Help her relax with deep pressure and toning.
- Help her learn to cross her body midline with her arms and legs.

Angie and Mike had figured out how to add some imaginative practice to these physical experiences. They used a folding futon in the dramatic play area to pretend to turn children into waffles. Half a dozen children at a time would come hurrying over anytime one of the teachers sat by the futon and said, "I'm hungry! I need to make some waffles." In addition to Danny and Maddie, many children climbed into the futon, often in groups of three or four, to be pressed inside the cushions. Children like Michelle who did not like to get inside became involved by helping the teachers close the futon and press down. Michelle still benefited from the deep pressure.

"Mmm . . ." the teacher would say with glee after pressing for a few seconds, "I think my waffle is ready." Some children loved to have the teacher and the other cooks spread syrup on them by gently massaging their arms, trunks, and legs. Others liked to hold hands and conspire to run away while the teacher pretended to cry, "Oh! My waffles!"

• • • •

The deep proprioceptive contact, physical challenge, muscle and joint input, organizing script, facilitated cooperation, added pretend element, and use of affect and humor all addressed plans for all the children. But as far as the class was concerned, "Waffles" was just one of their favorite games.

• • • •

Michelle loved to pile hats on her head. At first, Angie and Mike tried to connect with her by piling hats on their heads. One day, as Angie read the book *Caps for Sale* by Esphyr Slobodkina to a group of children, a lightbulb went on over her head. These two activities could be linked to help Michelle bond with her peers. She gathered up as many floppy hats as she could find. The next morning, she put them out in a basket in the house corner, where Michelle liked to play. When a child brought *Caps for Sale* to her to read, Angie led her to the house corner. As she read, she piled the hats on her head.

The children took the cue immediately. They became the monkeys and gleefully stole the hats when the monkeys appeared in the book. Angie used all her acting skills to display the peddler's anger at the monkeys when they refused to return the hats. The children squealed with delight at the chance to wield power over their teacher. And there, once again, the gleam appeared in Michelle's eye. She didn't join in on the first day. But Angie kept at it for several sessions. By the third or fourth time, Michelle was standing with her friends for a moment here or there, jumping up and down and squealing "Tzz! Tzz! Tzz!"

These embedded therapeutic goals had value for the entire group. They provided a script and props for developing interactive and symbolic play skills. And Danny and Michelle benefited from receiving goals and strategies inside group play.

Recommending Outside Support

The question of whether or not a child should be assessed by a practitioner with specialized expertise is very complicated. It draws teachers into the delicate area of raising timely questions without making assumptions or diagnoses. Sometimes a child is struggling and cannot find a way to thrive in a program. Sometimes a child will not reach certain very clear developmental milestones—failing to speak at all by age two and a half, for example. In these cases, it might seem as if everyone would agree that intervention would help. But for most children, there is no absolute moment when outside support is called for. A good early childhood program tries to advocate and promote each child's uniqueness. There are risks in looking at each child as a possible case for intervention. On the other hand, for children who can feel and do much better with early support, teachers and parents want to act quickly. It is impossible to balance these two considerations perfectly.

• • •

Angie and Mike asked Michelle's parents to meet with them to discuss their plan. They wanted Scott's and Catherine's expertise on their child to be part of shaping their work with her at school. The last time they had met, they spent most of the time discussing Michelle's life outside of school and listening to her parent's knowledge of her. This next meeting would focus more on Angie's and Mike's observations. Needless to say, Catherine and Scott seemed nervous. The teachers were nervous as well.

Before the meeting, the teachers reminded each other that they wanted to lead with clear information that would support their partnership with Michelle's parents. This information would come in two distinct parts: the teachers' concrete observations and questions, and, if her parents were interested, information about area specialists who would know more about Michelle's development than the teachers.

Angie and Mike made a point of starting the meeting by celebrating Michelle's new ability to stay happily at school without her mother. Michelle had clearly met the first, most important goal with flying colors. Michelle's parents told of how glad they were to be able to drive up to the building and have no trouble getting Michelle out of the car. She had stopped covering her ears protectively and was more relaxed in general.

"We thought she was ready for school," Catherine said, "but then we started thinking we had made a big mistake. We're just so glad that it seems like it will all work out."

"We really want to thank you for working so hard," Scott added.

The teachers could truly respond by thanking Michelle's parents in kind for helping them.

"We could not have done it without your help," Mike said.

This was not just idle talk. It was Scott's and Catherine's information about Michelle's strengths and interests and Catherine's direct assistance in the classroom that had allowed the teachers to find a plan that had worked.

That part of the conference was easy and enjoyable. The teachers were much more nervous about the next part. Sharing developmental concerns is never easy. We all naturally fear telling parents there might be something wrong with their child.

Angie took a deep breath. "So now we want to use the great support and insight you have shown us to think up some next steps. We've been keeping some notes and observations on Michelle that we want to share."

They gave out copies of their notes and went over them together. Scott and Catherine seemed sobered to see so many questions and challenges on paper, but to the teachers' relief, they did not challenge the picture of Michelle it suggested.

"Well," Scott said, "she definitely connects with us more at home than what you see here. But we've been a little worried ourselves."

"Spending all that time in the classroom," Catherine added, "you were both real honest with me about how her way of playing stood out from some of the other kids. And I couldn't help notice that snacktime and music time were tricky for her."

"So," Scott asked, "what are you recommending?"

"As you can see from our notes," Mike continued, grateful that Michelle's parents were facing questions head on, "we've written up some goals. We think we can build teaching activities and ideas that will help her move closer to her goals. But we also have some fairly significant questions. We're not sure we see her making basic connections, getting into routines, learning to talk and play with others. Since we all seem to share those questions, we wanted to be clear with you that as teachers, we can only provide certain pieces of the answers."

"We've been worried about it," Catherine replied, her eyes tearing up. "We've been meaning to ask you."

"I mean," Scott said, looking at the ground, "we're new to this. We don't know a lot about kids this age, or even what we're supposed to be doing at home. Maybe we haven't given her all the experiences she needs."

"In our experience," Angie continued, "what you do or don't do as parents isn't the main issue. All children develop from the top down. That is, they learn from the experiences they have, the messages people give them, and so on. But in our experience, they also develop from the bottom up—from their own internal wiring. Making eye contact, responding to language, getting into early play with peers, taking interest in group activities—these are things that we see children naturally developing in general, from the bottom up."

"Are you saying that you think she's not normal?" Scott asked quietly.

"We don't know. And that's the most important thing that stands out to us. It seems like you have similar questions."

"Well," Catherine said, "we have been wondering about her language. And I was surprised in the classroom. The other kids seemed to notice each other a lot more."

"It seems like a good time to get some more information about how she is developing. We do have some lists of specialists we can share with you," Mike replied.

There was a long silence.

"Well," Scott said finally, "I'm not sure what to say. But I think we want to do everything we can to help her be successful at school."

. . .

Parents go through a very intense emotional journey in discovering that their child has developmental challenges. This emotional journey must be acknowledged and respected. There is no way to hurry someone through it. Sometimes, as we saw with Michelle's parents, suggesting outside support gives voice to questions that parents have already asked themselves. Other times, parents need time to work through complicated feelings. (We explore the parents' journey more in chapter 11.)

It is important to remember that the decision to seek outside intervention is charged with emotions. We raise children in an isolated world in which parents often feel they have to do it all themselves. The thought of having a child evaluated for developmental differences can feel like a personal failure on the parents' part, the child's part, or both. At the very least, it can be frightening for parents to feel that they cannot give their child everything he might need. And the idea that a child is not typical, regardless of what a parent thinks or knows, is simply painful on its own.

Beyond that, parents have an understandable fear that once they step into the world of therapy, their child will be labeled and carry a stigma that separates him from his peers and makes him different in the eyes of children and adults everywhere. Finally, assessments and therapy require spending significant time and money, no small consideration in the delicate balance of contemporary lives.

Developing a Network of Support

Develop a network of support and build relationships with people and organizations serving families and children with special needs. Your key resources will be the regional agencies offering early childhood services for children under three and the local school district, which provides assessments for children over three. Learn how an assessment process is initiated so you can set the family on the right path. It is also useful to know private specialists who can either work with families or perhaps serve as free or low-cost resources to your program. These should include developmental pediatricians (a wonderful resource to be used as a starting point in determining a child's overall developmental profile), psychologists, speech and language therapists, occupational therapists, and physical therapists. You might also find some good resources at local universities. There may be parent support organizations in your area for families of children with special needs.

So keep these guidelines in mind when you consider offering resources for outside support:

- Be mindful of parents' emotional process in understanding that their child may have developmental challenges.
- Internally acknowledge your own fear and discomfort with the role of messenger.
- Ready yourself to support parents without taking their responses personally.
- Be honest about the limits of your own knowledge.
- Offer outside referrals as a choice, not as a condition or a command.

Deepening the Partnership with Families

Whether a child arrives in your program with identified special needs or questions arise after the child begins in your program, partnering with families can be one of the most complicated and intimidating aspects of inclusion. It is also the most important. Both teachers and families care deeply about helping children thrive. Both have expertise and perspectives that are crucial to supporting children successfully. And both teachers and families must work together in an atmosphere of trust and respect. So despite the charged feelings that everyone has around children's challenges, your positive and productive partnership with families is a crucial part of your plan for their children. In fact, inclusion is fundamentally about including all the important people in children's lives as much as it is about including all children.

Just as you read about the vital first step of building trust with children in the previous chapter, establishing a trusting relationship with their family is key. This is true whether or not you will ever have to raise concerns about their children. Recall some of the steps we described for showing children your trustworthiness:

- Observing and taking authentic interest.
- Getting to know each person as a unique individual.
- Listening and reflecting back what someone is saying, showing, or feeling.
- Using honest affect to create a sense of comfort and welcome.

This same list applies equally to your relationship with parents and families. But it can be challenging for many teachers. Many people in the field of early childhood education are more comfortable with children than adults. When questions or concerns arise about individual children, teachers and parents often have different perspectives. Janis Keyser, in her excellent book *From Parents to Partners* (2006), points out that both parents and teachers often feel a lack of respect from the world around them. Both have very difficult and isolated jobs. The understanding that we are all in this together can help us develop real empathy and affection for parents. We must try to take the lead in creating an environment in which different perspectives are viewed as positive, even necessary parts of the process.

It is also important to remember that parents can feel very confused and conflicted about their children's challenges. One moment they may feel that their child is struggling terribly and that immediate intervention is necessary. Days or even hours later, they may see a happier child whose strengths and struggles seem in healthy balance. So it is important not just to establish respectful trusting bonds with parents but to be sure that your individual relationship with each parent is developed to the point where each can hear your views, questions, or concerns about the child and will feel comfortable communicating as honestly with you.

Finding time to meet privately can be a major obstacle in family child care. If you want to talk with a parent about a child's challenges or suggest an assessment, do everything you can to make it a sit-down, hour-long meeting.

- Find a time when everyone can be present in a private space.

- Share e-mails or handwritten notes beforehand so that the parents know your observations and concerns and the importance of the meeting.

- Don't let parents push you into saying more than you want at drop-off and pickup. "We'll get the most out of it when we sit down and meet" should be your broken-record response.

- Make a plan for how you are all going to follow up: Another meeting? Written notes? Choose a method that works for the parent *and* for you.

- If you're not getting through to a parent on your own, find a resource person who can participate in the conversation. Is there city, state, or nonprofit support for early intervention, family child care, or families of children with disabilities? Their staff might help the parents understand.

- Make it clear that you like this child, see her strengths and progress, and are working hard with her. This will help you all through this challenging phase.

- See chapter 11 for more ideas.

• • •

Angie and Mike asked Danny's parents to meet with them in December to help put together their plan for Danny. As with Michelle, they knew they would need the expertise and collaboration of Danny's parents if their plan were to be successful. They were also aware from their communication with Danny's parents so far that the parents were worried about Danny's behavior and that they saw a somewhat different child at home. Despite lots of positive collaboration, Angie and Mike were aware that they did not see eye to eye with Danny's parents in many ways.

Angie and Mike had made a point of honestly sharing details of Danny's school experience with his parents from day one. They took care to show his parents that they recognized his strengths and to tell them about his positive and successful experiences, along with the challenging ones. They did not avoid being honest and open where Danny's overstimulation and aggression were concerned. When the bumping and hitting began happening on a daily basis, Angie and Mike began checking in with Danny's parents as often as they could, either at pickup time or via a short phone call or e-mail.

For this meeting, Angie and Mike could at least point to some success. Danny's aggression had decreased when a teacher worked closely with him, and with support he could stay calm for longer periods of time. They had some very detailed and organized observations and reflections, as well as the first draft of their plan. Although the teachers and parents did not completely agree in this case, Angie and Mike felt good about how they had laid the ground-work for a tricky meeting through careful relationship building and honest reporting. They had learned from past experience that they wanted to share any big surprises or the big problem or question before it was time to collabo-rate on an organized plan.

Sharing as much information as possible before the meeting was particu-larly important because today Angie and Mike wanted to be able to do a lot of listening. Although they had a lot they wanted to tell Danny's parents, they knew that they could not jump straight to their plan or ideas without honestly taking in what his parents had to say. Danny was different at home. His par-ents knew him better than anyone in the world. The teachers knew that the school's plan for Danny relied on his parents' point of view and their ideas as well as their support for whatever plan came out of the process.

Angie asked Danny's mother to start the meeting with her latest sense of how Danny was doing at home and at school.

"Well," Martha began, "at home he's doing much better. When I give him a time-out, he can calm down much faster. And he's starting to use more words. But I don't know about school. He's talking about children he likes, and when I talk to him about keeping them safe, he seems to get it. But I don't see him doing any better when I watch him here. It seems like he still pushes and hits everyone all the time."

Angie and Mike confirmed that Danny was still aggressive every day. They noted that he could play longer without head-butting, pushing, or hitting, and that he was doing much better with a teacher by his side to guide him. At this point, they went over their process to highlight what they had all observed and planned so far.

"We agree that Danny could use more support," the teachers concluded.

This gave Angie and Mike the chance to review their plan with Danny's parents. The strengths they had noted were very welcome at this point. The teachers could show Danny's parents details of what was going well and the connections between his strengths and his challenges. This helped them all see the big picture in a meaningful balance. Some of Danny's parents' ideas were already incorporated into the strategies, but Angie and Mike used this meeting to open up a more thorough, ongoing collaboration on goals.

Danny's parents brought up the question of limits again. "I don't know anything about the sensory diet," his father, Tony, said. "I don't know if that's right for Danny. At home, he needs limits."

Angie and Mike reassured Danny's parents that clear, consistent limits were a key part of the plan. They decided not to try too hard to describe the whole plan at this meeting. They made a note of the difference in perspectives and determined to try and listen respectfully to Danny's parents and learn what they could from their differing points of view about top-down limits versus more sensory-based, bottom-up strategies.

The teachers felt that Danny might benefit from therapeutic support. His difficulty with the classroom environment, his language, arousal, motor, and organization challenges, and the dramatic difference between how he behaved at home and at school suggested to them that their expertise as inclusion teachers might not provide all the understanding and responses Danny would need to thrive.

But the question of whether or not to recommend outside support for Danny was much more complicated than it had been for Michelle. In many ways, Danny was struggling harder than Michelle. But he also showed more basic language, interaction, and emotional reflection than Michelle. While they suspected that a speech and language therapist could support him in using language more effectively, and an occupational therapist might help him increase his ability to organize and regulate, they weren't sure he needed that kind of support to reach basic developmental milestones. They had worked with many children who settled into much more successful school lives after a few months or in their second year.

The teachers also respected the clear message of skepticism from his parents about supporting Danny by focusing on his internal temperament. His parents were honest about their feelings that the teachers should focus on behavior and limits. If Danny's parents were not ready even to consider the idea of therapeutic intervention, the teachers did not want to risk the basic parent-teacher partnership by pushing too hard too soon.

Angie and Mike had talked about this before the meeting. So they were able to sense that Danny's parents were not ready to address the question of development or outside support. They had decided in advance that should this be the case in the meeting, they would put that discussion on hold. For now, they would move forward with their own plans for support, and revisit both their plans and the question of intervention after a few more weeks. By then, the amount of progress Danny made (or did not make) would give them more information.

Angie and Mike had differing viewpoints from one another about the right balance where Danny was concerned. Mike leaned a little more toward Danny's parents' view. He felt that Danny was accustomed to adults setting clear verbal limits and giving him consequences when he lost control of his behavior. During one conversation, Mike confided in Angie that he had been a handful as a child. His parents were always angry at him, and his teachers had always described him as "smart, but rambunctious."

"I really needed limits," he told her. "And instead all I got was disapproval."

Angie agreed with Mike. She admitted that she could sometimes focus on problem solving and body strategies so much that she let things get out of hand. But she was still more inclined to focus on how guilty Danny seemed to feel when adults *did* set consequences when he was overloaded. She worried that the guilt and tension he felt over constant limits contributed to his becoming overwhelmed. And, she pointed out, they were both still concerned that Danny was seeking out their time and attention through these negative limits rather than developing his own initiative to play more successfully.

Angie had begun taking Danny out to the entryway with some friends, where they would lift and throw heavy cushions and crash into the couch. She felt that he seemed to be at his most relaxed and organized after these episodes. Mike agreed that the early attempts at finding a sensory diet for Danny were working. He just felt a little more strongly about removing Danny when he seemed to need a break and to be told "no."

Angie and Mike recognized that they had to find a way to reconcile the growing tension between their perspectives. They knew that they needed to figure out how to integrate them. They went out to a nearby café one night after work, hoping that a change of scenery would move their thinking forward. As they thought in a more relaxed setting, they began to see some creative ideas that had eluded them before.

First, they remembered some ways that expectations could be clearly laid out without using words or limits: they could choose materials that were more closed ended and suggestive, like simple board games, puzzles, or tools, like eyedroppers at the art table. These props suggested sequences and specific uses, which Danny seemed to like. Or they could add some patterns for building with the Legos. They could also keep the same materials for longer periods of time, adding just one or two elements at a time to make them more interesting or to advance the children's exploration. This would make the classroom more predictable and give Danny and his peers more ongoing definition and order.

Second, they could make their transitions and routines more explicit, challenging and engaging. Another teacher in the school was great at getting all the children involved at cleanup time by hiding different laminated shapes at different stations. She then gave each child a badge with one of the shapes on it and sent them off to find their jobs. When they did have to set limits after the fact, they could incorporate some body work, like wall push-ups. All of these techniques used ideas for outside definition and order but also helped kids find more organization and regulation on the inside.

They also thought about how to help Danny learn emotional regulation from limits and not just improve his behavior. (Remember, emotional regulation is seen as a fundamental milestone in the DIR framework.) Mike pointed out that he and Angie were often stressed by Danny's outbursts or aggression. When his tension went up, their tension went up. They realized as they talked that they could model calming when they set limits. They could show Danny with their affect how they expected him to regain emotional control. They could also use clear language with him to emphasize that he could play again when his body was feeling calmer, not just when he could keep the toys and his friends safe.

Angie and Mike each went home feeling much more relaxed and inspired. They both realized that by resolving their differing perspectives, they were moving into the next phase of their work with this class—reflecting on an existing plan and making necessary updates.

• • •

Inside/Outside

A debate—let's call it *inside/outside*—is common in inclusion programs. Some adults focus on the inside piece of the picture—the physical, sensory, cognitive, or emotional processes a child expresses as behavior. They feel that if adults can help a child feel more comfortable on the inside, then he will feel and act much more successfully. Others focus on the outside—the behavior of the child and the ways that adults respond, especially around expectations. If you make things clear, predictable, and orderly for children, this perspective suggests, they will feel better as a result.

It's easy for people to stake out these viewpoints as opposites: the inside camp thinks behavioral strategies are insensitive and neglect the roots of children's challenging behavior. The outside camp counters that its detractors create a vague and inconsistent atmosphere for children who need structure.

In our experience, however, successful inclusion requires seeing these two perspectives as linked, not as contradictions. Children need adults to help them become more comfortable with what they avoid and build self-knowledge and self-acceptance. And children need structure, limits, and order to help them meet outside expectations. But finding the right *balance* of inside strategies—sensory, physical, or emotional support—and outside strategies—organizing tools and expectations—is key to effective support.

In this chapter, you learned how you can build on your early engagement with children to make plans for support. You saw how lingering questions and challenges can inspire you to reflect on your knowledge about individual children by focusing on observable details and children's basic sensory profiles. You explored how this understanding can be turned into plans based on children's strengths and challenges. And you learned the process of setting up evolving goals and strategies to help children reach basic milestones. Finally, you considered some guidelines for when and how to recommend outside support and to continue supporting parents through this often difficult stage.

In the next chapter, you will read about how you can revisit and update these plans to keep pace with children's progress.

Chapter 7

What's Next?
Revisiting the Cycle

By late February, Angie and Mike had been following their plans for Michelle and Danny for almost two months. The winter holidays had made December rush by, and the process of working through the plan with Danny's parents and finalizing goals and strategies had taken longer than expected. But this was not unusual. As spring approached and Angie and Mike began to contemplate the last third of the school year, they felt their plans were starting to show some signs of success.

Danny was still making good progress in some ways. His speech was easier to understand, and he was expressing more of his strengths with concepts and imagination verbally. But much more than that, he wanted to use his words to connect with friends and get his needs met. He had developed friendships with two children, and he had been proud to get together with one of them for a play date in the park. Danny had learned to seek out the calming corner on his own to recharge several times a day. He asked for his choice chart and had become a pro at switching the activity tiles. He often followed his teachers' prompts to "stick with it for two more minutes" or "finish all the steps and then choose something else." And the frequency of his physical aggression had decreased significantly.

On the other hand, if a teacher was not nearby, Danny still became easily overstimulated. He could play independently with peers and materials for a few minutes, but then the needle just seemed to go into the red. He would push over block towers, crash into other children, or clap his hands over his ears and yell, "That's just great!"

The teachers had settled on a plan for removing him quickly but calmly. They used just a few words at a time to remind him of expectations and assure him that he was learning how to stay calm. And he was calming down faster and wanted to get back in the action.

Angie and Mike had a sense that Danny was accomplishing some goals from their plan while staying sort of stuck with others. Or more confusing, he was making some kinds of progress and staying stuck on many of the same goals. Despite their confidence in their plan, they realized it was time to revisit and revise.

Michelle, on the other hand, seemed to have reached a plateau. After her remarkable success with separation, she had learned to play happily in the classroom. She had begun to connect with her teachers, mostly through eye contact and parallel play. Sometimes she made the same fleeting connections with peers. But Michelle still preferred to spend most of her time on the margins of the classroom. She wandered in the house corner, gazing at pictures on the wall, or played in the sensory table with her back turned to the room. All the while, she kept up a quiet stream of talking directed at no one and imperceptible to anyone more than a few inches away.

Michelle's parents had accepted Angie's and Mike's advice to seek support from a therapist. At first, her parents felt that a speech pathologist would make the most sense. Angie and Mike had gently suggested that because questions about Michelle cut across several kinds of development, they might use the services of the public school district's early intervention unit. Here, an intake coordinator could supervise assessments from a speech therapist, an occupational therapist, and other specialists who could help see the big picture. Michelle was now on a waiting list for an initial visit.

In many ways, Danny and Michelle were opposites. Danny jumped right into the middle of the action and seemed to upset the apple cart. Michelle disappeared into corners. Danny's challenges stemmed from his desire to connect. Michelle seemed to want to withdraw. Danny was all too well known by his peers, who continued to seem afraid of him. Michelle's peers barely knew her.

But they had one very important thing in common. After responding well to the teachers' original plans, they both seemed to need something new, or something more.

●　●　●

As you know by now, the process of *Engage-Reflect-Plan* is a cycle. Even though we have separated it into a sequence of three useful steps, we have shown how each step happens in connection with the others. You reflect and even plan in the earliest stages of engaging. You engage and plan as part of an organized reflection. You engage and reflect with children and each other as you develop plans.

In this chapter, we examine how the larger cycle of engaging, reflecting, and planning goes around continuously. Once you complete a plan, you arrive back at the beginning—you engage with your students when you put a plan into action. You take play and support ideas and enact them with children on the floor. Just as with the early engaging phase, you observe and get to know children as you follow your plan. The balance of putting out and taking in is even more important as you try specific strategies. This time around, one of the things you observe carefully is how well strategies are working by asking some questions:

- How do children respond?
- Do they engage in the activities and experiences you planned for them?

- What are the signs that your plans are working or not working?
- What unexpected traps or obstacles came up for you, the children, and the environment?

And just as before, you must continually reflect on what you are observing:

- How do the strategies address goals once you put them in action?
- What new or changed information about the children do you need to take into account?
- How can you modify plans instead of starting over?

Finally, as you engage children with the different activities in your plan and reflect on how the plan is working, you return again to planning. This time, you want to organize your observations and reflections to make changes to your existing plan. As we shall see, changes to the plan often come from three kinds of observations:

1. What could you have planned better?
2. What needs to evolve as children become familiar with your plan?
3. What has changed about the children?

By paying close attention to these three questions, you can make sure that your plan is effective from the start. But more important, you can make sure that your plan keeps up with individual children and your group and does not become a dead end with limited benefits.

Progress—The Last Piece of the Puzzle

In the last two chapters, we presented three of the four key elements of a plan: strengths, goals, and strategies. In this chapter we add the fourth element: progress.

Strengths are important for helping children work from a place of comfort and competence. *Goals* define how parents and teachers want to help children grow. *Strategies* give teachers specific plans for helping children move toward those goals. We now come to the last piece: *progress*.

Progress is, in one way, the outcome of the entire process. You set appropriate goals, translate them into effective strategies, and a child makes progress. But progress never happens all at once or overnight. So it is important to think of progress not as the end of the process but as a key tool in the process. Taking detailed note of progress, or lack of progress, and adjusting plans is how you actually make the whole plan work.

Just as your first draft of an essay points you in the direction of your finished work, a plan starts you off in the right direction. A child's response to plans—and those of other adults, such as parents or colleagues—acts as the notes or comments in the margins of your draft. Your observations, reflections, and planning around a child's progress are the revisions you make to turn your first draft into a more effective work. For better and worse, though, a plan for a child, unlike an essay, never has to be finished. You constantly monitor progress to make continual revisions.

At this stage in the process, you have your first draft. It should serve you well and save you time and effort. As you engage, reflect, and plan around progress, here are some goals and strategies to help you keep a plan up to date and effective:

- Keep getting to know each child.
- Keep simple notes on specific goals.
- Keep simple notes on individual strategies and how well they work.
- Keep regular communication with all the adults involved in a child's plan.

Keep Getting to Know Each Child

Children, even those with developmental challenges, are constantly changing. Even as you make and enact specific plans for children, don't overlook the need to keep observing, engaging, and learning about each child. Take note of how a child's strengths are being expressed. Is she doing more in the same places? Has she added routines or steps to favorite activities? Has she become tired of favorites? Is she seeking new challenges with favorite materials or activities? Be aware of how a child's language, motor skills, social profile, emotional self-knowledge, and sensory profile are changing.

A number of tools will help you get to know each child and keep helpful information at your fingertips.

Keep Simple Notes on Specific Goals
As you put goals and strategies for a child into action, you want to observe details about how she is or is not moving toward those goals. For instance, if you have a goal that a child will begin to use her imagination, be sure to take note of what she pretends to be, how long she plays a pretend game, what she says, whom she plays with. If your goal for a child is to stick with activities for longer, you want to note how long she plays a monster chasing game in order to see if she is making progress. As we discussed in chapter 6, you want to capture details that you can observe, not judgments, generalizations, or guesses.

Keep Simple Notes on Individual Strategies
Just as you want to observe how a child is doing on goals, you want to also get a sense of how your individual strategies are working. You want to capture details. If you plan to use deep pressure to help a child get organized and calm early in the day, you want to be sure to note how often you have managed to do this, how the child responds, what he tends to do next, and for how long. Again, you will want to be able to compare details over time. You can also

note what got in the way and what prevented or complicated your strategy. Are you too busy with other concerns when you want to try certain strategies? Does the entire group try to get involved in a way that overwhelms things? Does the group's involvement change the plan? Does the plan interfere with transitions? Does the child avoid strategies? Does the child respond in positive but surprising ways?

Keep Regular Communication with All the Adults Involved in a Child's Plan

Just as honest, regular, two-way communication is vital to making initial goals and strategies, so the response, questions, and information from parents and other adults will play a big part in helping you monitor and update goals and strategies. Parents and teachers need to keep up particularly close communication to get a clear sense of how a child is responding to new plans both at school and at home. Teachers and parents can also inform each other of how a child seems to feel, what she says, and what this information might mean for keeping plans effective. And just as you find time to reflect together to make the plan, you must also find time and ways to reflect together to update the plan.

Update Goals Based on a Child's Progress

Vygotsky (1978) described teacher support as a kind of scaffold, a structure that children can use to reach their next level of ability or success. This is a very useful image for inclusion support, especially if you think it all the way through to the end. A scaffold is put up in order to accomplish a goal. Once that goal is met, the scaffold is taken down. Scaffolds we build to support children's challenges, however, are different from a painter's scaffold in one important way—they are taken down gradually, in an individualized and thoughtful series of steps. As children make progress, you will want to update your plans to make your support more and more discreet.

When developing goals and strategies, think of the least amount of support necessary. Of course, as we wrote in chapter 5, children with significant challenges will often need a high degree of support—a heavy scaffold—at first. But as we said in chapter 6, teachers want to use children's strengths to help them approach challenges in ways that set them up for progress. Even when they need significant support—to start and finish an activity, for example—you want to make plans with their independence in mind. And as they progress, keep thinking about how you can simplify, streamline, and integrate goals to decrease teacher support.

When you create early goals and strategies, be sure to think about how you, the parents, or the child will be able to measure that the child has met the goal. For instance, for Michelle's goal of separating with her mother, the teachers described concrete details of how she would behave when she progressed:

```
Michelle will say good-bye to her parents and get comfort
from the teachers daily. When she needs to cry, she will see
the teachers as her helpers and work through her upset in a
reasonable amount of time.
```

You can use the scaffold of support as a measurement tool. A goal can be considered met when a child can accomplish it without any extra support. At this point, it is time to reflect and come up with a new goal that flows from earlier plans. Just as school district Individualized Education Programs (IEPs) are rewritten yearly, you will want to rewrite goals on a regular basis.

When Danny began to play for longer periods of time with friends without always becoming excited or aggressive, his teachers revisited goal number two:

```
Danny will continue to form positive relationships with peers. He
will increase his ability to play and to play with friends for five
minutes at a time. He will replace physical aggression with words.
```

The teachers could see that Danny had accomplished much of what was written. His relationships with two individual children had grown. He had found ways of entering into play. He was using much more language, and he could play for more than five minutes successfully. But they also noted that Danny still needed a lot of support to meet the goal. So they rewrote the goal:

```
Danny will continue to form positive relationships with peers. He
will sustain cooperative and productive play independently and take
breaks if he becomes overstimulated. He will use safe and effective
ways to express himself and meet his needs.
```

Danny had accomplished goal one, which focused on the more basic goal of self-regulation. Now he was making progress on goal number two: developing positive relationships. So they updated their plan to focus on helping Danny achieve this goal in a more independent and sophisticated way. And they embedded the scaffolding concept—gradually removing teacher support—into the new goal. This is the kind of revision that you will find yourself doing all the time—changing the terms and details of a goal and focusing on the child achieving the same goal with less and less support.

This goes back to how you frame goals and strategies from the start. Recall how we wrote about breaking tasks down into bite-sized steps for both teachers and children. This approach sets up the process for effective revision. As you take a large, general goal and break it into chunks for both children and teachers, you set up a scaffold for yourself to track progress and make changes. When your expectations and methods are laid out in a clear sequence of manageable steps, you can track and analyze them with greater ease. You can also rearrange the chunks as you would a tower of blocks.

As you become more practiced at breaking plans down, revisiting and updating them based on children's progress, keep a few key goals in mind:

- Celebrate each small success and triumph.
- Collaborate to maintain reasonable expectations.
- Be prepared for new challenges.

Celebrate Each Small Success and Triumph

One of the hardest things about working with children with special needs can be the feeling that they are stuck and can't make progress. But one of the most valuable and rewarding things about working with children with special needs is the incredible satisfaction that you, they, and their parents feel when progress happens, no matter how small. Making mindful use of this sense of success, acknowledging and celebrating progress, is a very important part of the inclusion process. (Chapter 13 has more information about how this makes you a better teacher for all children.) The success is obviously part of your plans. But the celebrating—the acknowledging and reflecting on hard work and success—plays a huge role in ongoing progress.

First, celebration makes use of affect, which we have shown to be the key to helping children with challenges. Moments of high affect, positive or difficult, shared and defined by an adult, create powerful learning experiences and help children stay confident, alert, and open to more growth. As we have also discussed, plans and goals for children with challenges often have a lot to do with helping them learn how to read, express, and share emotions. What better time to help children work on this than when you have feelings of relief, happiness, pride, and mutual care to explore?

Finally, celebrating successes with families deepens your partnership with them on both emotional and practical levels. Teachers can make the most of this by structuring times and ways that they and parents can celebrate successes together. You will inevitably have several meetings with childrens' families to discuss roadblocks, differences of opinion, or ongoing struggles. You will be surprised how effective it can be to then devote a meeting just to talking about a particular success or triumph.

Collaborate to Maintain Reasonable Expectations

General goals can be relatively simple to recognize—a child's needs or challenges are right there on the surface much of the time. Strategies can be a little harder to figure out—you must match your observable goals for a child with your toolbox of teacher skills. But knowing how much progress to expect at any given time can be the hardest part of all about inclusion. There are many different measuring tools—a child's happiness and success in school and life, her ability to participate in her peer group, her readiness for kindergarten—and each one must be tailored to an individual child.

Sometimes it feels as if a child is making no progress, and sometimes it feels as if she has met goals overnight. Part of successful inclusion is knowing that this question—how much progress how soon?—is never really resolved. It is always a wide range, and that range is always shifting.

This is where collaboration plays such an important role. It is easier to keep focused on the most effective strategies when several perspectives are considered. Each adult—teachers, staff, and parents—can add a slightly different but connected thread of observation and opinion that helps you locate the right expectations for progress. Colleagues can help you know if a child is making more progress than you alone can see or if expectations need to be raised or lowered. They can also help you sort through your own feelings of hope and frustration and provide important reassurance and support.

Be Prepared for New Challenges

When teachers are organized, authentic, and reflective about making plans, children often make progress quickly. Nevertheless, we don't mean to suggest that children will not hit unpredictable obstacles or that a mindful plan will be perfect from the start. With each and every child and each and every plan, sticking points, surprises, and forks in the road will occur. As with inclusion in general, you must learn to have a curious and confident attitude about these progressive challenges. They are not a sign of overall failure or bad planning. On the contrary, you must learn to read surprises and glitches for what they suggest. Are they telling you that your initial plan could work better with adjustments? Are they telling you that a child is moving from his or her comfort zone and beginning down the path of positive growth? Or are they telling you that a child has made progress in a way that looks different from what you expected? Each of these different circumstances would call for different responses, but each different response would move your plans forward significantly.

As you have learned, many revisions to a plan are based on removing some of the existing support for a child. But this is not the only kind of change you will make as you monitor and update plans. Sometimes teachers decide that they need to make changes to their program—routines and transitions, how they divide their time among children, how they divide the children into different-sized groups. Some monitoring and updating can focus on the physical environment as well.

• • •

Michelle no longer needed moment-to-moment support. She had established a pattern of solo play, moving around the room, speaking softly to herself throughout the morning. The teachers had learned to sing to her to communicate important information, such as a transition. She allowed some fleeting connections. When Angie or Mike found time to get down at her level and follow her lead, she made momentary eye contact once or twice. They could only make out a word or phrase of her self-talk. "Oh no you don't!" was common. She also liked to name letters with the teachers at the writing table and watch as they wrote them down.

The problem was that she was so self-sufficient and inward focused that teachers found it hard to interact with her at all. The three-year-olds were in full swing. It was a particularly demanding group, and not just because of Danny and Michelle. Angie and Mike realized that Michelle's mother had not only offered support for separation—she had also been Michelle's play partner. Without her, Michelle was becoming less connected and her play less purposeful. And Michelle still did not have a very developed relationship with her teachers.

The teachers and parents had made a plan for Michelle as soon as she began the program. The plan had focused on one main goal—to help Michelle become comfortable with school, peers, and teachers and be able to separate from family. One key strategy—asking Michelle's mother to provide support—had helped them meet their goal. Following Michelle's interests had helped create more and more fleeting connections. But now Angie and Mike realized that she needed new goals and strategies.

They returned to their observations:

- Michelle liked to play with letters and costumes.

- She sometimes accepted play partnering from teachers if teachers entered into her theme gently.

- If a teacher could help bring another child into the play, Michelle sometimes took interest.

- Michelle had participated in the routines and transitions of the day when her mother cued and helped her.

- Michelle had been far more engaged with teachers, peers, and the program when she had one-on-one support.

Angie and Mike wrote two new goals:

- Michelle will increase her interest in connecting with teachers and peers. She will respond to others with expressions, gestures, or words.

- Michelle will increase her independent participation in play, transitions, group times, and routines.

As they used their observations to come up with strategies to meet these goals, Angie and Mike noticed something right away: one-on-one support from an adult seemed to be a common thread in Michelle's success. Angie and Mike felt confident they could each partner with Michelle for one or two short episodes a day. But they did not feel they could offer her the kind of constant support that she seemed to need for the next few months—especially at group time.

Danny's latest goals and strategies also suggested that the group could use some extra staff for a month or so. He loved going out to the couch with a small group for heavy lifting and crashing. After these short pull-outs, he appeared more calm and organized in the classroom, at least for short stretches of time. Sometimes Mike would try to take a larger group outside for some extra yard time so that Danny and a small group could work in a quieter, less crowded classroom. During these small-group sessions in the classroom, Angie often started with some kind of organizing motor experience, such as giving Danny and his friends turns bouncing on a hoppity-hop ball or building an obstacle course. She would follow this with some supported calm play at the manipulative table. But any curveball—if a child needed to go to the bathroom, for example—could make these plans difficult to achieve.

Extra Support in the Classroom

Whenever we give presentations or talks to fellow early childhood educators about our work with inclusion, the problem of limited staffing comes up over and over. Creating schedules that provide enough coverage and give staff time to take breaks, talk to each other, plan, and communicate with families is almost impossible.

We have also found that for children with challenges and inclusion classrooms in general, the right amount of staff is one of the most important elements for success. Throughout our inclusion experience, we have made efforts to bring in extra teachers, sometimes for three weeks, sometimes for an entire year, when we felt it could support strategies for a child's goals.

Previously we discussed how you must take on the curious, problem-solving perspective that defines inclusion to solve practical challenges. This is especially true where staffing challenges are concerned. In fact, there are many more ways to find people than there are to find time! Early childhood or special education students, community service programs, parents, and other members of your staff can all be sources of creative staffing.

Early childhood education is badly understaffed and undercompensated in our culture. Even in the easiest, smoothest group of children, teachers can rarely offer an ideal adult-child ratio. As we push for effective staffing for one child or one group at a time, we begin to push back against inadequate standards. We advocate for improved quality in programs and higher priority in our culture at large. Chapter 13 speaks to this cultural issue in more detail.

. . .

Angie and Mike spoke with their director. All of them were familiar with the process. They had worked with extra teachers to support a few other groups over the years. They decided to bring in Alexis, a teacher who taught half-time in one of the afternoon classes. She was currently making up some extra hours doing administrative work. It would, as always, be a stretch for the budget, but they felt that the class needs were the highest priority. They also felt it would be most effective to use a teacher who knew the program, its staff, children, and parents, and who had some experience with inclusion.

In order to manage a full day of teaching, Alexis would have to take a break during the last half hour of the morning. She would not have any time in her day to meet with Angie and Mike. But Alexis could at least use their observations, questions, goals, strategies, and progress to get up to speed. They checked in via e-mail to make a plan for sharing the workload.

The three teachers devised a plan that they thought would make the most effective use of the new staffing pattern. During open choice time, they decided that Alexis would spend most of her time working with the children who needed the least support. This would free Angie and Mike up to work with Michelle and Danny, one-to-one, in pairs, or in small groups. They could all work in the classroom, or one of them could also work with small groups in the area by the couch for ten to twenty minutes. Alexis could also help one teacher take eight or nine kids to the yard so that Danny and some of the expert players could work in the classroom.

During group times, Alexis would switch her focus. While Angie or Mike led the group, Alexis would focus on providing support to Michelle or Danny. Danny needed gentle, supportive physical containment and verbal cues in order to participate with a calm voice and body. Michelle seemed to benefit if a teacher sat behind her and used verbal cues and even props to keep her focused. Planning for Alexis's role helped Angie and Mike better understand what both children needed at group time.

The plan was designed to be both specific and consistent, on the one hand, and flexible and responsive, on the other. All three teachers would have a clear idea of what they intended to do, but they would also have the freedom to tailor their roles to the opportunities that arose in the moment.

● ● ●

Support teachers can work with core staff in many ways, but in the most basic relationship-based inclusion model, they offer support to the entire group. Because the main teachers in a classroom have the most knowledge and experience with individual children and plans, extra teaching support offers them the chance to put their plans into action. Not only is this approach the most practical and effective, but it also reflects the message of inclusion: all the teachers support all the children. Relationships are the foundation of inclusion, so it is ideal if all teachers in the classroom form relationships with all the children, rather than just those who need extra support. Likewise, it is a subtle but very real goal to help the children see all teachers as important members of the classroom community and for all teachers to model an authentically equal and respectful partnership.

This circles back to the goal of effectiveness. As the support teacher gains the trust of all the children and learns how each one likes to connect and play, she will be more and more able to help children with challenges to connect and play with peers.

Of course, this isn't always easy. When teachers have a long-term relationship with one another, they have developed a level of comfort and camaraderie. They collaborate in ways that a new member of the team cannot learn overnight. Even (or perhaps especially) teachers who run a classroom alone face these same challenges. And as was true with Angie, Mike, and Alexis, teachers rarely have much time to share the vital information or make a basic plan, let alone get to know each other, before integrating a new member. Knowing that a new teacher will be only a temporary partner can discourage colleagues from devoting energy to building a new team.

Despite these challenges, it is our experience that when support teachers work with all the children and rotate through roles with the permanent teaching staff, children make more progress. First, doing so downplays the sense of difference surrounding a child with challenges. Second, when the support teacher has relationships with all the children, and all the children recognize her as one of the teachers for everyone, it opens up opportunities for the support teacher to help foster connections between children.

Whenever you have the opportunity to bring extra support into the classroom—colleagues, trainees, aides, or volunteers—it is important to set at least a clear goal of working as a team. This includes making sure that new adults know the basics—the names of all the children and parents, the routines and schedules of the program, the expectations and agreements of the class, and the approach to curriculum and development. Adding new staff also requires that support staff be given clear orientation to the teachers' knowledge of and plans for as many children as possible. Sometimes this requires catching up on the floor while teachers work together. But this is also one very important reason to make plans for children that can be shared in writing.

There are, however, times when one teacher needs to devote attention or support to a single child. If a child needs a high level of continuous support to maintain basic participation, such as a child with physical disabilities might, or if a child needs constant supervision to keep her peers physically or emotionally safe, teachers should and do decide to provide ongoing one-on-one support. In the latter case, this kind of support is sometimes called *shadowing*: a teacher stays within arm's reach of a specific child, like a shadow. Even in these cases, we have found that it is both possible and preferable to move beyond the old model of teacher and paraprofessional with permanently divided roles. Even when children need this level of support, all teachers in the classroom can often learn to provide it and rotate through the shadow role. The child receives constant attention or support, but not from the same teacher all the time.

This again illustrates a key benefit of the inclusion model. As each teacher works with specially trained support staff or outside specialists and learns the necessary skills and techniques for supporting one child, each broadens her qualifications to serve more children in the future.

Once Alexis joined the class, Angie and Mike found that they could work directly with Danny and Michelle much more often. Mike was able to use floortime techniques to follow Michelle's internal play in the house corner without interruption. He had learned to use very little language with Michelle as he engaged in play with her. When he did want to get her attention verbally, he sang. They had grown to understand that Michelle responded to singing much more than to talking. The also had noticed that Michelle responded to being silly. One time, as Mike sat across from Michelle at the table in the house corner, she dropped a plastic potato chip into a toy teapot.

"A potato chip in my tea!" he sang, making a surprised face. "Yuck!"

Michelle stopped sorting the food for just a moment and looked him right in the eye. For a fleeting moment, she lit up and smiled. When she turned away, he could hear her mumbling, "Oh no you don't . . . yuck!"

With just a little extra time to engage, Mike was able to use his affect to show high interest and curiosity in the materials that Michelle explored. Michelle seemed to pay attention when Mike reflected interest back to her. This didn't just increase Michelle's inclination to connect and notice others, it also seemed to encourage her to stick with play scenarios for longer. In addition, she started to put a few constructive or imaginative steps together into a more organized sequence.

Similarly, he was able to get other children in the class to sit with him and Michelle as she lined up materials. Sometimes Mike would enlist the expert player to put a piece of toy food at the end of Michelle's line of letter shapes.

"A-B-C-D-E-F, Cheese!" he would sing.

Most of the time Michelle would silently push the food aside and keep working. But the other children could be counted on to giggle at the song. This would cause Michelle to look up and once again, momentarily show a gleam in her eye.

Angie could now work in the block corner with Danny and his two best friends with fewer interruptions. She could help them plan and organize the pretend ideas behind their building and negotiate spatial challenges in ways that helped them keep the play going. She could encourage Danny and his friends to negotiate on the details of their creations and help them dictate signs to label the parts of their spaceships or factories. And she could embed some of the elements of Danny's sensory diet, such as using deep pressure to help the kids pretend they were blasting off, or using weighted bags for seat belts.

As Mike did with Michelle, Angie could use the expert players to help Danny turn his pretend ideas into purposeful play. When Danny seemed poised to push over the spaceship his group had built, Angie could herd up all the players and give them stickers to make control buttons. She could get a friend to help question Danny about where the spaceship was going, what they saw out the window. Most of all, she could show great curiosity and enthusiasm for their ideas and honestly help them celebrate successful and satisfying play with high fives and verbal congratulations. They would often use the classroom camera to take pictures of their work before cleanup time, which helped them all feel more flexible about this often tricky transition.

One of the biggest surprises about the new staffing pattern was how much each child in the group seemed to benefit from the small-group work one teacher would do outside the classroom. Angie found that a simple formula worked well with Danny during pull-outs. She would bring him out to the couch area with his two closest friends. They made good partners not only because Danny liked them but also because they were very patient and open to working with him. They could help Angie scaffold the play for Danny with their social sophistication.

First, Angie would recruit the boys to make a crashing pit by piling large cushions and pillows onto the couch. This gave them some heavy work and proprioceptive input and also helped Danny connect to his peers through structured collaboration. She would use simple cues like "Ready, set, go!" or a starting line made from masking tape to facilitate the play and keep Danny (and his friends) focused. She found that by engaging him in the planning, setting clear rules for positive physical connection, and encouraging a circle of start, run, jump, crash, return to start, she could help Danny satisfy his urge for deep input without his becoming overwhelmed.

After a few rounds of running and crashing, when Danny seemed to be at a comfortable level of arousal, Angie would introduce a pretend theme. "Are we going to be race cars or rocket ships?" she would ask.

"Race cars!" Danny often replied.

"The race is starting!" she would then call out. The crashing game with the pillows and couch was then transformed into a racetrack. This time, after calling "Ready, set, go!" she would add, "Oh no! There are rocks on the racetrack!" Sometimes the children would steer around them. But most often they crashed all the same.

"Bring in the tow truck!" Angie would call at that point. "Danny," she would say, "We need the tow truck! Go rescue your friend!"

Danny loved to take on the strong helper role. His friends loved to lie on their backs and let Danny haul them out of the pillows.

As before, this sequence of play encouraged Danny to make positive, structured connections with peers and to physically connect through heavy work. The added dramatic theme also gave him some practice enacting an imaginative sequence and connecting to his peers through pretend themes as well as physical activity. Angie would use the affective elements of the pretend theme—danger, fear, urgency, heroism—to help Danny stay organized and involved. She used her own voice, body, and face to model affect and capture Danny's interest, as well as to point his attention to the imaginative and social cues embedded in the game. Sometimes she also had the team give each other hugs to add even another element of positive connection and physical contact.

Whenever Danny became defensive or overstimulated, Angie remembered to use limits as a chance for him to build self-knowledge. She also used these times to help his friends understand what was challenging for Danny and how he was working on it.

"Danny is working on using his words to tell you his ideas," she would say. "His ideas are so important to him, and he loves to play so much, but he still forgets sometimes. You can remind him to use his words. And let's all try to listen carefully to his ideas. I know you can all work together to make your game fun and to get what you need."

● ● ●

In this small-group play, everyone is having fun, working together, and increasing their arousal through proprioceptive play—a happy playtime for all. More positive independent peer play may follow this kind of proprioceptive small-group play with a teacher, either immediately or over time.

Even if everyone doesn't press their hands together, this activity calms a small group before they re-engage with their whole class.

• • •

When Angie felt it was time to return to the classroom, she made a point of staging a transition from a high to a low level of stimulation. She gave a two-minute warning. She gathered the group together when the two minutes were up and sometimes engaged them in a small fingerplay exercise like "cut the pickle—get a tickle." This focused their energy on a smaller field and on fine-motor rather than gross-motor expression. She gave clear expectations and descriptions of what to expect.

"We're going back to the classroom," she would say. "We have to bring our engines down to the classroom speed."

She would lead the group in a few deep breaths and have them push their own hands together. Sometimes she would have a short conversation with them to choose an activity—often she would use the choice chart. Finally, she would pick a way to go back to the classroom that offered proprioceptive input and challenge, such as hopping like frogs or combat crawling. Sometimes, if Danny recognized that his engine was running high, he would choose to spend some time in the calming corner.

The three or four children who would join Angie or Mike out by the couch loved to jump and crash and seemed to collaborate and cooperate more naturally in the quieter, less crowded area. The children who remained in the classroom also seemed to relax and focus now that the room was less chaotic. With two teachers in the room to work with nine or ten children, everyone seemed to get more time to advance their ideas, work with a teacher, explore space freely, and have control of materials. Everything seemed more relaxed.

Alexis turned out to be a real partner to all the children. She had a natural feel for using space and materials to support each child's sensory exploration. She would help them build forts out of pillows, where she would encourage two children to squeeze in together. She would rig sheets up to the climbing structure to make pirate boats with a built-in hammock. She taught them how to sing partner songs like "Row Your Boat," where children would hold hands and pull each other back and forth. And being used to working with the older class in the afternoon, she had naturally high expectations around routines and physical challenges. This led to a lot of collaborative work among the children when she stepped back to have them move heavy things out of the way at cleanup time.

At pickup time one day, Angie received a clear message about how well the new plans were working. Luke's mother, Mary, looked up from the sign-out board with a big smile.

"Luke is really into Danny these days!" she said in a friendly whisper. "I just can't believe it. He talks all about the tow truck game and how Danny is nicer now." They both laughed.

Mary continued, "He says he wants to have Danny for a sleepover."

"Whoa," Angie replied. "That's even better than an invitation to a birth-day party."

"I know!" Mary replied. "It's really great to see him go from worried to so happy. He's really proud to have a good buddy."

"They do really like each other. Luke has done so much to help Danny learn to relax and play."

"Well," Mary said, "you guys really got him into shape too. I have to say, I'm amazed."

Effective Pull-Outs

Pull-outs refer to a practice in which specialists visit programs to remove children for one-on-one therapeutic support. Some therapists also practice the opposite model—*push-ins,* where they work with their clients in the children's classroom.

This model has several potential drawbacks. Intermittent and unpredictable visits can interrupt play for a child, which is often a core classroom goal. Providers from outside a program often have different information, skills, plans, and methods than classroom teachers, causing confusion and sometimes resistance on the child's part. Special attention through push-ins or pull-outs also mark children as being different.

In a relationship-based, inclusive setting, pull-outs refer to the process in which a classroom teacher works with pairs or small groups outside the classroom. (Or, as we have seen, a large group leaves the classroom and a teacher stays behind with a small group.) The small-group pull-out is a much more natural extension of a child's typical experience. In fact, it happens all the time, even where challenges or plans are not present. Think, for example, of how the Reggio Emilia model (Malaguzzi 1998) or the Project Approach (Katz and Chard 2000) emphasizes collaboration between teachers and small groups. As we have discussed elsewhere, when these kinds of natural pull-outs are part of everyday classroom life, teachers can embed individual goals and strategies in ways that feel like play to the children.

There are endless ways to embed children's individual goals in small-group work.

Lifting gives good proprioceptive input.

So does sumo wrestling. The props are large T-shirts with pillows sewn into them.

Who is having more fun—the children throwing the pillows into the loft or the children throwing them out? Both are getting muscle workouts.

In this simple vestibular activity, these children can travel all over the world.

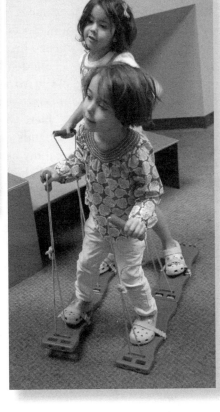

We're not sure where these children are going, but it will take a lot of work and cooperation to get there.

• • •

There were still many times when the teachers felt bogged down by the basic management demands of a busy classroom. Angie and Mike often felt frustrated to look up from performing three tasks at once and see Michelle once again at the writing table all by herself, lining up letter stamps. Some days it felt as if they didn't interact with her at all. They particularly dreaded the last half hour of yard time, when Alexis would depart for her break and they would be back to two teachers again.

On one such busy day, Mike sat on the rim of the sandbox a few minutes before the end of the morning. Three children were competing for his lap, waiting for Mike to help wipe the wet sand off their feet and tug their socks and shoes on. Mike was well aware that he had only a few minutes before he had to help the children gather together and walk inside for lunch. The faster he tried to whip socks onto tiny feet, the more they seemed to cling and stick to wet toes.

Suddenly he felt a tap on his head. Perhaps he felt it three or four times before he noticed, so focused was he on getting that last shoe on before the call for lunchtime. Whether it was the first or seventh tap on the head, he eventually looked up. Michelle was standing over him, dangling a sandy, water-soaked paintbrush into Mike's hair. She stared off at some point on the far horizon, singing to herself.

Mike's first response was irritation. It was hard enough coaxing these socks and shoes onto six feet at once! The last thing he needed was another distraction, especially in the form of a soggy, filthy brush on his head. He instinctively opened his mouth to ask Michelle to stop.

Suddenly, Mike remembered a strategy they had planned for Michelle—*Join in Michelle's self-initiated play to make connections. Use high affect and humor to extend her verbal and nonverbal communication.*

Here was a chance. Mike quickly shifted gears. "Oh no!" he said, putting his hands up to his face and making a dramatic expression of fear. "Don't paint my head with the yucky brush!"

Michelle stopped singing to herself and looked down into Mike's eyes. Her face remained blank. After a moment, she turned and took a few steps away. A moment later, however, she turned and wandered back. This time, she was looking right at Mike, the brush held high in her hand. She came in fast and started painting Mike's head again.

"Oh no!" Mike said again, repeating the gestures and expression, "don't paint my head with the mucky yucky brush!" This time, Michelle looked into Mike's eyes the entire time, and her face lit up with a mischievous smile. She turned and ran ten paces away, then wheeled around and looked at Mike expectantly.

"No! No!" Mike said, repeating the expression and gestures. Michelle's face lit up again and she let out a small laugh.

"Mucky yucky!" she said.

"Don't paint my head with the mucky yucky brush!" said Mike.

Michelle squealed and came running at Mike with the brush. She crashed into Mike, squealing with laughter.

And suddenly, here was Danny, climbing out of the sandbox, wrestling with a huge bucketful of sand. He weaved and crashed right into Mike.

Michelle's plan flashed into Mike's mind again: *Michelle will engage in more back-and-forth interactions that last longer with teachers and peers.*

And then he remembered a goal for Danny: *Danny will continue to form positive relationships with peers. He will increase his ability to play, and play with friends for five minutes at a time.*

"Danny!" Mike said, keeping up the tone of melodrama. "Michelle's going to paint my head with the yucky brush!"

Danny sized up the scene and he, too, broke out in a mischievous grin. Michelle looked briefly at Danny, turned, and ran off.

"There she goes, Danny!" Mike said. "But I know she's going to come back and paint me!"

Sure enough, Michelle turned around at the same spot. "Mucky yucky!" she yelled.

"No, Michelle, no!" Mike called out with the same expression and gestures. This time Michelle jumped up and down, consumed with excited giggles. Danny smiled and laughed as Michelle came careening back and laid the brush into Mike's hair yet again. When Michelle ran off, Danny followed her. They turned around together at the same spot and ran back to Mike in unison. This went on several more times until the group went inside for lunch. (Some of the kids just went inside barefoot, and Mike put their shoes on after they ate.)

The 50-Percent Solution

Putting a plan into action is the core of successful inclusion. Children need repeated exposure to experiences and activities that build and evolve as they respond and progress. But as Michelle's and Danny's teachers discovered, thinking of goals and strategies is much simpler than finding a way to regularly fold them into the seemingly endless list of things that teachers must do in the classroom. Teachers can't help but feel that they are only doing a fraction of what they set out to do for individual children. Sometimes teachers can feel that they aren't doing anything at all, that a plan has just fallen off the map.

The most important tool to remember regarding successfully implementing plans is that *you will always feel like you aren't doing enough*. There really is no way to put plans into action as fully as you can imagine them. As with so many things about teaching, you can envision a great deal, down to many exciting details, but you can only actually do a percentage of what you can imagine.

The good news is that you usually don't have to do it all to help a child make progress. In our experience, children make significant advances around goals when teachers put even half their strategies into action half as often as they intend to—the 50-percent solution. The key is to come up with good goals and strategies, understand the big picture and the individual parts, and revisit the plan often.

Just formalizing your knowledge and ideas for a child sets an effective process in motion. The observation-based assessment process of Descriptive Review, developed at the Prospect School in Vermont by Patricia Carini and many others, emphasizes that sometimes just watching and thinking more deeply about a child seems to inspire growth and progress. It pushes teachers to better recognize and support what a child can already do and deepens the basic supportive collaboration between children and teachers (Carini 2000).

And although it is not pleasant to feel that you are not doing enough for a child, you can learn to use these feelings in productive ways. Mike's frustration about his work with Michelle and Danny allowed him to recognize a teachable moment and fueled his excitement about bringing in strategies from the teachers' plan. You can learn to see even your guilt or frustration as a useful cue to adjust the plan, keep trying, or even give it a break, rather than as a sign that you are failing.

Understanding your own feelings and trying to stay relaxed about putting plans into action are important tools. As we discussed in the opening chapters, your tone and affect play a large role in supporting all the children in your care. Mike was able to make the most out of a surprising, spontaneous opportunity because he was able to recognize and reflect a relaxed, curious, playful frame of mind himself. It was his receptive, positive outlook toward partnering with Danny and Michelle that allowed him to see how the moment connected to strategies for both of them. Most of all, it helped him remember to be joyous and enthusiastic about the children's positive interaction. Just as you must keep some faith in an individual child's potential to grow and thrive, you must keep a sense of faith in yourself and give yourself the benefit of the doubt in order to work effectively.

This raises the most important point of all about adjusting plans. Implementing plans consistently is only half of the successful equation. Allowing for surprises and being willing to adjust and improvise is the equally necessary other half of the cycle. This is the real 50-percent solution. You must learn to feel your way into the proper balance of planning and experimenting, leading with existing ideas and going with the flow of play. As you work to strike the balance, you will find that the two sides feed into each other: applying strategies in a systematic way will create new experiences and learning for children, which then creates lots of surprises and new possibilities, which teachers then incorporate into the plans and strategies and so on.

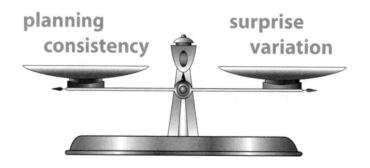

The 50-percent solution requires a balance between planning/consistency and surprise/variation.

• • •

Working with Parents—Revising, Revisiting, and Updating

The school district's early intervention team began its evaluation process in March. Michelle caught a bad cold during the week that she was to be seen by a speech therapist, and her family was out of town in early April. Nevertheless, she was seen by an occupational therapist, a speech therapist, and a psychologist. The psychologist, who also doubled as the intake coordinator, visited the school to observe Michelle in the classroom and meet with her teachers. By then, Angie and Mike had a well-developed plan to share.

It was mid-April when Michelle's mother took Mike aside at pickup time. Her voice caught as she spoke.

"The early intervention team sent us their report. They say she has Pervasive Developmental Disorder. They call it PDD-NOS."

Mike could see that Catherine had been surprised by the news. They set up a time for later in the week when both parents and both teachers could sit down to meet.

"We had been worried about her," Scott said as they looked over the reports together. "We thought maybe she needed some speech therapy. But this took us by storm."

"Do you think she is on the autism spectrum?" Catherine asked.

"I think the behavior and challenges they saw look consistent with what we all have observed," Mike replied. "But we also understand how you are feeling. I think we would all agree that she could use some extra support learning to relate to people outside her family and reading affect. That is consistent from our observations to theirs."

"I know it is a hard idea to think your child may be seen as developing atypically," Angie added. "And the thought of being involved with therapy and intervention—every parent we have worked within the same situation has needed time to figure out their take on that. But it's important to remember that even if she is in a range of atypical development, she still has the same strengths we all see in her. She is still the same girl she was before."

"Let's take it one step at a time," Mike said. "Let's look at what they recommend and compare it with what we have already been doing. We can help you make a list of questions about their report and their recommendations. Let's see how we can combine our work and this latest round of knowledge to make a coordinated plan."

Michelle's teachers and parents reviewed the reports. Her parents pointed out some areas where they felt Michelle was generally more competent than she appeared in the reports. Angie and Mike acknowledged that at home she was more connected, organized, and verbal than at school. Her highest levels of competence—her strength with letters, her imaginative skills, her ability to organize herself, her capacity for joy, her full verbal range, her connection to her family—were not reflected in the district's evaluations. The teachers also tried to help Scott and Catherine begin to make useful sense of how Michelle seemed consistently challenged in group settings.

Angie and Mike explained that the next step would be to have a team meeting in which Michelle's parents, teachers, and the district specialists could all sit down together to coordinate an integrated plan of services. The district would normally write up an Individualized Education Program in which everyone could collaborate on setting goals for Michelle's developmental progress for the upcoming year. But since the school year was almost over and it was likely to be June before the meeting could take place, Angie and Mike made an alternate suggestion. They offered to see if the coordinating psychologist would come to meet with the teachers to make some suggestions for adapting the program to meet goals. This could at least bring some immediate benefits from the evaluation process while Scott and Catherine reflected on the upcoming IEP and the prospect of individual therapeutic intervention.

Unlike the situation with Michelle and her parents, Angie and Mike had decided not to push the idea of outside support for Danny when they had last met with his parents. Because his challenges revolved so much around over-stimulation, everyone had hoped that with the right balance of external limits and sensory body support, he would be able to regulate more consistently as the year went on. In addition, Angie and Mike had felt that they needed to continue building their relationship with Danny's parents by responding to their feelings that Danny mostly needed limits. They had decided that if Danny continued to struggle with stimulation and aggression into spring, it would strongly suggest outside support. It would also form a stronger foundation for revisiting the issue with his parents.

They now felt that that time had come. Danny had made consistent progress yet had continued to experience consistent challenges. He could go for several sessions playing successfully with much less teacher support. But everyone had noticed that he also had begun regressing into yelling and head-butting for several sessions in a row. Angie and Mike had been able, with a third teacher's support, to maintain a physically and emotionally safe classroom. They were quite proud of how they had kept two very challenging plans in balance while they served the needs of the entire group. But that didn't mean that Danny didn't hit or push anyone anymore. Some children, even his friends, still felt anxious about him. Other parents still brought up concerns. And Danny's parents, despite being focused on behavioral strategies, continued to express concerns as well.

Angie and Mike sat down with Danny's parents in April, around the same time that Michelle's family received the district's evaluation. As always, they used their latest observations to note Danny's most recent progress. His parents added that he was having friends over and was thrilled to develop relationships with peers.

"But," Martha added, "it still seems like every time I pick him up, he's crashing into someone or tackling them. It seems like he just can't get it together at school."

"He definitely is still physical and sometimes aggressive," Angie confirmed. "And he is often able to use his words, stay calm and organized. I think we all feel like both things are true. We feel like it was a good call to focus on containment and limits. I think we can see that he recognizes and responds to clear boundaries."

"Yes," Mike added. "It really helped to bring in what worked at home."

"So what can we do now to help him get over being so rough?" Tony asked.

"There are a lot of options," Angie said. "We want to put our heads together again to use his latest progress at home and school to update our plan. Your input has helped us adjust the recipe all along, and we think it's time to do that again."

Angie took a breath. She and Mike had carefully thought through the wording of the next part. "There are also some other supports available outside the program. Let us know if you have any interest in pursuing that avenue. We can help you explore different options if you feel it might be effective."

"Do you mean like a psychiatrist?" Tony asked.

"There are actually several different kinds of therapeutic support out there," Mike answered. "But none of them would be like an old-fashioned psychiatrist."

"Like, would he have a tiny couch?" Martha joked. This let some of the tension out of the room.

"Well," Angie replied in the same spirit, "I think we would all agree that asking Danny to lie still and talk about his challenges would be the last thing he needs!"

Angie and Mike went on to discuss the possibility of speech therapists.

"My sister-in-law's niece was in speech therapy," Martha said. "It helped. We had actually talked about that."

The teachers then went on to describe what an occupational therapist and a physical therapist do, and how they might give useful information about Danny. They reminded Danny's parents of the sensory integration concepts they had discussed all along and explained how these kinds of therapists could address them. When they had finished, Danny's parents sat in silence for a moment.

"Well," Martha said at last, "I'm not sure. I want to think about it some more."

"I can see speech therapy," Tony answered. "He could use some help with his diction. But the other stuff is hard for me to get my head around. I mean, he runs and climbs and rides his bike. His brother just taught him to slam dunk, and he aced it. He doesn't look like a kid who needs physical therapy."

"I guess what we've really been wondering," Martha said, "is whether this program is just too big and free-play for him. Maybe he just needs more structure, like you've been giving him with Alexis in the room."

Angie and Mike decided to leave the discussion at this point. They agreed to get some written resources to Danny's parents, to help them gain some more understanding of sensory integration, and to revisit the question of outside support in a month. In the meantime, Danny's parents tentatively resolved to arrange a speech and language evaluation.

Angie and Mike also decided to make some modifications to their own plan, based on their conversation with Danny's parents. They developed some strategies for helping the other children in the program better understand Danny's challenges and feel more empowered by offering their support.

They had some meetings with children in the block corner to discuss safety issues. Pushing and hitting came up, and the teachers embedded messages about Danny's behavior in a broader discussion of individual goals. Some kids were working on dismantling block towers without pushing the pile over. Others were working on using their words to negotiate different ideas. Others, including Danny, were working on sharing space safely. The teachers wrote down many of their words and ideas. The children who participated in these discussions helped the teachers take some pictures of safe and successful play and challenging situations, such as conflicts and unsafe structures. Angie and Mike enlisted a parent with good computer skills to help turn these words and pictures into a short story, "Keep the Block Corner Safe!"

They also thought repeatedly about Danny's mother's question. Was the program partly responsible for Danny's challenges, at least in ways that could be modified? At first, Angie and Mike had responded defensively (but only between themselves). It seemed as if Danny's mother, like any parent of a child with persistent challenges, was looking for a way out, something outside her child that didn't require the pain of recasting their picture of him or the stigma of a diagnosis. Angie and Mike's commitment to relationships and inclusion eventually led them to try to see what was true and useful about her comment. And as they looked around the room, they began to feel that she might have had a point.

Danny had responded well to the calming corner they had built with pillows and cushions. Perhaps the room needed a broader rethinking along those same lines. They decided to look for several areas that could be enclosed and defined better, in which one or two children could find privacy, quiet, and containment. They also added some dividers and partitions that would help children work together but with clearer separation from each other. Some were made from a spare table or a large piece of cardboard. They also noticed that their classroom furniture arrangement created several dead-ends, open spaces, and natural circuits. Children tended to run around the circuits and avoid the dead-ends. They rearranged the room to create clearer pathways to the newly organized workspaces and to absorb the open spaces into table and floor areas with more defined uses.

By March, the teachers, now a team of three, could survey the new room with satisfaction. The new space, and their newly adjusted plans for the children in the class, promised to make the last few months of the school year exciting.

· · ·

In this chapter, you learned how plans must be constantly reviewed and updated. As teachers observe the initial effectiveness of their goals and strategies and how children respond to them, they return to their plans to make effective changes. You saw how progress forms the final element in a successful plan for supporting children with challenges. As children learn to meet goals with little or no teacher support, teachers must rewrite goals or create new ones. If children do not make timely progress, teachers must reassess their original goals. We explored several examples of how changes to curriculum, activities, and even staffing patterns or room design can help keep pace with children's changing needs and abilities. In the next chapter, you will learn how to support children as they go through transitions within their program or to a new program.

Many of the photos in this book are intended to give you ideas about involving children's bodies and sensory systems more in your curriculum—both in their play and in their work. Here are a few more examples to inspire you.

Vestibular

Sit and spin toys are a great, inexpensive way to offer a vestibular experience in a space of any size.

Sitting on the scooter board and moving by pulling on the rope is the kind of high-challenge, vestibular, proprioceptive activity children love.

A balancing activity is good for the vestibular system.

Monkey bars are good for both the vestibular and proprioceptive systems.

Tactile

Teachers use dozens of familiar tactile materials all the time.

Adding some new tactile experiences for children to a teacher's tool kit is always a good idea.

Proprioceptive

A piece of elastic fabric is a simple, inexpensive, portable tool for surprisingly satisfying proprioceptive input.

Including heavy building materials in the classroom is a good way for children to get proprioceptive input.

Calming/Regulation

Fish tanks have long been used as calming influences in classrooms.

Blowing bubbles is also a common calming activity.

Blowing pretend bubbles can work just as well. This is a good activity to help children transition into a focused group time. A pretend pop at the end makes it especially fun.

If sitting and reading or listening to books isn't calming enough, a child can always sit in the blue egg chair and pull the cover down for some privacy.

Chapter 8

Transitions: Supporting Children and Families

The summer after Michelle's first year was busy with activity. Her parents and teachers took two important steps to continue to support her:

1. They collaborated with the school district's early intervention team to write an Individualized Education Program (IEP).
2. They met with teachers from the school's four- and five-year-old class to make a support plan for Michelle's move to a new classroom in fall.

Angie, Mike, Michelle's parents, and the school district's early intervention team—the coordinating psychologist, a speech and language therapist, and an occupational therapist—met at the district's early intervention office in June to write up an IEP for Michelle. Angie and Mike gave a short overview of her school history. Their plans made it easy for them to reconstruct her experience, their goals and strategies, and her progress to date. They also were ready to make a small push for significant occupational therapy services. Scott and Catherine told the teachers several times that they felt so much more comfortable having Michelle's teachers present during the early stages of working with the district.

The district was at first more inclined to emphasize psychology and speech and language services. The teachers were able to draw upon their successes to advocate for a stronger body component to the plan. They brought up detailed examples of how much more responsive, receptive, and organized Michelle could be with focused attention on getting her level of arousal and affect up, like the paintbrush play, or with proprioceptive input, as in the waffle game. As a result, the district agreed to include occupational therapy goals and services as well.

Incorporating Relationship-Based Goals into IEPs and Individualized Family Service Plan (IFSPs)

Those of you used to participating in the development of IEPs and IFSPs may be aware that the goals and strategies influenced by sensory integration and the DIR functional emotional milestones may not be the kind of language typically found in IEPs. And yet the goals we want to work on are often related to those useful lenses. Below we offer some samples of what an IEP might look and sound like if a DIR perspective were included. Sensory goals and strategies could be included in a similar way.

The following IEP goals, adapted from Monica Osgood and Lauren Blaszak's "Sample Individual IEP and Program Outline" (2003), might have been appropriate for Michelle as she moved through her early childhood years:

- Michelle will improve her ability to sustain attention in a one-on-one setting to 60 percent.

- Michelle will maintain 10 verbal circles of interaction with an adult.

- Michelle will maintain 5 circles of interaction with a peer with adult facilitation.

- Michelle will improve her ability to sequence original ideas in her work and interactions, without using scripts, up to 60 percent.

Angie, Mike, and Michelle's parents met with the teachers in the four-year-old class later in the month. Scott and Catherine began the meeting by sharing some good news—Michelle was now so connected with one little girl that they had begun meeting at a nearby park once a week.

"It's so nice to just sit on a bench with another parent while our kids play!" Catherine said.

In this upbeat mood, the teachers and parents began to review the short transition document that Angie and Mike had prepared to summarize the most important information for their colleagues in the new classroom to know. At the meeting, they were able to flesh out the document and answer the new teachers' specific questions. In particular, the new teachers raised a question for the first time: What did Scott and Catherine want to do at the end of the following year, when Michelle's class graduated from the program and went on to kindergarten?

It was a busy summer for Danny and his family as well. His parents scheduled a speech and language evaluation, which took the better part of June. It was July, almost up to the end of Angie's and Mike's time with Danny, before the results came back. The evaluation confirmed what the teachers and the parents had observed all year. Danny was at or above age level for concepts and receptive language, in the low end of average in mechanics and pragmatic speech, and below age level in articulation. A line in the evaluation stuck out to all the adults: "Results of many of the assessment scales are not as clear as with some other children, owing to Danny's resistance to sitting still and responding." Danny's parents decided to follow the recommendation in the evaluation for speech and language services once a week.

Martha, Danny's mom, reported to Mike that the first few sessions were difficult. "I don't think she gets him," she said of the speech therapist. "She wants him to sit across from her and do all these drills. He just doesn't want to do it. She gave me a lot of things to help him practice at home, like blowing bubbles and drinking through a straw. If I make it fun and don't make it look like therapy, he'll do it at home. But he really doesn't want to go to her office."

Danny, much more than Michelle, seemed acutely aware of the upcoming change. He had always been very observant, even sensitive, about how school was organized and the expectations around him. When Angie and Mike had visited the four-year-old room with the class in June, Danny had clung to the back of Mike's legs the whole time. After the visit, he had burst out running and yelling in the yard, pushing children and kicking over sandcastles. When Angie removed him, he dissolved into tears and climbed into her arms. "I no go to new class," he told his teachers and parents on more than one occasion. "I stay."

Danny's parents were also nervous about the transition. Danny was one of the oldest children in the group—a late February birthday. Some of the younger children had the option of staying in the program for two years after this. But children Danny's age always moved on to kindergarten after the four-year-old class. Danny displayed many of the expected pre-academic skills for kindergarten already: he wrote most of the letters in his name, recognized many letters and even words, could count to thirty, and drew pictures of faces and cars. But he showed these skills at home much more often than at school, where he remained focused on physical exploration and pretend and social play. Socially, physically, and emotionally, despite much improvement, he still experienced a high level of challenge.

Supporting Children's Transitions

This chapter examines a universal aspect of working with children with challenges: how to support them when they move on to a new setting. As we saw with Michelle and Danny, there are transitions within a program. Children move to a new classroom or teaching team. These transitions are in many ways easier because they take place under one roof. The children know the general setting and are often familiar with the new teachers and space. And teachers within the same program work—or should work—from a common approach and knowledge base. They can also communicate about children all the time and can plan for smooth transitions. Danny's story reminds us that for all children and families, and particularly for children with challenges, these in-house transitions are still significant and can be the source of much apprehension.

Then, of course, there is the much larger transition to a new school. For children who display challenging behavior and for their families, this is an enormously complicated and daunting process. In fact, it is becoming more complicated and challenging for all children. In many parts of the country, children don't automatically move together from preschool to their neighborhood public school. Families often undertake a significant school search, and children scatter after preschool to several different public or private elementary programs. Standards of school readiness and the pressure on schools to prepare all children to reach uniform learning standards have risen over the past two decades. Kindergarten, once viewed as a gentle, play-based transition into the school setting, has become much more demanding in terms of behavior and academic achievement.

For children assessed with special needs, the end of the preschool years becomes a time when families must choose one of several paths. Will their child be able to manage a traditional school setting? Does she need more time in preschool? Are there inclusion classrooms in local public schools, and will they work for their child? Does their child need a special education setting? Does the existing plan for their child—whether limited to their preschool or coordinated between school and outside services—do enough to prepare her for elementary school?

Because the process of moving from child care or preschool settings to elementary school contains so many variables, child care providers, teachers, and administrators can't know all the answers to these questions. We can, however, use the principles and practices of relationship-based education to set up a process of support through this challenging step when we

- Help families know their legal rights.
- Build relationships with local kindergarten and elementary programs.
- Create a transition document.
- Participate in or arrange a transition meeting.
- Provide individualized support for each family's unique transition.

Help Families Know Their Legal Rights

Under the Individuals with Disabilities Education Act (IDEA), if a child has an IEP or an IFSP, the law requires that a transition plan be written for children moving from preschool to kindergarten. Specifically, the IEP must be amended. Families must be given information about transition processes and further placement options. The child must be prepared for the changes. The child's pertinent records must be sent to the receiving placement.

You should become familiar with the service agency in your community responsible for providing IFSP and transition services. If a child in your program does not currently have an IFSP or an IEP but you think the child might qualify, recommend that the families begin a process to have their child assessed long before the transition to kindergarten. Of course, the family's place in their journey will determine if this is possible. But having an IEP in place will allow families to access more support for the transition and the next placement.

Build Relationships with Local Kindergarten and Elementary Programs

Relationship-based education, as we have seen, is all about tailoring the fit between school, child, and family. Because the transition to kindergarten now involves more and more choices, preschool programs can play an important support role in the choice. You can accomplish several things by getting to know your local public, private, and parochial school programs, teachers, and administrators. First, you can provide details to families about the curriculum style, school culture, and priorities of individual schools. You can also help elementary schools get to know your families, and in some cases, even advocate for children. Keep in mind, however, that you want to follow a family's lead and provide the kind of support they request. If the family is already receiving services, they may also have a transition coordinator assigned from their service provider (whether the provider is the school district or some other entity).

Following up on a child's progress in the elementary setting can be particularly useful. Besides furthering the relationship benefits discussed above, doing so also furthers your ongoing understanding of a child's development. This is vital to your process of learning. It tells you a great deal about how to support other children and families through the transition process. It also sheds light on how the expectations in your program fit into a child's long-term process of learning and maturation. As a result, you learn about your program and your teaching as well.

These ways of providing support are all important, but they also take place on a broad level. That is, they happen outside the context of your plans and your direct work with children and families. Let's look at how you can use the ongoing processes from the previous three chapters to support families through the transition to a new program by creating a transition document.

Create a Transition Document

If you have followed a course similar to Angie's and Mike's with Michelle, you will have amassed pages of notes, your own SGSP plan, and possibly a school district IEP. You can boil these down to a simple, short document that families can use to help provide continuity during the transition. Ideally, a child's new school will want to make use of the volumes of knowledge, insight, and teaching strategies you have developed during a child's time in your care. You will want to make sure your report is concise yet covers the important information.

While any child could benefit from this kind of transition support, you would realistically only prepare this kind of document for those children whose challenges have led you to use the *Engage-Reflect-Plan* cycle to create an SGSP document.

To be most effective, the transition document should focus on a few key elements. It should emphasize a child's strengths and learning preferences. These will translate in the new setting in material ways and help build a positive relationship between a child and her next teachers. The document should summarize challenges or goals. It should focus on a simple digest of the most current, effective teaching strategies for the child. Here, it is important to consider that primary school programs tend to focus more on the child bending to the community rather than the other way around.

Finally, the transition document should contain the most current information about that child. During this process, schools cannot take in a child's entire experience in your program. However, if you maintain contact with a school about a child, it can be helpful to reconstruct what was challenging at first and how it became easier. It is important to focus on where a child is at the end of the process more than on the process itself. The transition document can act as a brief narrative and practical supplement to a formal IEP or IFSP.

Families may want to use your transition document in different ways. They may want you to forward it to a school. They may want to discuss it with their child's new teachers. They may want to keep it to themselves but use it as a kind of script for sharing information in their own way. Or they may want to review it and then keep it on hold. Depending on how their child adapts to a new setting, they may just leave it in a folder for future reference.

Remember that families often have justifiable concern about attaching a label to a child and prejudicing schools and teachers. Families understandably want kindergarten to be a fresh start and a chance for their child to fit in more seamlessly in a mainstream class. This will be especially true when a child has made good progress in your program. Nonetheless, it is up to a child's family how the transition document fits into the actual transition. How do you communicate this to families? That is part of the next strategy for providing transition support.

Participate in or Arrange a Transition Meeting

As we saw with Michelle's story, once a child has a support team that extends beyond school and parents, it is crucial to set up regular systems of communication to coordinate services. But even if the team for a child consists of teachers and parents, it is useful to conduct periodic team meetings for children with articulated challenges and plans. This way, you can set aside time to share detailed information from all the important adults about a child's progress, and update goals and strategies together. When a child prepares to move out of your program, the team meeting focuses on transition support. If a child receives a school district's IEP, the district's early intervention team will conduct a meeting to review and rewrite the plan after six or twelve months. They may also coordinate all of the transition meetings.

At this meeting, you might write, revise, or share a transition document. Often you will do some of each. It saves time to prune your current plan down to a succinct draft of the document before a meeting. This makes it easier for others to give input and helps you build the final version. As we have seen throughout the process, you want to keep up a fluid cycle of reviewing what you have done, sharing responses, and updating plans. Discussing the transition plan also feeds back into adjusting current goals and strategies for the remainder of a child's time in your program. Transition meetings sometimes cover plans for presenting a child's challenges to teachers, children, and families in a new setting and partnering with new teachers for maximum support.

And, as always, don't forget to celebrate successes. This is especially important during transitions to kindergarten. The competition, lack of power, and volume of unknowns in the kindergarten search cause intense anxiety for families. They need to hear encouraging information in order to stay positive about the change and to do their best to hold onto what curiosity and confidence they can.

In some cases, teachers in the preschool program can arrange a transition meeting with the new kindergarten teachers. A visit to the new site to discuss the new program in the actual program space can be very effective. See the suggestions included in the ABCs of Sending Programs in the section below for more transition suggestions.

Provide Individualized Support for Each Family's Unique Transition

As children and their families move to a new program, they will begin again at the *engage* part of the cycle. You can play a significant role in helping children, families, and staff at the new program learn about each other, get to know each other, and become comfortable with each other. In this way, you are setting up a positive engagement in the new relationship for everyone. They all focus on one of three aspects: On the one hand, the suggestions help the child and parent reflect on their departure from the current program, what is the same or different in the new program, and what the new program will be like. On the other hand, they do their best to set a positive foundation for the new relationships that will be forming. Finally, as much as possible, they draw on the strengths and resources of the family and child, empowering them to lead the way in the transition. The support you provide during the transition is in keeping with your relationship-based, inclusive principles and approach.

Let us return to Michelle and Danny to see how the teachers and administrators tailored their transition approach to these two children and their families.

. . .

The environmental changes that Angie and Mike had made to the room had shown several benefits. When the open circuit and meeting area disappeared, Danny and several of his peers stopped running around the room as much. The clearer pathways seemed to support Danny's growing ability to choose activities and stay with them in a productive sequence. The teachers were able to move through the room more comfortably, thanks to improved space and organization of the individual areas. In particular, Danny and his friends were better able to remove blocks from the shelf and build large structures, and the teachers could still sit and join them. All the children seemed to take advantage of the closed-off, partitioned areas the teachers had created. Danny and his friends loved to pile into the pillow boxes and pretend they were vehicles. They were together in a cozy space, away from the distractions of the rest of the room, but they were also separated into their own vehicles.

Angie, Mike, Danny's parents, and the four-year-old teaching team met in early July, before Danny's family went on vacation. As in Michelle's transition meeting, Angie and Mike updated their plan into a one-page transition document of goals, strategies, and progress. The teachers and Danny's parents presented a consistent picture of his strengths and challenges. They all endorsed the importance of clear expectations, organizing supports, and limits. Angie and Mike made a gentle push for the sensory diet activities. Danny's parents did not join in, but they did not object.

Danny's parents did report, however, that the speech and language therapist was not working out. Angie and Mike consulted their lists of resources. Eventually, they helped Danny's parents choose a new speech therapist who used a more play-based approach in her office. Danny's parents seemed very relieved to report that he liked the new therapist better and worked with her cooperatively. But the new therapist lived twenty minutes further from Danny's home than the first therapist.

"He's so tired after his appointments, and then he just goes crazy in the car," Martha reported. "We're both exhausted by the time we get home. Sometimes I wonder if it's doing more harm than good."

Everyone noticed, however, that his speech was becoming easier to understand. Angie and Mike watched closely to see if his improved diction led to improved confidence. Would he be more relaxed and willing to use his words?

It was a difficult time in which to tell. Luke, Danny's closest playmate, was away on vacation for two weeks during Danny's early speech progress. Danny's family also went on vacation after two weeks of speech therapy. By the time they returned, Angie's and Mike's class had only three weeks left before they transitioned to the four-year-old class.

When Danny's family returned from their vacation, Danny experienced his most dramatic period of regression to date. Not only did he begin yelling and dumping almost perpetually, he was frequently aggressive with his closest friends. On one occasion very near the end of the summer, he pushed Luke off a spaceship they had built from big blocks, leaving a large lump on the back of Luke's head. Luke's mother's concerns about Danny, which had evolved into a robust appreciation of Danny and his place in the group, became an issue once again.

Angie and Mike met with Danny's parents the following week. Martha burst into tears. "I just don't know if anything has worked," she said, shaking her head. "Every time I think he's improving, something like this happens and I realize that he isn't any better. He isn't any better."

Angie and Mike knew that Danny had indeed made progress over the course of the year. They understood that some of the current challenges even reflected growth and progress on Danny's part. But they did not pursue that angle. They made time for active listening at first. They carefully wove some of Danny's progress into the process of acknowledging and validating Danny's parents' frustration and worry. They made plans to speak with Danny's speech therapist to try to coordinate his school plan with therapeutic services. And over the next week, through a series of conversations and e-mails, they finally made a strong recommendation that Danny's parents consider occupational therapy. Danny's parents still had very mixed feelings. But they tentatively agreed to schedule an evaluation.

In late July, just weeks before he was to move on to the new class, Danny's parents surprised everyone at the school with an announcement. They had decided to move Danny to a different program. It was a small, private pre-kindergarten program that was part of a K–8 school. Danny could move straight from the pre–K into the elementary program.

"Honestly," Danny's mother confided to Angie, "we thought it was our best shot at getting him into kindergarten. But they are also much more structured. They start the day with a meeting, and they use more of a Montessori approach. I think it might be a better match for him."

At first, Angie and Mike felt defensive. They had worked so hard and had seen Danny grow so much. It seemed like sabotage. They knew that Danny was very aware of and sensitive to transitions. They worried that the disruptive effects of moving to a new school might outweigh any advantages the new program could offer. They all felt that Danny was on the threshold of real progress. The evaluation with an occupational therapist was still pending. The teachers felt that if a stronger therapeutic component could be put in place, Danny could keep moving from strength to strength.

Angie and Mike had used their focus on relationships to develop a supportive partnership with Danny's parents. After a day or so of complaining to each other and making dire predictions about Danny's future, they renewed their commitment to respect his parents' expertise and do what they could to support their decision.

Although there had always been differences between the school's perspective on Danny and his parents' view, Angie and Mike had learned to take his parents seriously. This had led to successful modifications in the environment as well as effective use of limits. It was likely that Tony's and Martha's feelings about a smaller, more structured program were, at least in part, correct. Regardless of who was right or wrong, the teachers knew that Danny and his parents needed their real respect and support. It would not help them to become bogged down in differences.

Danny's parents declined to have a full transition meeting. They felt busy enough just pulling off the transition. But they did readily accept Angie's and Mike's offer to create a transition document to help his new teachers get off to a good start. Angie also had a series of phone conversations with Danny's new teachers. They were able to talk about more details and examples than could be contained in the transition document, and the teachers at the new school were able to ask questions. Angie worked hard to strike a delicate balance. She gave the kindergarten teachers honest reporting of what had and had not worked well for Danny in their program. She also provided an honest confirmation of Danny's parents' reasons for the switch. Without hiding or changing important facts, Angie was able to portray a unified effort between the teachers and Danny's parents rather than sow doubt or confusion.

Angie's and Mike's class said a quiet but sincere good-bye to Danny on the last day of school before the August break. Danny's parents and his teachers felt that too much attention or celebration might overwhelm him. But everyone agreed that some kind of ritual was needed to define the transition and to show Danny what an important place he held in the school community. His friends made him some pictures and wrote him some notes at home. These were compiled into a journal that was presented to Danny but not read out loud at school. Danny's parents had enlisted him to make chocolate chip banana muffins for his last day. The class presented him with a paper crown and the school scrapbook at the end of music time and then adjourned quickly for the special snack.

Danny bounced around a little, crashing into children. But he also sat through a short discussion of summer plans at group time. He volunteered that he was "taking a spaceship to my new school," smiling from ear to ear. He sat next to a friend at snacktime and told jokes. He put his arm around his friend a few times but did not push or hit him. This was particularly encouraging, given that he had been so unsettled during his last weeks of school. He seemed to take real pride in his peers' and his teachers' respect and affection for him. He ate three muffins.

Danny's final departure from the classroom was surprisingly low key. He packed up his lunch box at the end of the morning and helped his mother clear out the artwork the teachers had collected in his cubby. With a moderately loud "See ya!" he marched out the door.

Angie and Mike were waiting by the school's front entrance. When Danny saw them, he climbed up into his mother's arms and buried his face in her shoulder. Angie and Mike couldn't help but think of that first day he had come into the classroom, when he also used his mother as a shield. They each wished him well in an upbeat and cheerful tone. Since he kept his face tightly against his mother, Angie and Mike patted him gently on the back and sent him on his way with a quick request that he write them a note to tell them about his new school.

A week later, Angie and Mike went out to dinner again after work to review their work with Danny and to try to make sense of his transition. They reminded each other that even a good inclusion program is only one program. Some children do need a different kind of structure, teaching style, or physical environment. They also talked at length about how, despite the importance of early intervention, children with challenges and their families have a lifetime to put together a toolbox of skills and strategies. The process takes time. They pondered the central paradox of inclusion: sometimes, the more urgent the case for intervention seems to be, the more crucial it is not to push too hard. Finally, they thought about how hard it is to help families find the right kind of outside support and how there is often a lag time between a family's decision to get help and a child's reaping the benefits of help. Danny's case reminded them that the riddle of how to support a child doesn't end with one evaluation or the start of therapy. Sometimes the riddle only begins then.

Angie and Mike finished their work with Michelle by blending in the goals from her IEP with their existing plan. The transition document included strategies for helping Michelle use more language to respond to teachers and peers, stay organized with activities, and allow peers into her play. As is often the case, these therapeutic approaches were focused on skill building and behavior modification and came from a one-on-one, adult-to-child perspective. It was up to Angie and Mike to fit them into their more relationship-based, play-focused group setting. They did notice that the extra structure and language that the district specialist provided drew a positive response from Michelle and furthered everyone's goals.

Michelle, unlike Danny, did move on to the four- and five-year-old class. In late November, her new teachers held another team meeting with Michelle's parents and therapists from the district. There was much good news to share. Michelle had eased into the new class with confidence and enthusiasm. She had showed no signs of the separation challenges of the previous year. The teachers had been able to work Michelle's therapeutic goals and activities into the more challenging, project-based curriculum in their class. They presented the entire group, or small combinations of children, with activities built around some of Michelle's language and relationship-building work. Michelle was sometimes able to take on a leadership role in these activities, showing friends how they were done or providing help to one partner.

At the suggestion of her therapy team, the teachers had used photographs to make a social story for Michelle called "Playing with My Friends at School." The first page contained snapshots of each child in her class. The rest of the book recreated the sequence of the day and showed specific play episodes and skills. The captions described play strategies, elements of relationships with peers, and even common feelings in play. Michelle appeared in many of the pictures. She used this book at home and school to deepen her growing ability and inclination to participate in class life.

Social stories are intended to help a child make progress on a specific challenge. The stories share important social information in a scripted, sequential format and outline positive steps a child can take toward mastery of the challenge. For a more detailed understanding of social stories, we recommend Carol Gray's *The New Social Story Book* (2000). At The Little School, we have adapted Gray's approach. We have used social stories for individual children's challenges. We have also used social stories to help a child make sense of an experience, routine, or transition. We have also used these stories for an entire class. These are the steps we use to make a social story:

- Set the scene.

- List relevant positive things about the child.

- Share the child's goal in child-friendly and manageable terms.

- Point out what the child is doing that works better and/or outline the desired action. Make the goal sound appealing and attainable.

- Finally, summarize by acknowledging the child's efforts.

For illustrations, we sometimes use real photographs, draw stick figures, or have the child illustrate the story. Each main idea is presented one page at a time. We work to tailor the story to the level of comprehension of the child it is created for. Some stories are very, very simple, while others are more complex.

Michelle had made significant progress. She used language spontaneously to join in table activities, negotiate with peers for materials or space, even to make the occasional random joke. With teacher support, she could join in spontaneous dramatic play. But the teachers also made a point of encouraging her to work with groups on acting out stories or other scaffolded imaginative activities. Michelle responded particularly well to these structured activities, as she did to games like Duck, Duck, Goose or Candyland.

She had begun to play with two or three regular partners, and even spoke of them occasionally at home. She sat and listened through morning meeting, although she did not yet spontaneously contribute comments. She had developed a habit of bringing favorite music for dancing, and she showed great aptitude with rhythm instruments. Many children followed her lead at music and movement time. They sometimes even called her "Dancing Queen," the title of one of her favorite songs.

Scott and Catherine planned to send Michelle to a typical elementary school. The district's early intervention team felt this could be a possibility. She would probably be able to secure paraprofessional services for some in-class support. Everyone agreed that this would be crucial to making a mainstream setting work. A lot would depend on how much progress she made over the fall. Still, everyone was confident enough that Michelle's parents put their neighborhood school at the top of their enrollment form in February. In April, they learned that she had been accepted.

The teachers and the school district's early intervention team—the coordinating psychologist, a speech and language therapist, and an occupational therapist—met in early May for a transition meeting. They began by reviewing Michelle's IEP. She had made progress on or met all of her goals from the year before. Michelle now regularly engaged in short verbal interactions with teachers and friends, often around symbolic play. She loved to play with dolls. She had ongoing friendships with three other girls. She participated in routines and stayed with the group through the transitions of the day. She enjoyed taking part—variably and in her own way—in teacher-structured games and motor activities.

Some types of abstract thinking and language were still coming slowly. She still spent significant amounts of time playing on her own. And much of her success still happened in a context of close teacher support. But everyone agreed that she had made as much progress, if not more, than they could have hoped.

The early intervention team reported that it looked very possible for Michelle to have extra support in the classroom. Everyone agreed that she would take the placement in her neighborhood school. The team reviewed the transition document that Michelle's teachers had prepared. It included a plan for her current teachers to work with the early intervention team to help prepare her kindergarten teacher and her aide for effective support. The district team agreed to schedule a meeting at the kindergarten in June, before the end of the school year. Because the document detailed Michelle's strengths, preferences, and progress, her aide and teacher would be ready to help her get off to an effective start. Finally, the four-year-old class teachers and the new kindergarten teachers pledged to try and do an e-mail check in October to keep track of Michelle's progress in the new school.

The four-year-old teachers held a "Moving On" ceremony on the last day of school for those children leaving for kindergarten. Angie and Mike sat with Scott and Catherine for some of the ceremony, drinking sparkling water from a paper cup. It was one of the first times that all four adults had been able to be together without a business agenda. They laughed about the outfit that Michelle had picked out for the occasion—red ruby slippers, jeans, a striped leotard top, a Snow White dress, and a plastic tiara. The teachers couldn't help noticing the contrast between the drawn and sober family they had first sat down with to talk about their daughter's difficulty saying good-bye and the people with whom they now shared an easygoing social event and a joyous milestone. Michelle waved her hands and talked to herself a few times during the graduation, but she also giggled and whispered to her neighbor and held her head up proudly as she stood to accept her diploma.

"I know I don't need to say this," Catherine whispered to Angie as the morning ended, "but I'm just amazed to see this. It's been such a wild two years!"

"I couldn't have said it better myself," Angie replied.

"I know we've said this a hundred times," Catherine continued. "but thanks."

"Thank you too."

Epilogue—Danny

It was Halloween afternoon. Mike parked his car and hurried into the market to buy two bags of candy. How ironic—he had just sent a letter to the parents in his class about holidays, sugar, and health, and here he was rushing to buy candy for trick-or-treaters! He was running late. His sister was coming over with her three-year-old daughter, who wanted to show off her costume to her favorite uncle before going out.

As Mike picked through the remains of the store's candy section, he felt a hand on his shoulder. He turned around to see Martha, Danny's mother, smiling. They embraced warmly. Mike looked hopefully around for Danny, but Martha was alone. They chatted quickly but joyously. Perhaps they were both surprised at how happy they were to see each other.

"Danny's doing okay," Martha said, still smiling but reserved as well. "He's in the kindergarten class, and they really like and appreciate him. He does a lot of the work well, but he still gets in trouble for yelling. Same old Danny," Martha laughed.

"And the aggression?" Mike asked.

"He still hits sometimes, but it's much better. Oh, and by the way, we did get the OT evaluation," Martha continued. "They say he's undersensitive to vestibular input and has problems with proprioception, which I still don't understand. But Danny wouldn't cooperate with them. He was really nervous, and he just wouldn't do a lot of what they asked. You know how that is." She looked down. "I don't know."

"How's he doing with the more academic stuff?"

"He's writing some letters, but they're worried about his academics. We're thinking about the public inclusion program. They like him where he is now, but they don't do as good a job as you did with the one-on-one plans. You know, it's always been hard to know what to do for him."

Mike remembered his recent conversations with Angie. "I think you're doing it. You are feeling your way towards the right recipe. It's going to take time. It's hard to see with Danny, but he has come a long way."

"Well, that's thanks to you guys," Martha said. "It really is. I know a lot of preschools would have kicked him out," Martha said. "I can't imagine what he'd be going through right now if you hadn't stuck with him. You know, he still talks about you all the time."

Epilogue—Michelle

Angie dropped off her 12-year-old son, Tyler, in front of the auditorium at his middle school and drove around to park the car in the school yard. Children from several middle schools were presenting holiday songs, and the place was mobbed. Angie filed into the auditorium with the herd, looking for Tyler on the stage and an empty seat at the same time. In the dim light, she found herself staring at a little girl with a thin blonde ponytail, sitting on her mother's lap and playing intently with a small figurine. After a moment, her vision and her memory snapped into focus. It was Catherine and Michelle. Michelle's hair and legs looked twice as long as the last time Angie had seen her.

"Shell, look who's here!" Catherine said. Michelle looked up. At first her eyes drifted to Angie's face and off to another vantage point in an all-too-familiar fashion. But a moment later she looked back into Angie's eyes and smiled, looking down to her little doll in what seemed to be shyness.

"Who's that, there?" Angie asked, pointing to the figurine.

Again, Michelle didn't answer right away. After a pause she said, without looking up, "This is Miss Lang."

"That's her teacher," Catherine whispered.

"Oh, you brought Miss Lang with you. Does she like holiday music?"

Michelle looked right into Angie's eyes. She smiled with a suspicious yet mischievous gleam in her eye. "Miss Lang is always busy!" she said. "She has a worksheet for me."

"Do you like being in Miss Lang's class?" Angie ventured.

Michelle was once again absorbed in her pretend play.

"Michelle," Catherine said. "Teacher Angie asked if you like Miss Lang's class."

"Oh, yes." Michelle said, still looking down.

"What do you like?" Catherine prodded. "You like the math station."

"I like the math station," Michelle repeated. "I did a hundred yellow blocks."

"Have you made some friends?" Angie asked. Her mother repeated the question gently again, but Michelle did not respond.

"What about Lorna?" Catherine persisted.

"I like Lorna," Michelle answered, manipulating the doll's arms. "Sometimes she's bossy."

Angie and Catherine laughed at that.

"It's going pretty well," Catherine said. "Sometimes I want to send her classroom aide to you and Mike for some boot camp. But he does a good job. Miss Lang likes Michelle—she calls her the math champ."

"She always had a knack for order," Angie said.

"Oh my goodness, Angie, you wouldn't believe it. Scott says she's going to be our ticket out of here! We never realized what a head she has for numbers. And, you know, some of the writing work is a little hard for her. And she still wanders sometimes. That aide is getting his exercise! But everything is manageable. And she's really happy. She really gets along with the other kids."

Angie looked up to the stage, where Tyler was waving from the back row. "I should try to find a seat!" Angie said, feeling a pang of guilt for ignoring her own child.

"Say good-bye, Michelle," Catherine nudged.

Michelle looked Angie right in the eye again with the same playful smile. She held up her doll. "Miss Lang says, 'Get back to work!'"

Angie blew Michelle a kiss and hurried back up the aisle. She managed to find a seat just as the lights dimmed. She could not help stealing one more glance at Michelle and Catherine. Michelle was still absorbed in her own world with her doll. Then, as the spotlights framed her ponytail, she lifted her head up to the world around her.

• • •

In this chapter, we discussed techniques for supporting children with challenges as they make transitions. You learned how transitions within your own program can be significant and provide opportunities for support. We focused on the very complicated challenge of supporting a child's transition out of preschool into kindergarten. Building relationships with local elementary schools, creating transition documents, and holding transition meetings can add structure to your plans for helping children make the transition smoothly. Finally, you read how each child and family requires individual plans for transition support. Sometimes families leave your program in surprising or even frustrating ways. But you can still partner with and support them with respect and care.

In the next part of the book, we will consider some broader ways that children, teachers, administrators, and families can build an inclusive community based on honest and effective relationships.

Some of the ideas and activities we have introduced you to involve props and materials. Some of these materials are familiar and some may be new. Let's take a closer look at props that might be used at circle time.

Different seats help children with different kinds of challenges attend.

The seating option on the left offers some core support and tactile input. The one on the right offers a little tactile input.

Fidgets help some children attend and distract others. Check items for recycling to find some good fidgets.

Weights give a little proprioceptive input and are calming to some children.

A variety of textured balls are a great addition to regular balls and might make a good circle time activity.

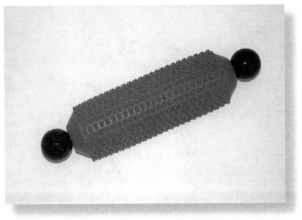

This tactile rolling pin isn't so much for circle time. But since it can be used by a teacher or a child, it seemed a good tool to share.

Here are some props that provide children with vestibular experiences and different experiences of their bodies in space: tipping chairs, hoppity hops, therapeutic "eggs," sit and spins, and the good old-fashioned rocking horse.

Part 3

The Wider View

Chapter 9

Creating an Inclusive Children's Community

A few children and a teacher sit around a table. Their arms are stretched to the middle of the table, and the teacher encourages the children to compare the varying shades of their skin. One little boy with very pale skin has poor articulation and is having a hard time making himself understood.

Another little boy, with darker skin, says to the teacher, "You can't understand what he's saying."

The teacher, without missing a beat, says, "That's right. Corin is learning to make his mouth work, just like you are learning how to keep children safe. We are all learning something!"

And indeed we are.

This vignette actually takes place in The Little School's teacher training DVD, *Relationships: The Key to Teaching and Learning in the Early Years* (Little School 2004). Lisa, the teacher in the vignette, has been teacher to Corin, the pale-skinned boy, and Jordan, the dark-skinned boy, for two years. She knows much more about them than the color of their skin. Like Mike and Angie in the previous chapters, Lisa knows these boys' strengths and interests, developmental profiles, families, life experiences, and challenges. At the time this actual classroom scene was filmed, Jordan was indeed learning how to keep people safe. He was a boy of passionate feelings, and sometimes when he was upset, he became aggressive. He had verbal and cognitive strengths, great social leadership skills, and a good heart. Jordan was the son of a single mom. He was a biracial child, and his skin color was different than his mom's, his teachers', and many of his classmates'.

Corin also had some trouble with aggression. At the time of the vignette, his challenge to communicate, express his newfound cognitive skills, and feel powerful among his peers was causing him some frustration. Corin was very engaged in the life of the classroom and life in general. He had some developmental challenges, a little sister, and a supportive mom and dad.

When Lisa chose to respond to Jordan's comment about Corin's speech, she did so with all of this knowledge. She chose her words carefully. She wanted both boys to feel supported in the challenges with which each was currently struggling. She was communicating that she was there to support them and that she hoped they would be there to support each other. And in her matter-of-fact way of responding, she also communicated her acceptance of each of them and of anything that might arise for them in her classroom.

This ability to choose just the right words for just the right purpose is not a superhuman ability. *It is the ability of an open, reflective teacher who has committed herself to creating an inclusive children's community in her classroom.*

Acceptance, Acknowledgment, Respect

One common and universal desire we all share is to be accepted for who we are. A classroom where a teacher consistently responds to every child, regardless of circumstances, with acceptance, acknowledgment, and respect is an emotionally safe classroom. In an emotionally safe classroom, children will be comfortable asking for what they need, taking risks, learning from experience, working on their challenges, and offering care and support to other children.

Two universal principles apply to all children—*our differences make us who we are* and *a child cannot be known separate from her context*. It is the specifics of a child's profile, family life, and life experience that must be affirmed for the child to truly feel accepted, acknowledged, and respected. In the very brief descriptions of Corin and Jordan above, it becomes clear that for these children to feel affirmed, the teacher must look at what the environment, curriculum, activities, and materials say about these children and their lives. She must be ready for whatever comments, emotions, and conversations the child needs or wants to have with her. The child must know that whatever he shares will be greeted with an honest, authentic, accepting response.

For a community of children to be receptive and affirming to a child with special needs, they must feel affirmed themselves. Thus, any inclusion teacher must deeply reflect about the acceptance, acknowledgment, and respect she shows in her classroom for all of the important aspects of each child's many identities. The teacher must be equipped to see the world through each child's eyes. The teacher must also attempt to understand how the child relates to his family structure, race, ethnicity, culture, gender, and developmental profile.

Even if she has not yet learned about each child in the classroom, a teacher who thinks, feels, and speaks the language of acceptance, acknowledgment, and respect will be creating the emotionally safe atmosphere that leads to the culture of inclusion.

Playing a game or doing an art project with photos of classmates helps children learn more about each other.

This child is painting a portrait of herself from a photo projected onto the wall by an overhead projector. Through this activity, children learn a lot about themselves. The painting activity is part of a long series of activities in which children learn more about their own and their classmates' physical differences and similarities. These same photos are cut up into parts and made into a display of everyone's eyes, noses, and mouths. The questions "What do you notice?" and "Can you match these face parts to your friends' faces" provoke a lot of interest and discussion.

The Language of Inclusion

What does this language sound like? Here are examples of the kind of language a teacher in an inclusive classroom might use. The examples each relate to one of four of our guiding principles:

- *Bodies Matter:* "We are ready to sit for a quiet meeting, but your body doesn't look ready. Do you want to push the meeting benches across the room for us? After your muscles do some work, it will be easier for your body to sit quietly."
- *Brains Matter:* "Hold on! Xander is trying to tell us something, and it looks like his brain needs a minute to think. Let's wait."
- *Emotions Matter:* "You are so sad about saying good-bye to your mom that you are not ready to play with friends yet. Why don't we put up a curtain here for you so you can be alone until you feel ready."
- *Relationships Matter:* "Charla is playing with lots of children, and she usually just plays with you. That's hard for you. I can't let you hit Charla or the other kids, though. Let's sit here and think together about what else you can do."

In each comment, notice how the teacher acknowledges something that is real for the child. Take note of how respectful the teacher is. And look for how the teacher makes an accepting place for the child's individual needs within the classroom. An emotionally safe, affirming classroom is not one where limits are avoided. It is one where teachers can acknowledge the desires behind the aggressive or negative behavior even when they can't accept the behavior. Offering acceptance, acknowledgment, and respect is one essential way you create a classroom culture in which children are likely to be accepting and supportive of each other.

There is another simple way you can create that accepting environment. When we discussed the wisdom of using the universal principle of a strength-based model in chapter 2, we wrote, "Using one's strengths as the foundation for growth breeds joy, motivation, enthusiasm, and optimism." The more you can point out each child's strengths and positive behavior, as well as the strengths and positive behavior of the class as a whole, the better everyone will feel.

Children Can Do It Too!

With your coaching, children can provide the same kind of acceptance, acknowledgment, and respect to each other that you offer to them. You become the role model. The children learn how to speak to each other from listening to you. You can also coach them directly by making suggestions about how to relate to their peers in specific situations. Coaching children in this way has at least three benefits:

1. It increases the emotionally positive, affirming atmosphere in a classroom.

2. The children learn the language of positive affirmation and respect to take with them as they grow.

3. The children experience how good it feels to make others feel good, contributing to the likelihood that they will become lifelong, positive community members.

Using the same examples from above, here are some ways you can get the children more involved in the active creation of a positive, inclusive community:

- *Bodies Matter:* "We are ready to sit for a quiet meeting, but Lupe's body looks like it is not ready to be quiet yet. Any ideas? Your friend Mitzi suggests getting our muscles ready by pushing the benches over. Do you like that idea, Lupe? Do you want to invite some friends to help push? I bet some other people's bodies aren't ready to sit yet either. Lupe and Mitzi, thank you for helping *all* of us get our bodies ready to sit still."

Getting through this dialogue and taking the time to have some children push benches across the room might take some time away from the meeting. It is possible, however, that children might learn more from thinking about how to get their bodies ready and helping each other than they would learn from the meeting:

- *Brains Matter:* "Hold on! Xander is trying to tell us something, and it looks like his brain needs a minute to think. Can you help your friend Xander by being very, very quiet?" And after Xander shares, "Did it help your brain work better when your friends stayed quiet? It did? Now we know another way we can help each other's brains to work. This class is good at helping each other."

With the first few comments, the teacher has modeled how seriously she takes children's individual needs. In her reflective questioning, she has reminded the children that brains work differently. The final comment affirms the social behavior she is encouraging:

- *Emotions Matter:* "You are so sad about saying good-bye to your mom that you are not ready to play with friends yet. Why don't we make a curtain here for you so that you can be alone until you feel ready? Shall we ask your friends to help make the curtain? Hey everyone, Katya needs your help!"

The teacher lets Katya know there is nothing wrong with having sad feelings or expressing them. She lets her know that friends can help when you feel sad. And she provides an opportunity for the children to be altruistic:

- *Relationships Matter:* "Fiona is playing with lots of children, and she usually just plays just with you. That's hard for you. But I can't let you hit Fiona or the other children. I know some other children in the class have had just this problem. Would you like me to have them come tell you how they handled it?"

Again, the teacher affirms the feeling but places a limit on the behavior. And she again offers the other children a way to help. This time they can help by sharing their experiences.

Children, like adults, want to feel involved, helpful, and powerful. That is why they will often respond positively to this kind of coaching. You can see how this kind of positive involvement among children creates an atmosphere in which all children, including those with special needs, will receive valuable acceptance, modeling, and feedback from their peers.

You can influence how children see each other with what you say about their peers and how you say it. When children hear *you* speak respectfully to other children about their challenges, they respect those children as well. They feel sympathetic to the children and their challenges. It is often useful to let children know about each other's goals, challenges, and strengths. In chapter 7, Angie explained to Danny's friends that when he got disruptive, it was because he was trying so hard to convey his ideas—"Danny is working on using his words to tell you his ideas. . . . You can remind him to use his words. . . . I know you can all work together to make your game fun and to get what you need." Angie framed a way for Danny's friends to understand him in a positive light. Instead of thinking of him as just disruptive, they also saw him as someone who was struggling to explain himself. And they could help him! (For more examples of teachers using the accepting, supportive language of relationship-based inclusion, see appendix A.)

Communication: A Key

We all know that communication is a key factor in helping people get along with each other. But how often do you make communication the topic of conversation in your classroom? Because some children with special needs communicate differently, to create an inclusive atmosphere, it is important to help children learn all of the ways people communicate with each other. They communicate through their words, their gestures, their body language, their facial expressions, and their noises, cries, and shouts. Sometimes people communicate through a drawing, a picture board, a communication book, or a voice output communication aid. Children will be intrigued to explore these different kinds of communication and identify how each one works. If children learn to pay attention to the many different ways people communicate, their social skills will undoubtedly benefit. And the child who uses methods other than verbal language will fit right in.

Look for the various ways you can explore and play with communication in your classroom. Try a snacktime when you communicate only with gestures. Look at pictures of faces to guess what they are trying to communicate.

Listen to recorded voices saying the same words but with different intonation and intent. Guess what the person is trying to communicate with each version. These kinds of games will be fun and challenging for all. And they will be wonderful skill-building practice for your children with communication challenges.

Support a variety of communication styles in your classroom. This will benefit all children and will especially support children learning English as a second language and children with various communication challenges:

- Have plenty of visual cards available to allow children to express needs and desires for everything from what kinds of materials they want to play with to when they need to use the bathroom.

- Have visual cards available that express emotions so that children can use these to express how they feel when words don't work.

- Develop a rich common gestural language for your classroom. Perhaps children or teachers can put their hands over their ears to signal when things get too loud. Drawing in a deep breath can signal that everyone needs a deep, calming breath.

- There are many signs and sign phrases from American Sign Language about practical and emotional matters that make very useful shared classroom gestures.

- Make use of music to convey transitions and other important information. Music is an open communication channel for many of us, including many children with special needs.

Sometimes a teacher being in tune with a child's gestures can make that child feel more understood than any conversation ever could.

Creating an Inclusive Children's Community • **163**

Give children honest feedback about their communication skills. When a child speaks for so long that the other children get bored and drift away, point it out to her. "You have a lot of ideas for play. But your friends can't listen so long. What if you just told them one idea at a time?" Similarly, when a child speaks too loudly or too softly or gets too close for her peers' comfort, help her see the effect. "Let's ask Kyu why he isn't answering when you speak to him. Sometimes when people don't answer, it is because they can't hear what is said." As long as this feedback occurs in the context of your respectful, supportive acceptance of the child, it will be welcome information.

Children are motivated to improve their relationships with their peers. This same motivation is useful when you give children feedback about the communication styles of children with special needs. "Mira, Sasha is knocking your blocks down because she wants to play and doesn't know how to start. Can you show her a way?" Mira's irritation might turn to pride as she helps Sasha build blocks with her. If Mira learns that Sasha pays attention when Mira gets right up to her face and speaks loudly, she will feel even more successful. Children like to connect with other children, and they like to be given the tools that empower them to do so.

Sometimes for conversation to flow, a child may feel the need to literally hide part of himself. If you look at this through an accepting, inclusive lens, this is an easy enough accommodation to make. This girl certainly seems to be taking this different form of communication in stride.

Giving children feedback about their own communication styles is one way of providing them with useful feedback about themselves. Children are open to this kind of feedback because it helps them get what they want in the world. Communication tips can help them figure out how to play and make friends. Children are also open to feedback about their sensory profile, learning, regulatory, and arousal styles. This kind of information can help them figure out how to be most comfortable in the hustle and bustle of a peer community, as well as the demands of a learning environment. Just as you might find it valuable to learn that chewing gum during a meeting helps you pay attention, a child might welcome a weighted lap cushion during a circle time. We encourage you to give feedback and explore their individual profiles with the other children.

Sensory Styles

Hopefully, by now you have learned how useful the sensory lens is for looking at children. But the usefulness of this approach doesn't end with its application in *understanding* children. Information about the sensory-arousal-regulatory system is made for putting it into action—literally. Think back to chapter 5, in which Danny's teachers were coming up with goals and strategies to help him in the classroom. Many of the goals centered on responding to Danny's sensory-arousal-regulatory system. By addressing Danny's sensory system, the teachers hoped that Danny would be more physically, mentally, and emotionally organized and receptive. He would be able to take advantage of all of his strengths and talents to learn. The sensory support the teachers brought into the classroom to help Danny benefited *all* of the children.

Individual support creates community strength. Addressing children's sensory-arousal-regulatory needs is clearly valuable for children with special needs. And it is valuable for *all* children. We all have sensory systems. Some of us can benefit from techniques like fidgets or a weighted lap cushion to help us pay attention at meeting times. All of us can benefit from calming, organizing techniques, such as taking deep breaths or using our muscles to lift heavy objects. Embedding practices that address the sensory system into the daily life of the classroom helps all children bring their best selves to be ready to learn. Embedding these practices also supports the creation of an inclusive classroom. If several children are wearing lap cushions at a meeting, or all of the children take deep breaths when it is time to make the transition from a rowdy activity to a calm activity, the sensory supports you are supplying to children with special needs will not stand out. They are just one of the sensory-supported gang.

This child chose to take his chewy outside with him. It doesn't seem like it interfered with his play.

These children chose to wear headphones. The headphones don't seem to be interfering with their day either.

A little physical activity in the middle of a meeting time wakes up everyone's attention.

Sensory tools help people pay attention at circle time too. They are available to anyone who wants them.

Two children here chose fidgets, while another child chose a weighted yoga bag for extra proprioceptive input.

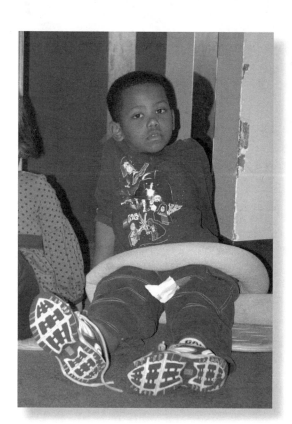

This child chose a weighted snake.

When sensory tools aren't available, children create their own. Because of all of the muscles in the jaw, biting offers great proprioceptive input!

In fact, these kinds of supports become part of the curriculum. Just as teachers discuss communication as an ongoing topic of conversation, so teachers and children regularly discuss issues and strategies for just right sensory input and arousal and regulation practices. These are pretty heady concepts for preschoolers, but they are surprisingly easy to translate into intuitively understandable language. For example, in the narrative about Danny, the teachers talked to him about how his engine was running. They helped him learn that when his engine felt high, the calming corner would be a good place to go to help his engine feel just right again.

Embedding sensory supports throughout your classroom will certainly make your classroom a better place for children with special needs. It will also make your classroom a more successful classroom for all of the children. When we discussed the principle *Bodies Matter* in chapter 2, we asked the following questions: "What if we used what we know about the body as a foundation to support children's academic, social, and emotional learning?" "What if responding to the needs of a child's body became the magic key to ensuring that a child was ready to learn, play, and interact?"

Embedding sensory supports throughout your environment and throughout your day may be just that magic key. By incorporating knowledge about the sensory system into your teaching, you become a more effective teacher for all children.

Emotional and Social Skills

A relationship-based inclusive classroom makes learning social and emotional skills a central aspect of the learning goals, curriculum, and experience. Some of the skills children need to attain are internal skills, such as emotional regulation. Some of the skills children need to develop are interpersonal skills, such as conflict resolution. Children's ideas and attitudes about conflict, about differences of opinion and perspective, and about how communities work are important to the learning process as well.

Emotional Self-Regulation

Preschool teachers spend a lot of time helping children identify and express their feelings. And indeed, feelings do matter. They guide us throughout our lives. At some point, however, all of us need to learn that we can't just let our feelings come out willy-nilly, expressing them in any form that feels right. Crying every time your boss corrects you just doesn't work. Blowing up at your spouse every time you get mad creates a lot of bad feelings. Raising your voice to the police officer who pulls you over may lead to something even worse.

In our experience during the last twenty years of teaching, it seems as if more children are having difficulty with regulating their emotions. And certainly if you look at all of the stories about road rage, air rage, and widespread incivility, it seems as if adults, too, are having more difficulty regulating their emotions.

What do we mean by emotional regulation? Think of how you feel when you get very, very angry with someone. What does it feel like in your body? Do your fists clench? Stomach tighten? Do you feel blood coursing through your head? The reactions may vary, but these are all signs of emotional flooding. When we are emotionally flooded, the amygdala part of our brain is in charge, and we can't access the higher thinking levels in our cortex (MacLean 1990). In other words, it is all feeling, action, and reaction. No room for calm, considered thought. When our amygdala is in charge, we aren't able to solve problems verbally with someone, make good decisions, or even take in and understand what someone is telling us. We are just flooded with feeling.

As the DIR functional-emotional milestones teach us, in order to engage, a person must be calm and regulated enough to take in information (Greenspan and Wieder 1998). When a child is emotionally flooded, he will not be able to do most of the things you want him to do. He won't be able to learn, take in your guidance, talk things over, or respond to problems. So to make sure a child will benefit from your guidance or the classroom experience, make sure that he is emotionally regulated.

This can make your life as a teacher complicated. Suppose a child gets angry and knocks all of the puzzles children have been working on to the floor. Naturally, as a teacher, you want to let the child know that this isn't acceptable behavior. You also want to let the other children see that the child isn't just going to get away with destroying their work. So you walk quickly over, shake your finger, and set a limit in a loud, stern voice. But the child, already emotionally flooded, experiences the quick walk and loud voice without even taking in the actual words you are saying, and he really loses it. He starts running around the classroom knocking everything over. Now you are left in the position of chasing him and physically forcing him to stop. In his current state, he may resist and start hitting, kicking, and even trying to bite you. The situation has gone from bad to worse.

Not all children react this way, but some do. Some of the children who might react this way may be typically developing children with very intense emotions. Some may have home environments that haven't helped them learn how to get back in control when flooded. Children who have had early emotional trauma often have brain wiring that doesn't support emotional regulation (Koplow 1996). And this is also true of some children with special needs.

So what do *you* do? Think about your own reactions when you are upset. What helps you calm down when you are really angry? For most people, being by themselves is a big help. Some people calm down while moving (walking works for Cassie; cleaning works for Leslie). Others just like to sit still and breathe (Todd). But all three of us also calm down if someone we care about can just calmly sit with us, not saying too much. When people are very upset, they often cannot take in advice.

These same methods work in a classroom. The calmer we can stay, the more of a container we can be, the more likely the child will be able to calm himself. In chapter 6, Angie and Mike realize that, as often happens, this reaction is happening in reverse. As Danny gets tense, they mirror him by getting tense too! So they make a decision that when he gets tense, they will get calm.

You would use the same technique with the out-of-control puzzle guy from our example above. You might walk over more slowly, squat down, and say in a calm, steady voice, "I can't let you knock the puzzles over. You seem really upset. Let's pick up the puzzles together." Your upset child might be able to mirror your calm to get back in control (instead of having you mirror his out-of-control feeling with your loud voice and quick movement). If your modeling isn't enough, you might need to let the puzzles sit for a while so you can help him try some of the calming techniques from the repertoire you have developed as a class. Until he is calm, he will not be able to understand the negative impact he has had on his peers or help repair the situation.

If regulation and emotions are frequent topics of conversation in your classroom, the children will all understand that the puzzle thrower needs time to calm down. They will not look at this as unfair, special treatment. It is a class understanding that it is never good to act from that flooded place. With this understanding in place and the tools to calm down rooted in the classroom curriculum, children with difficulty will get the support they need from peers and teachers. Again, limits and consequences are not forgotten. They come after the child is calm. Hopefully, by the time the puzzle thrower leaves preschool, he will have learned acceptable emotional responses. And everyone in the class will have gained valuable tools they will use for the rest of their lives.

Techniques to Calm Down and Regain a Regulated State

- Deep breathing.
- Getting in touch with heart rate and body sensations.
- Sitting quietly with a trusted adult.
- Sitting quietly alone in a nook or calm area.
- Looking at books quietly alone.
- Rocking in a rocking chair.
- Swinging in a hammock.
- Doing something to get the "mad" feelings out: tearing paper, pounding on a pillow, stamping feet, pounding in the sand area outside, running around outside.

While some children become calm by being contained in a nook or on someone's lap, others do not need to be touched and regain control more easily in the freedom of outdoors.

Conflict Resolution

Conflicts often cause our emotions to rise. To help children learn to resolve conflicts, teachers must teach the skills of emotional regulation. In addition, teachers must give children the actual tools for conflict resolution. Finally, *ideas* about conflict will also influence how children approach conflict. A key message to offer about problems and conflict is that both are inevitable. Everyone encounters problems many times a day. Any people who work together, play together, or live together will sometimes have conflicts. Sometimes we even have conflicts with strangers.

Because conflicts and problems are inevitable, one of the most important parts of your job as a teacher is to provide children with a full conflict-resolution toolbox. For all children, you first want to make sure that everyone is regulated or calm enough to solve the problem. Are they ready to listen and think of solutions? When everyone is ready, you can support a process in which each child says what she wants, listens to what the other person wants, and brainstorms solutions until the children find one on which they both agree. This method is exactly the same method many adults use to mediate their conflicts.

Gaining conflict-resolution skills takes time and repeated experience. A teacher can be the bridge and help children with different styles and skill levels until they are ready to solve problems on their own.

With repeated experience, children can take on this task of conflict resolution by themselves. What an empowering feeling!

Creating an Inclusive Children's Community • **173**

Many children with special needs may have even more difficulty resolving conflicts and solving problems. They may need simpler tools, different tools, and more patience. It is important to make sure that every child participates in conflict resolution and problem solving, regardless of the challenges their special needs present to the process. Problem solving is a very necessary, basic social skill. DIR's functional-emotional milestones teach us that by learning to problem solve—with materials, in play, or with people—children are moving up Greenspan and Wieder's (1998) functional-emotional ladder. They are enhancing their social, emotional, *and* cognitive development.

If you use the *Engage-Reflect-Plan* process to figure out how a child with special needs can participate in problem solving, there is no end to the solutions that can be found. Remember that part of the process will not simply be figuring out how the child with special needs can participate but how the other children can participate as well. Conflict resolution is by its nature a collaborative effort. Keep in mind that many of the ideas that you develop so that children with special needs can participate in problem solving will work for many of the other children.

Here are a few examples of obstacles children with specific profiles might encounter and how you can adjust the problem-solving process for them.

Manuel is on the autism spectrum. He has difficulty completing the circles of communication that are part of the third functional-emotional milestone. Manuel loves to play with trains, and another boy, Sámi, comes along and takes most of the train cars away. Because Manuel cannot communicate for himself, you may need to respond on his behalf. But make sure not to leave him out of the process altogether. Use what you know about Manuel.

"Sámi, I saw you took the train cars. I know Manuel usually plays with all of the cars!"

Use Manuel's facial expression if that is helpful. "Look at Manuel's face. Usually he is smiling when he plays with the trains. Now he isn't. How do you think he feels about you taking the cars?"

Use Manuel's gestures. "I see Manuel is flapping his arms. He got upset when you took the cars."

This might be a time when you can motivate Manuel to open a circle of communication. Getting those trains back is high motivation! "Manuel, I can see you are upset. Do you see where the train cars went? Can you let Sámi know that you want them back?"

Again, use Manuel's gestures. "Sámi, Manuel is reaching his arms out. He's letting you know he wants the train cars back."

Rosie has cerebral palsy. She has the capacity to complete circles of communication and is an excellent problem solver. It takes her a while to get her words out, and children need to pay close attention to understand what she is saying. Because she is in a wheelchair, she can't move around the classroom as quickly as the other children. In her situation, you need to scaffold the skills of the other child. When Sámi comes over to take the trains from Rosie, you need to intervene quickly before he moves away.

"Wait! Sámi, you have to check and see if it is okay with Rosie if you take the trains."

When Sámi asks and looks like he's ready to leave before Rosie can answer, step in again. "Hold on. Give Rosie a chance to answer."

If Rosie's answer is hard to understand, reinforce her words as part of the problem solving. "So Rosie says she doesn't want you to take the trains. What happens now?"

"Oh, it looks like Rosie has an idea. Come closer so you can hear."

Here's another example. It is difficult for George to get his words and thoughts out. It is also hard for George to quickly process what is being said. George needs you to slow down the process. He might need you to repeat what is being said in a simple way he can more quickly absorb. And he might need your help in translating the intentions in his brief words.

"George," says Kamila, "I really need those trains right now. We are making a city and we are looking for a way for people to get around the city. We have tracks but no trains." George looks lost.

"So, George, Kamila is asking for the trains." Wait many seconds. When Kamila tries to break in again, stop her: "Hold on, Kamila, George is thinking." Wait several seconds again. "Do you want to give Kamila the trains?"

"Play" is George's response.

"You want to play?" you ask, trying to figure out his intention. He nods.

Kamila responds quickly. "Well, I don't know if you can play because we already have a bus driver for our city. I'm the firefighter, and we have a train conductor already."

Again, re-word her information and help him along. You can also buy him some time by your attentive pause after you ask your question. "Who do you want to be, George?"

If you keep your eyes glued on him while you wait, Kamila might too.

"Tracks," says George.

"You are thinking about the train tracks." (Wait a few beats.) "Do you want to put the tracks together?"

George nods again.

"Okay, you can be the construction guy and put all the train tracks and buildings together," says Kamilah. She takes George's hand, and off they go together.

Notice that in all three of these examples, you show your respect for the children by not taking over for them. You may need to translate, based on their facial expressions, gestures, or telegraphed language, but they are very much in the driver's seat. You have not skipped over them to tell the other child how to treat Manuel, Rosie, or George. They remain in charge of their peer interactions.

If you have good visual communication props or have developed a good gestural communication in your classroom, such tools might be very useful in conflict situations for the children described above. A gesture that is universally understood to say "Stop that!" in your classroom or a picture tile with a symbol for "I'm mad" would probably get a lot of use.

Zora, James, and Karyna have just started playing a game involving pirates. Karyna has great difficulty when she can't lead all aspects of the play.

She is generally bossy and inflexible. At first the children liked her as a leader. But lately, they haven't liked her at all.

"Here's the ship," says James. "I'm steering."

"Yeah, and there's some bad guys! Let's chase them," Zora chimes in.

"No, we have to build the ship," says Karyna, "so we have to stay on the island. We all have to go search for wood."

"Nah. Let's chase the bad guys, James." And with that, Zora and James run off.

Is Karyna rigid in her play with her peers because she has special needs or because this is her personality? Either answer might be correct. The answer also might be something in between. Karyna might have a sensitive sensory system. Because she often feels overwhelmed and out of control in her daily life from all of the sensory input, she tries to take control whenever she can. Whatever the reason for her challenges, she needs some honest coaching from you.

In your most sympathetic voice, you can say, "James and Zora had an idea for the pirate ship. You wanted a different idea. It is fun to get friends to try your ideas. You like that—and James and Zora like it too. It is no fun when your friends go away. I wonder how it would feel for you to play their idea. I'll try it with you, and afterward we can see how it felt." By offering to join the play, too, you might be able to encourage her to try a new way. But it might take Karyna a while to learn new play skills. A social story, such as the teachers used with Michelle in chapter 8, might be a useful tool here. The story can describe encounters with friends in which problems occur and how good everyone feels when the problems are resolved by using everyone's ideas. Karyna needs a clearer message than most that listening and compromising are part of friendship.

And what about the child who always gives in, who never sticks up for himself, like Timmy in the following example?

"Timmy, I want those train tracks!"

"Sure," says Timmy.

"Timmy, you can't be the captain of the pirate ship. I want to be the captain."

"Okay."

"Timmy, you can't have any blocks. We're using them all."

And Timmy walks away.

You might miss Timmy in a classroom. Because he is so agreeable, he makes things easy. But as with Karyna, you don't need to understand why Timmy doesn't stick up for himself to do something about it. He deserves to see what it feels like to get his way.

"This time, you say your idea first, Timmy. I bet your friends will want to do it your way!"

Because the children are in a classroom culture in which everyone is trying to help each other, they probably will.

Emotions Matter

Why are children likely to help each other when the classroom culture is a positive, supportive one? One of the reasons is because children like to be powerful. It is a powerful thing to help someone else. It feels good. But children may not cooperate for this reason alone. You must understand that to gain children's cooperation to work on their own challenges, to follow your limits and guidelines, and to invest in problem solving and conflict resolution, the starting point must be the children's own emotions. They need to know that they will get what they want by working with you. A child who is feeling sad about what a classmate said will engage in problem solving if he thinks doing so will make him feel better. An angry child will engage in problem solving if she thinks that by doing so she will be heard. The child willing to calm her body at circle time does so because she anticipates that the conversation and songs at circle time will engage and delight her.

We wrote at the beginning of this chapter about accepting, acknowledging, and respecting children's feelings as a way to validate them and bolster their self-concept and self-confidence. Making room for feelings in the classroom has an even more basic purpose. Children, like adults, are motivated when they care and when they want something. If your classroom is set up to help children get what they want, they will follow you anywhere. And that includes into higher motivations, such as generosity of spirit, self-discipline for the sake of the community, and learning for the love of learning!

In an accepting, supportive, inclusive environment, children step forward to help each other in all sorts of ways. In simple ways such as

. . . helping with a shoe,

. . . opening a food packet,

. . . pushing your friend up a slope,

. . . or helping stretch out her leg.

Or children might be there for their peers when they need a little support

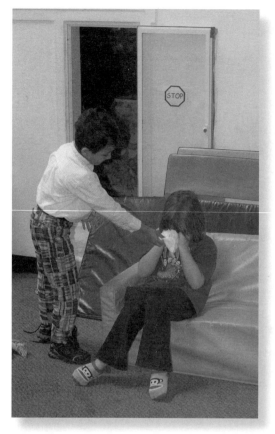

. . . by offering them a tissue,

. . . coming over to check on them,

. . . or just plain being there.

Symbolic Play

Many of the tools and concepts we discuss in this chapter can also be learned through play, especially symbolic play (also called *imaginative play* or *dramatic play*). In fact, children use this kind of play to symbolize the dramas that happen in their lives, internally and externally. Could all that play about bad guys, monsters, and fires be helping children think and talk about all those emotions raging inside? Could they be exploring how scared and powerless it feels to be a small child and what they can do about it? Could they even be exploring how angry they feel sometimes and how scary that feels? Could they be acting out all their aggression in their play, so they don't do things like knocking over the puzzles?

And what about family play? Are children modeling their parents, reenacting the roles of being nurtured and nurturing, the experiences of being soothed and cared for? Are they showing what it feels like to soothe and care for someone else? Similarly, in kitten or puppy play, are children exploring emotional regulation when those pet owners create a calm, ordered container for any wild impulses? It is hard to get too out of control when you are on a leash.

Playing out their aggressive ideas meant so much to these boys that they spent a long time making their props. In these times, when children have a hard time separating real-life aggression from aggression in play, figuring out how to allow them to work out these important issues through play is a challenge. The real and media violence that surround children makes it even more confusing for teachers. And yet, if children are truly to work out their inner conflicts and grow in their cognitive and emotional development through play, early childhood educators must figure out how to make a safe space for the exploration of aggression through play.

Recognizing the value of symbolic play and actively supporting it also help create an inclusive children's community. Look around your classroom. You'll see plenty of examples of how important symbolic play is to the emotional, social, and cognitive development of all children, especially children with special needs.

Here are several different ways to support children who have more difficulty engaging in dramatic play:

- Narrate the play.
- Become a player yourself so you can help the child who has difficulty following the play.
- Scaffold and intercede with the group when necessary, all in the context of the play.
- Structure the acting out of familiar stories or themes so children with special needs can learn these themes in the structured context and then translate them into less structured settings. (In chapter 6, the teachers used Michelle's love of hats to get her involved in group play by acting out *Caps for Sale*.)

All of these methods are invisible to the children. They will not see that you are providing help to individual children who may have difficulty. Scaffolding children's ability to participate in dramatic play ensures that those who have more difficulty will be able to participate with their classmates in this all-important aspect of life in the classroom. Children who have braved monsters, fires, and earthquakes together, who have been each other's mommies or babies or brothers or kittens, feel a bond that would be hard to explain to an adult. Offering every child the support she needs to participate in dramatic play (without making it obvious to the other children) allows the child with special needs to be part of the heartbeat of the children's culture, the culture they create and share with each other, in which adults are just other players.

Walking in My Shoes

Some of the tools you use to scaffold children in dramatic play are also tools you can use to help them participate in other classroom interactions. "Walking in another's shoes" or "seeing through another's eyes" is developmentally challenging for preschool children. Doing so can be especially challenging tasks for children with special needs. Like self-regulation, this is another practice that can become part of the daily curriculum and conversation of the classroom. Simple narration of what is happening can help children learn to see other points of view. Simulations of typical classroom dilemmas using persona dolls, puppets, or toy animals are another good way to see a situation through another's eyes. Asking questions is a third tool:

- "How do you think she was feeling when she stomped away?"
- "What was he trying to do when he brought that chair over to your bus and sat down?"
- "Do teachers and parents ever feel sad? Why? What do they do about it?"

By "walking in another's shoes," all children can begin to learn the important social skill of empathy.

Sounds Like We All Have Different Ideas

Not all conflicts are over toys or who gets to be the bad guy. Some are about ideas that come up in conversations. Is broccoli delicious or disgusting? Is it okay to watch a lot of television? Are you a baby if you still like stuffed animals? Who sides with the troll in "The Three Billy Goats Gruff" and who sides with the billy goats? Do people go to heaven when they die? Can boys marry boys?

These are all conversations that have caused strife between children in our classrooms. We have developed a standard way of responding that underlines the values of our accepting, inclusive classroom, in which everyone is different and everyone needs to keep each other's feelings safe.

"It sounds like we all have different ideas about that. It's okay to have different ideas. Yarina, you believe X, and, Kai, you believe Y. You both believe different things."

Because we are a diverse community, we want families to know we respect their desires to impart their own values to their children. We have a few additional factual phrases or practices we add when the topic is especially charged, like what happens to people when they die or if people of the same sex can marry. When there is factual information, we impart it. (At the time we were writing this book, for example, marriage of same-sex couples was legal in several states.) But we also have developed some special language that goes beyond the factual. For example, "Different families believe different things about that. Some families believe A, some families believe B, and some families believe C. You may want to go home and ask what your family believes." And then we make sure to give families a heads-up about the classroom discussion of the day. We have rarely had a family who has had a problem with this approach.

In some cases, one might personally want or hope children will develop a different opinion than their family's. But that is for a different developmental stage in their life. At the preschool age, it seems most appropriate to let children know that different families have different ideas and to find out what their own family believes. If children grow up with the idea that people have differing ideas about things, one day they will realize on their own that they can have a different idea from their family's. At this developmental level, finding a way to explore and respect all sides of an issue in a way that is comfortable for our families seems the right way to go.

This language of "everyone has different ideas" has its limits if it bumps up against someone's universal need for respect and acceptance. For example, if a child in our class said "Having black skin means you are dumb," we would emphatically reject the notion.

Similarly, beliefs can surface that adversely affect our children with special needs: "You're a baby if you can't talk." "You're a baby if you wear a diaper." "There's something wrong with you if you can't walk." There are situations in which we would not simply say that different people have different ideas. But we *would* be able to help children learn about the variety of individual difference through our response. "I can't let you say that. That doesn't keep Molly's feelings safe. Some people learn to talk when they are babies. Some people learn when they are older. Some people learn two languages when they are babies. Some people never use words to communicate but always communicate through their gestures and facial expressions. Right now Molly is using her face, body, and sounds to communicate."

Community Strength through Individual Support

That last comment about Molly represents an overarching message we give to children about differences. We have identified several important messages to convey to support the creation of an inclusive classroom:

- Everyone learns skills at different times.
- Everyone learns in different ways.
- Everyone is learning something.
- Everyone has strengths. Everyone has challenges.
- We can use our strengths to support each other. We can get support for our challenges.
- Sometimes to help support someone, the whole community will bend toward that person. That means the whole class might give up what it wanted or planned in order to help someone out.
- Sometimes to let a classroom community go on with what it is doing, a child must bend to the community.
- When we work together and support each other, we can accomplish great things.

These kinds of messages help a child with special needs to be accepted, embraced, and supported by her peers. These messages also help all of us to feel accepted, embraced, and supported. Here we return to our basic principles: *We are more same than different. A reflective teacher committed to openness and active learning can be an excellent inclusion teacher—with a little help from the community. Individual support creates community strength.* And everyone in the community benefits.

In the game of Busy Bee, bees fly to a flower, where they find a partner. The partners match various body parts on each other's bodies (here, chin to chin and ear to ear) and then, at the teacher's signal, fly off to another flower and find a new partner. Being partners with children they are not close friends with is challenging for some children. Touching is hard for others. But all the children are motivated to make the game work, building connections while they play.

Children are paired for many different kinds of activities. Teachers start off pairing children with a high degree of comfort with each other. Over time, they partner children with less familiar peers. "How to greet your partner" and "how to care for your partner" are activities practiced when children are getting used to each other. Partner time is especially useful for children who have difficulty connecting with peers. After being paired to explore a particular part of their classroom together, these two classmates are certainly looking forward to partner time!

Caring for the environment and the larger community empowers children and makes them feel good. Children can help with many of the real kinds of work that happen in the course of a school day. Much of it involves asking them to use their muscles—all the better for organizing their sensory systems for the learning activities that follow.

We use visuals, techniques, and tools to help children learn to pay attention, follow directions, and learn academic skills. Why not use visuals, techniques, and tools to help children learn what it means to be a good community member?

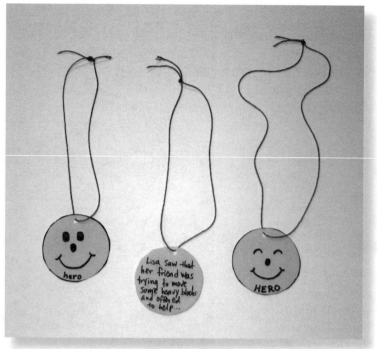

In this class, children receive hero badges when they do something out of the ordinary to help a classmate. They take their hero badges home, where family members can read about their heroics on the back of the badge. At the beginning of the year, the teachers nominate children for hero badges. As the year goes on, children nominate each other.

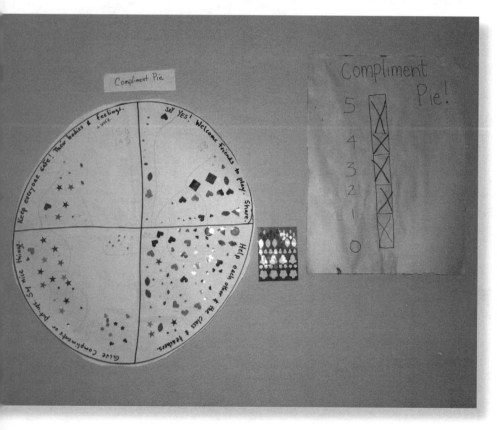

In this class, children and teachers decided on some ways they wanted to try to treat each other. They put a sticker on the compliment pie every time someone acted in one of the agreed-upon ways. When they got to 100 stickers, they had a dance party.

In this class of three-year-olds, every time a child made another child feel good, the children would put a marble in the Sam Can. The Sam Can was a big motivator and had a significant impact on a group that had been having a difficult time together.

• • •

In this chapter, we have suggested how you can create a classroom culture in which all children, including children with special needs, will feel accepted, respected, and included. Through your outlook, actions, and language, you can be the model for acceptance, acknowledgment, and respect. You can offer children the lifelong tools of communication, problem solving, and symbolic play to get their own needs met and to meet the needs of others. Sensory supports can be embedded in the classroom as aids to all children. We have explored the importance of emotions and emotional regulation and provided different techniques children can use to master emotions. You have also read about how important it is for children to gain self-knowledge and be able to see things from different points of view. Within all of these topics, we have looked especially for ways to support children with special needs. But we have returned again to the concept that we are more the same than different. The techniques that support children with special needs are techniques that help many children.

In the next chapter, we take the idea that we are more the same than different to another level by exploring a number of questions: If children need acknowledgment, acceptance, respect, and support for their sensory systems and emotional regulation to learn, what do teachers need to do their jobs well? Could the needs be the same? Do adults in a working environment need the same kinds of communication and problem-solving skills as children in a classroom? In a workplace in which people get support for their individual needs, does that individual support lead to a strengthening of the entire staff community? And most important, how can we support the teachers who are supporting the children in our classrooms?

Young children love nooks for privacy. Sometimes children also need nooks and private places because their sensory systems get overwhelmed. Having a private place to cut down sensory stimulation and regroup gives these children a chance to stay regulated, positive, and able to follow routines and teachers' directions.

Be as flexible as you can about allowing children to create these safe havens. A cubby makes a good space.

Private places can easily be created by putting pillows and blankets inside a climbing structure or by simply piling pillows together.

This is another child-created private space. Here, the child employed both big blocks and the big block storage shelf.

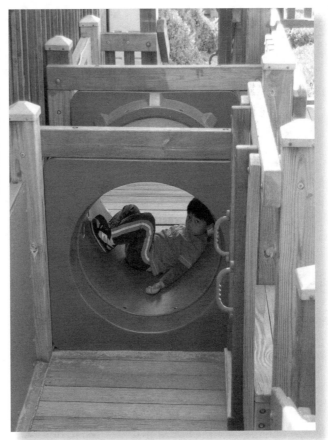

Don't forget to build private places into your indoor and outdoor spaces.

Otherwise, children may create some private places that you'd rather they didn't!

Supporting Teachers

One year, we had a boy in our classroom who was just out of control. When he got upset, he knocked toys over. Sometimes he'd knock another child over. And when teachers tried to stop him, he would hit or kick. Early in the year, he bit me. His parents were getting a divorce, and neither of them paid attention to what we told them. I didn't think I should be put in that situation. I told my supervisor I wasn't trained to be a punching bag and wouldn't work with this boy. My supervisor talked to my coworkers and told me I didn't have to be the one who dealt with him when he was upset. Another teacher volunteered. That teacher told me she thought this child was really upset about his parent's divorce, and she felt bad for him. My supervisor arranged for a psychologist to do a workshop about children in crises. What the psychologist said made sense. When I went back to work with the child, things went a little better, but only for a short time. My supervisor let me call the psychologist and ask more questions. I asked my coworkers if I could spend some one-on-one time with the boy. He started choosing to be with me. We'd play these games he made up, and it seemed to help. My coworkers gave me the credit for how he was changing. I started getting interested in children with emotional trauma. I took some college courses, and now teachers at my school ask me questions about their challenging children. They ask me to help them. I'd have never made this leap if my supervisor and coworkers hadn't been so patient. I will never forget that. Now I'm embarrassed about how I behaved. I learned a lot more than just how to work with challenging children. Now, when I see a child or a teacher balking about learning something new, I give them some rope. I try to give them the same gift of patience my colleagues gave me.

—**Anonymous**

Creating an Inclusive Staff Community

Hopefully, we have made a case thus far in this book for how relationship-based inclusion best serves children across a wide developmental spectrum. But does it best serve those of us who work in the field of early childhood education? We have heard teachers, providers, and administrators raise concerns and questions about implementing a relationship-based inclusive environment:

- "How do I think about each child in this kind of depth? I'm overwhelmed just planning my curriculum and filling out my paperwork."
- "I have a small family day care home. When I am the only educator, how can I do special activities for one child?"
- "If I'm giving time and attention to individual children in my class, what about the rest of the children? And how do I explain it to parents?"
- "Paying teachers for time to reflect and plan for individual children, and time to meet with parents. . . . I just don't know if the budget can handle it."
- "I just don't feel like I am equipped to do this."

Hopefully, we give satisfactory answers to these questions throughout the book. In this chapter we are more interested in the question above: Does relationship-based inclusion serve those of us who work in the field?

Despite the challenges, fears, and anxieties, relationship-based inclusion can have a *beneficial* impact on its practitioners. Relating to children and their families in this way brings professional satisfaction. And the rewards can go far beyond that. If the same principles and approaches that govern the work with the children and families are applied to the staff, it transforms the workplace. Think about it: Who wouldn't want to be part of a work community in which

- Everyone tries to understand and support each other.
- Being inclusive and welcoming are values embedded in everyday practices.
- Colleagues rely on each other's strengths to lead the way whenever possible.
- Colleagues recognize each other's limits and find reasonable ways to respond to them.
- Everyone believes that growth is possible at any age and understands that, even for adults, development occurs through a combination of maturation and experience.

Everyone—teachers, support staff, and administrators—benefits when the relationship-based teaching philosophy permeates the entire culture of the community. We all are empowered by having our strengths acknowledged and our challenges supported. We feel excited by the quality of the work we are doing together. And we feel satisfaction at the recognition and appreciation that comes our way. *Individual support creates community strength.* As each staff person is supported and does a better job, the quality of the entire program improves. The workplace becomes a setting that adds to the pleasure and meaning in our lives—and that makes us happier people.

But how do we get there as a staff? What do we need to learn to treat each other so well?

Start with the Children

The first principle, *we are more same than different*, is useful when thinking about the differences and similarities between children and adults. Whether you work alone or with others, spend some time thinking about what you want for children. Make a list of answers to the following questions and others that you might think of:

- How do you want children to be treated?
- How do you want them to feel?
- What do you think they need to grow and thrive?

Now look at your list. Is there anything on that list that you wouldn't also want for adults to help them flourish? When you take a step back and look at how ideally adults should be treated, it provides an important wider view. If you do this same activity together as a staff, it will get everyone on the same page and provide a set of principles to guide the adult relationships in the community.

Continue with Each Other

In order to put these positive ideas into practice, you need to keep in mind the second principle: *our differences make us who we are*. To learn about the differences, you will need to build relationships with each other. Everyone builds relationships all of the time at work, some better, some worse. In a relationship-based approach, when you build relationships, there is a more conscious aspect than often happens when you throw a group of people together for eight hours a day doing hard, important work.

Part of the work is just the usual getting to know each other and finding out each other's likes and dislikes, joys, and sorrows. But there are other elements as well. You need to find out about each other as professionals, know what you each do well and what you are not as good at. You want to take a realistic, nonjudgmental approach to what you find, recognizing that everyone has strengths and everyone has challenges. Part of this discovery can include getting to know each other's learning styles, sensory profile, and temperament. This way, you learn, for example, who always needs to hear something said at least twice, who is a great note taker, who has a hard time speaking up, and who will take up all of the speaking time at meetings.

As staff members learn this information about themselves and each other, they learn how individuals can support and be supported. The person who takes great notes repeats her notes at the end of a meeting to support the person who needs to hear all of the information twice (and anyone else having trouble listening that day). At meetings, you go around the circle to share ideas about an important topic. That way the person with difficulty speaking up gets time and space to do so. And the person who talks a lot will take a long turn.

By learning and thinking about each other in this way, each person gets to reach her best professional potential. We also learn to have compassion for children's individual differences. We see that there are fair and reasonable ways to accommodate weaknesses and use our strengths to support each other.

We can also incorporate the knowledge we have about the sensory system and arousal into the way we conduct our staff meetings and staff trainings. Everyone learns and pays attention in different ways. The techniques we use in the classroom also improve staff meetings.

Staff Meetings through a Sensory Lens

- Include regular movement breaks. These can be organized movement breaks in which teachers lead each other in their best classroom arousal/organization activities.

- Bring in crunchy or chewy food or something to suck on at intervals. All of this heavy jaw action wakes people up.

- Provide a variety of seating options—chairs with back support and feet on the ground, lounging chairs, bouncy balls for those who need more vestibular input to pay attention.

- Have alluring fidgets available.

- Include music or playful activities to get people's arousal levels back up.

- Make sure people are actively participating, not passively listening. Asking people for input wakes them up.

- Share roles. People who want to lead, plan, facilitate, take notes, or be timekeeper should do so. Involvement not only brings buy-in on everyone's part but also keeps people engaged and alert.

- Supply visuals for your visual learners and kinesthetic activities for your kinesthetic learners.

- Repeat critical information for your slow-to-process learners.

- Use the strengths of each staff member to help each of them absorb the critical information.

• • •

People are not just their temperaments and sensory profiles. The third principle tells us *a person cannot be known separate from his or her context.* Each staff member came from somewhere and was influenced by family, culture, background, and experiences. If colleagues reflect on these influences and share reflections, coworkers will know where each person is coming from. Communication will be more effective. Hurt and angry feelings may be avoided. Through discussions with each other, each staff member will develop a wider cultural lens. Teachers will be more likely to consider how the cultural and family context influence the children in their classes.

Not only can colleagues avoid hurt and angry feelings by getting to know each other; learning about each other can also shed light on how to solve other kinds of problems. Angie and Mike had a difference of opinion about how much Danny should be disciplined for his aggressive behavior. In fact, they weren't having much success conquering Danny's aggression with either method they used. Mike shared that his belief in the importance of limits came from his own childhood experiences, and Angie shared her beliefs. This broke through some kind of stuck place for them. Soon they were able to work together to come up with creative, effective solutions to Danny's aggression. Sharing where you are and where you came from is not only a technique to make everyone feel good. It is a tool to allow people to broaden their own and others' perspectives so that they can do their best thinking, decision making, and problem solving.

When is the time to learn about each other? All the time! Yes, the usual daily exchanges, lunches together, and occasional social events are important. But professional meetings can also provide opportunities for coworkers to learn about each other.

When an administrator decides to make this personal learning process part of the professional conversation, she makes a statement to the staff about the importance of relationships. The administrator needs to be aware of privacy issues. Staff should not have to share anything they feel uncomfortable sharing. The purpose of personal learning is to become a better team of professionals, and each person can decide for herself what personal information furthers that goal. As long as the administrator respects privacy and injects these kinds of personal learning conversations only briefly and occasionally, they make lively, interesting meetings.

Administrators can set a relationship-based tone at the beginning of any staff meeting, staff evaluation, individual supervision or coaching meeting, curriculum, or planning time. The reflective question presented for discussion should fit the purpose of the meeting. If the staff has been under unusual stress, a reflective question may be the only item on the agenda. This kind of personal learning provides a nice change of pace. Keep it brief. The question might be discussed in small groups for five minutes and then shared with everyone, or individuals might each be given ninety seconds to answer. Movement or creativity could be woven into the mix. Here are some sample questions to get you started:

Questions to Start Off Any Professional Meeting

- How are you feeling about your work life right now?
- What made you go into teaching?
- What is your current professional inspiration or goal?
- What are personal interests and passions that you can bring into your classroom or workplace?
- Who was your favorite teacher and why?

- What is your favorite childhood play memory?
- What values influence your teaching? Where do you think these values came from?
- How does your cultural heritage influence your teaching?
- How does your learning style influence your teaching? How can your colleagues support you?
- How does your sensory style influence your teaching? How can your colleagues support you?
- What do you need from us to be a better professional?
- What skills or dispositions do you have to offer the staff that you would like us to know about?

Questions to Start Off a Staff Meeting about Individual Children

Before talking about an individual child, it might be useful to get people's personal perspectives out on the table. One of these questions could be helpful:

- How does this child make you feel?
- Whom does this child remind you of?
- In what ways are you similar to this child?
- In what ways are you different from this child?

Relationship-Based Inclusive Staff Development Trainings

Consider starting off staff training with a quick personal sharing about the topic at hand. Again, use facilitation techniques, such as small-group sharing or reporting out in quick, creative ways to keep things moving and efficient:

- For a workshop on sensory profiles, have staff fill out a checklist that describes their own sensory style; have them share what influences them the most at work.
- For a workshop on working with parents, have staff describe what was most important to their own parents about their children's education and what would have made their parents feel most comfortable in a school setting.
- For a workshop on individualizing, have staff describe a time in their education when they could have used individual support.

When tackling shared problems, start or end with personal sharing. We can offer you some examples that come from our personal experiences at The Little School.

- We had an intractable problem with facility upkeep and order. We started the workshop off with staff reflections on cleanliness in our homes growing up and how those expectations affected us today. Starting off with this sharing opened people to look at the problem at The Little School in new ways.

- For a workshop on communication, we ended with staff sharing something in writing that they wanted colleagues to know about their communication style. Below is some of the written information people shared with each other. Notice that these staff members have clearly spent some time learning about their own sensory and learning styles.

Sometimes I speak without thinking—put my foot in my mouth—so please forgive me and give me a chance to backtrack and say what I really meant.

I feel most comfortable communicating when I've had time to evaluate, process, and organize my thoughts. I also like to write things down—that way I can read it and make sure it's how I want it to be/sound.

Sometimes it takes time for me to form an opinion. . . . I need to process things for a while first. . . . I sometimes tend to find myself in agreement with whoever is giving their opinion at the time.

I can get very excited by discussion with all you smart thoughtful people. Sometimes my arousal level gets very high and while listening, I start talking and interrupt! I wish I didn't do this and am trying to stop it—but old habits are hard to break.

Taking a Look at Ourselves

Obviously, this work takes a certain amount of personal reflection and sharing about one's professional self. Even in this regard, teachers have individual differences. They don't all need to relish or spend time looking inward or sharing reflections. Even those who shy away from these modes because of temperament, culture, or experience will find value enough to stretch themselves to make the process work. This is no different from messy people trying to be neater or quieter people trying to speak up in meetings. Remember: *Sometimes an individual bends to the needs of the community*. Staff members who find this easy should appreciate the efforts of colleagues who are stretching themselves to participate in self-reflection.

One place almost all people need to stretch is in being able to identify and acknowledge their mistakes and shortcomings. Not liking to admit we are wrong seems to be a universal trait, at least in our current shared culture. And yet to serve a wide range of children well, we constantly need to be able to step back and examine the daily schedule, classroom environment, even our behavior as teachers. To create the kind of adult community we want, we need to step back and examine the ways we have acted toward our colleagues and the part we have played in unproductive interactions. To gain this challenging skill, we need to treat ourselves with as much patience, understanding, and reassurance as we treat children who are trying to learn something difficult. We have to accept any progress we make, imperfect though it is. With the commitment to learn from our mistakes and a patient, accepting attitude toward ourselves, growth will occur.

We have seen this growth so consistently that we felt comfortable turning it into a principle: *A reflective teacher committed to openness and active learning can be an excellent inclusion teacher—with a little help from the community.*

Help from the Community

Sometimes the community bends to the needs of an individual. What kind of help can you expect from your workplace? Of course, each setting has different workplace rules, expectations, and abilities to support staff. From the discussions below, you might be able to figure out what is possible in your reality.

If we could always be the perfect employees, fulfilling every expectation of our workplace, it might be nice, but we would be automatons, not humans. Humans have lives—our spouses get sick; our own children get in trouble; our parents die. Balancing the obligations to our lives and the obligation to our workplace is a tricky, ever-moving target. This is especially true in our own country, where family life and needs receive less and less public support and where we lag behind many other countries in government support for important family issues such as child care, elder care, education, health care, and family leave (Heymann, Penrose, and Earle 2006).

Despite these challenges, staff members in a relationship-based workplace come together to try to recognize the reality of their lives in reasonable ways. Coworkers cut them some slack when they are going through a hard time. When a fellow staff member is in crisis, others might donate their paid personal time to that person when she has run out of hers. They take turns making meals when a colleague is laid up. They celebrate everyone's family triumphs.

And ideally the institution can be flexible within its means as well. Someone gets a salary advance to get through a tough financial crisis. Another person gets some time off to attend to serious family business. Supervisors try to work with staff members to find a reasonable compromise between their need to be at home with a sick child and the center's need to have dependable employees. If this kind of attitude and support can be created in a workplace, it should not be taken for granted but actively appreciated and applauded; this kind of workplace environment is a rare thing in this country (Heymann, Penrose, and Earle 2006).

What other kinds of workplace supports should you expect? Can you raise your voice because you have a fiery temperament if the flip side of your personality is your wonderful enthusiasm? No. Can you avoid certain parents because they intimidate you? No. Yet if you are a committed, reflective teacher who honestly asks only for what you need, who knows what kind of individualized approach your colleagues and workplace can accommodate? You won't know unless you ask. The following vignette provides an example.

Eva, Leigh, and Harry had worked together for several years in a four-year-old classroom. Eva and Leigh were highly organized; Harry was not. Eva and Leigh could always remember what individualized plan was in place for each child; Harry couldn't. Eva and Leigh knew just what needed to happen each day; Harry didn't. But Harry was a caring, warm, insightful presence for children, parents, and teachers. Everyone liked him, including Eva and Leigh. Generally, they all got along. And when things were going well, Harry often helped the children spearhead large, spontaneous, fun projects that added much to the life of the classroom.

But things hadn't been going well for a while. Harry's wife had been on bed rest for months and couldn't lift their young child. Harry's housing situation was uncertain, and his dad was sick. He came to work late most days, and his energy was low and distracted. Eva and Leigh were sympathetic to his situation and didn't want to make him feel worse by mentioning his lateness or distraction. But they both really cared about the class, and their concern and resentment built until they knew they had to do something.

They spoke to the program director. The director suggested that she facilitate an open conversation and problem-solving session among the three. During the meeting, Eva and Leigh started with their acknowledgment of what a tough time it had been for Harry. Then they shared their concerns. Although a few specifics surprised Harry, for the most part he was not surprised. He knew he hadn't been giving his all. And he acknowledged how hard it must be for his colleagues to carry much of his share.

Once the situation was acknowledged by all, the problem solving began. It became clear quickly that there was no institutional solution to the lateness. Everyone was needed at 8:00 a.m. to set up the classroom. Harry committed to finding a way to be on time. Harry also talked about what a somber mood permeated the setup time. None of the three of them seemed happy to be there in the mornings. Harry suggested a little upbeat music. Leigh and Eva agreed that this might be fun.

They also talked about Harry's difficulty in remembering how they were supporting individual children. The program director remembered seeing a curriculum-planning sheet that had a column for what kinds of individual support different children needed during different parts of the day. Eva and Leigh quickly figured out how to add a similar column to their weekly planning sheet. They told Harry they would post it in the closet, and it would be Harry's responsibility to read it each morning. Eva mentioned how excited the children were about dragons and wondered if Harry might raise his work energy by figuring out how to create a classroom dragon with the children. Harry loved the idea. The meeting ended with Harry thanking his colleagues for their support during his difficult time and for their honesty now. Eva and Leigh both seemed relieved and gratified.

Problems Are Inevitable

Anytime people are working or playing together, problems are inevitable. This is something we teach the children. Conflict resolution and interpersonal problem-solving skills are necessary life tools for adults as well as for children. Unlike the generation we are raising in our inclusive, relationship-based schools, we may not have been given the guidance to develop these skills ourselves. Without them, a work atmosphere can turn sour from gossip, resentment, and grudges. This causes low staff morale and reduced quality of care for children. Many of us take workplace resentments home with us. We spend our time away from work caught up in these negative feelings. Problems at work seep into our personal lives.

For all of these reasons, it is important that everyone in the work environment take responsibility for her own style in conflict situations. The staff as a whole needs to come up with some methods, structures, and agreements for how to handle conflict and the strong emotions that arise when people are working with children. If we didn't care so much about the children, we wouldn't react so strongly.

Children aren't the only ones whose emotions matter. We have to create professional spaces and forums within our workplace to allow us to express our emotions safely. We need to get these feelings taken care of so we can bring our best professional selves to the children who need us so much. Supervisors must communicate that it is okay to come to them if a staff member needs to vent or share. When a teacher brings a difficult situation with a family or child to their attention, supervisors should remember first to ask how the situation made the teacher feel. Then they can begin problem solving together. If there is a traumatic situation at the center, mental health professionals can be made available to the staff.

Time for sharing emotional states can be built into staff meetings and other formal times when the entire staff is together. The following list provides some quick ways for people to share their emotional states:

- Ask each person to say just one word that describes her current emotional state.

- Ask everyone to describe her current emotional state with a facial expression. Each person can then take a minute and look around the room at all of the faces.

- Have each person make one body movement or gesture that describes her current state. Perform all of them at the same time for a group expression!

- Suggest that each person name one song title, movie, or television show that summarizes her current emotional state.

Showing Appreciation Helps

And now we start to circle back to the issues, dilemmas, anxieties, and fears that opened this chapter. Serving children at widely disparate developmental levels is a skill that can be mastered. It is exciting and rewarding. But it is not easy. It becomes even more challenging when we expect teachers to enact thoughtful individual plans for many of the children. Add to that the expectation that the teacher maintains warm, informative relationships with each family, and you have a teacher with a lot on her plate. Again, there are many inherent rewards, but the job is challenging enough that teachers will need more than those. What can colleagues do to tip the balance from challenging to rewarding? And what can supervisors, directors, and administrators do?

Think about the strategies we have discussed thus far:

- Reflect on how we treat each other.

- Share our strengths, passions, challenges, needs, and cultural and family contexts.

- Support each other when we need to.

- Use good conflict-resolution and problem-solving skills.

All of these strategies will help. But none can be used as frequently as recognition and appreciation.

Coworkers and supervisors need to develop as many ways as they can to recognize, value, and appreciate the contributions everyone makes. It can be something as small as how much you liked someone's circle time. Or it can be as large as how much you respect someone's integrity and generosity. Both will mean a great deal.

Showing appreciation is especially important if people are having a hard time with each other or have constructive criticism they want to give. Here's an example of how showing appreciation can work. One teacher really wanted to share her seasoned observations with her new-to-the-field colleague. But she had a hard time giving constructive criticism, so she suggested they start their daily meeting by naming something positive they had noticed in each other's teaching that day. With these kinds of positive exchanges in the bank, constructive criticism became easier to share.

Family Child Care Note

Even if there are only two of you in the workplace, some of the more formal approaches suggested in this chapter might be helpful. They provide a forum for issues that are difficult to discuss in a more casual way:

- List each of your strengths and challenges.

- Discuss the kind of support each needs for your challenges.

- Answer the "getting to know each other" questions.

- Agree upon a method for how to resolve conflicts that arise. Follow it.

- At the end of the week, share five things you each thought the other did well. Doing so will send you into the weekend with a smile.

Many family child care providers work alone. What do you do then? You need to figure out where you are going to get recognition and acknowledgment. The children aren't enough.

- Do the child care families appreciate you?

- Do relatives or friends acknowledge your work?

- If not, find someone with whom to talk about your work who can tell you what a good job you are doing. Maybe it's another provider. Many family child care professionals have support groups with other providers in their area.

- Announce a Family Child Care Professional Appreciation Day at your family child care setting a few times a year. Put up a posterboard on which families can write what they appreciate about you. They might even take the hint and bring you cookies or flowers!

And what about support? Again, maybe it comes from

- Your child care families.

- Relatives or friends.

- Other providers.

- If not, look for or form a local association of family child care providers.

- Local resource and referral agencies offer support and technical training for family child care professionals.

Leading the Way toward Change

Not everyone works in a professional environment that is open and willing to improve upon the work relationships in these ways. If you work in such a setting, this limits your options, but it does not make you powerless to effect change. You can act on many of the strategies and approaches suggested in this chapter as an individual. For example, you can

- Publicly reflect on your classroom practices.
- Show your appreciation for your colleagues and supervisors whenever possible.
- Publicly take responsibility when you think you have contributed to poor communication.
- Ask for help when you need it.
- Offer understanding to colleagues going through a difficult time.
- Respectfully communicate your point of view when problems arise.

In these ways, you serve as a model for your fellow professionals. Other people may begin to take up some of the same practices. Before you know it, there may be more openness on the part of the staff to begin discussing how you would all like to treat and be treated by each other.

The Special Role of Supervisors

In early childhood settings, the boss may have different job titles—executive director, owner, supervisor, program director, lead teacher, or principal. Are you a person who holds power over others in your professional setting? If so, this section is especially for you.

Yours is a difficult position, to be sure. Sometimes it is an isolating position. The relationships you have with all of the people in your workplace are tempered by your position as their supervisor. Your professional relationships are affected by the power and responsibility you wield over others.

Reflecting on this aspect of your job is important and revealing. It might lead you to realize what *you* need to ask for from those you supervise. You might begin to move toward a more relationship-based approach by sharing your own strengths and challenges with your staff. We hope this might also lead to the kind of compassion and understanding for your position that you try to extend to your staff in their roles.

Use a Strength-Based Approach

You play a special role in determining if a relationship-based inclusive approach will be successful. In many cases, you may play the key role. It is the leader who often determines the kind of support individual staff members receive. And it is the leader who can offer staff opportunities to develop their strengths. Take time to notice these strengths and look for professional growth opportunities for your staff. Is one of your teachers ready to lead an in-service training? If her in-service is successful, is she ready to submit a proposal to make a presentation at a conference with your support and mentorship? How about your most visual teacher? Does she get to create schoolwide displays, take photos, and offer ideas for your Web site design? Is your most experienced teacher ready to be an observer in other classrooms, using her knowledge to mentor other teachers? It is you, the leader, who will set the atmosphere for work relationships and for how much time and energy is spent creating a healthy, collegial work community.

Working with Teachers When Challenges Arise

Most important, you, the leader, will determine the responses to the challenges that arise for early childhood teachers as they implement a relationship-based inclusive approach. For this important role, you need to remain sympathetic, understanding, and realistic about what teachers can accomplish. Suppose they tell you that a particular class of children is impossible or a child too much to handle? Then you need to engage with them in a serious way. Teachers need to know that they can openly discuss their teaching challenges without suffering any adverse consequences. They need to know that they can expect a receptive, supportive response. Your task is to create a positive partnership in which your teachers know they can come to you with their problems.

A process like the one listed below can help teachers learn to perceive and solve problems better. This makes them more valuable employees. And it takes care of their emotional needs at the same time. When teachers bring you a problem,

- Give them a few minutes to describe the situation any way they want.

- Then have them tell you what happened again, but this time just sticking to the facts.

- Next, talk about their emotions. Sample questions include "How do you feel?" "What are you worried about?" and "How will you feel seeing this child or parent tomorrow?"

- Finally, help them get clear about the difference between their feelings and the reality of the situation. Try not to give them the answers. Ask leading questions. Is the problem really as big as they think? Is their frustration causing them to see the child as more challenged than he is? Is their coteacher really inadequate, or does she just have a different style?

- After these steps, the teacher should be ready to problem solve or to take in your solution.

What about the opposite situation? You perceive a problem with a particular child or classroom, and the teacher does not see it or admit to it. You can use the same techniques a teacher might use with a parent to build a shared view of a child:

- Tell the teacher your general concerns.

- Ask her to observe and note specific topics; tell her you will do the same.

- Meet to share your observations. Hopefully, they coincide. You can move on to planning and problem solving.

- If not, do one more round of observations and note taking. Perhaps ask another teacher or specialist (trusted by both of you) to observe as well. Again, hopefully this will yield a similar view of the problem.

- If not, tell the teacher that given the difference of opinion and your responsibilities as the supervisor, you are both going to have to go with your understanding of the situation. You are still going to problem solve and plan together. Part of the plan will address why the teacher might be seeing things differently than you and the other observer. You and the teacher will both be in a research mode about this particular part of the problem. Maybe you will discover that in fact the teacher is seeing something that others are missing. Maybe you will discover that a belief the teacher has is clouding her observation. Using your differing perspectives as a research and discovery opportunity should keep the teacher invested and feeling respected even though she needs to work on something she doesn't identify as a problem.

Once a teacher asks you to get involved in challenges with a child or classroom, the options are numerous. Sometimes teachers just need another eye, ear, or perspective. Directors or teachers from another class can listen to the teacher's concerns and come to observe. Sometimes an outside observer may be able to see that approaches that worked for so many other children don't work for this class or this child. Helping teachers reflect on the classroom elements and the particular children might be enough to set things back on the right track. Regular, built-in time in which teachers can problem solve with peers and supervisors makes this process easy. If that is impossible, teachers must know that a reflective, effective, emotionally safe process that includes them will be put into place when they contact their supervisor.

Seeking Additional Support

Some problems cannot be solved by either in-house observation or reflection. Many programs have a mental health consultant who can come in to observe a particular child or class. Perhaps an occupational therapist, speech therapist, or physical therapist might be a better observer in certain situations. If you work in a setting that does not have this kind of built-in support, professionals in private practice often enjoy working in early childhood settings. They might even donate their services because they are so enthusiastic about working with teachers (or because the school's endorsement might bring them more clients). Either way, the children win.

Sometimes the most effective way to respond to a situation requires bringing an additional adult into the classroom. The teacher can then focus more fully on a particular child or a particular group challenge. For example, if a child becomes very aggressive and typical methods are not successful, the teachers and administrators should reflect on and make a plan for the child. The plan should include a teacher or an adult physically close enough to the child to respond quickly when she becomes aggressive. With the support of reflection, planning, family consultation, and the additional adult, it's possible to significantly reduce a child's aggression within weeks.

Does this feel like too much support going to a specific child or class? Is it an excuse for or enabling poor behavior? Think back on the stories of Danny and Michelle. It is interesting that in our national culture, we believe in remedial classes, tutors, and other kinds of academic support. Yet at the same time, we don't believe that children might need or deserve additional scaffolding to overcome social or emotional problems. Scaffolding behavior while teachers figure out how to best make a classroom work for a child makes sense. This kind of investment also allows a child time to gain self-awareness and self-control. Emotional scaffolding could be an investment that yields more long-term, significant gains than many popular academic supports. It is also an investment in teachers. Giving teachers the needed support to serve all children in their class increases their confidence, competence, and sense of partnership with you, their supervisor.

Focusing this much effort on a specific child or class and bringing in another adult costs time, energy, or money—sometimes it costs all three. And time, energy, and money are in short supply in most programs.

Here are a few suggestions for low-cost solutions to bringing an additional adult into the classroom for a period of time. These adults will not count toward licensing ratios. They may need to be fingerprinted or otherwise vetted, depending on state or local laws. They aren't trained professionals who can do the work of educators. But they can read books to children, play with them, and give them a little extra attention to allow teachers to focus on the area of greatest need.

- Graduate or college students in related fields.
- Retirees.
- Family members of children.
- Extended family members of children.
- Existing staff, temporarily reassigned.
- In some cases, it might be appropriate to use a family member of the child who is having challenges.

Listening to teachers, being available, and following through with action and actual supports when required are all necessary. Teachers need to know that you are willing to step in when necessary. With that support, they are willing to take on the issues, challenges, fears, and anxieties that accompany teaching in a quality, relationship-based inclusive classroom.

Strengthening the Teacher-Family Partnership

Teachers also need to know that administrators have their backs when it comes to their relationships with families. This does not mean that you can't acknowledge when a teacher has made a mistake. But the goal for any intervention or action should be to strengthen the family-teacher partnership. The teacher may need some additional training in some area, but that does not mean she does not deserve respect for what she is bringing to the situation. Sometimes a director can help a teacher and family see each other's strengths and gain more sympathetic insight into each other's challenges. That alone would increase the likelihood of a strengthened family-teacher partnership.

Relationships Matter

The quality of work relationships and the way individual employees are treated make a significant difference in people's ability to provide quality care and education. Sometimes teachers, administrators, families, board members, or funders want to diminish the value of this touchy-feely stuff. We can't let them. Our children are depending on us to uphold the truth that individual differences matter in our workplaces and our classrooms. If we insist upon the recognition of relationships, emotions, and individual experience in our workplace, this recognition will naturally flow into our classrooms. We help our workplaces when we introduce a relationship-based inclusive approach in our classrooms. And we help our classrooms when we introduce a relationship-based inclusive approach in our workplaces.

· · ·

In this chapter, we discussed how adults benefit from a relationship-based inclusive work setting. Just like children, adults can achieve more when they are appreciated and known for themselves. We have shown ways for colleagues to get to know each other better and learn each other's strengths, challenges, background, and passions. We provided examples about ways for coworkers and supervisors to show support for each other's professional efforts and personal life challenges. We have recognized the inevitability of conflict and the importance of open communication and problem solving. We have examined how an individual teacher can attempt to change the culture of a workplace and how a supervisor can lay the foundation for relationship-based inclusion to flourish.

In the next chapter, we attempt to understand the journey a family takes when their child is challenging or is diagnosed with a special need. Through our empathy and understanding, we can see more clearly what families will need from us in our family-teacher partnership.

Chapter 11

The Journey of Families of Children with Special Needs

Having a child with autism has completely changed the way I see the world. I don't take perception for granted anymore. I'm constantly aware of loud sounds, harsh colors, unexpected noises. Things that you or I would barely notice will upset or distract him. Or something might mysteriously strike him funny, and pretty soon everybody's cracking up. And when he learns something new and looks so proud—there's nothing like it. So I try to let him explore the world at his own pace. It's taken a while to get here, and a procession of teachers and therapists along the way. Some were inexperienced, and some were brilliant. Some warm, some self-righteous, some intuitive. Some were unbelievably clueless. Like our son, I don't think we were always as openly receptive to them as we could have been, yet we registered every word and nuance. The thing that always separated the educators we relied on from the ones we dismissed was a genuine appreciation and respect they had for my child. Whatever they may know, not know, do right or wrong, however much training they have—respect is never negotiable.

—Susan Etlinger
Parent

Because early childhood teachers are often the first people outside the family to spend significant time with a child and because of their knowledge of child development, teachers are often the first to identify to families that their child is challenging or has challenges. This often involves suggesting to families that their child might benefit from an assessment—a simple sentence that does not convey the very emotional journey teachers and families travel before and after this event.

Although this chapter is about the family's journey, it begins by examining a little of the teacher's journey. In this way, you can understand more about what happens between the two.

All over the country, teachers (and administrators) have shared similar hopes and fears with us, the authors, about their relationships with the parents of children with challenges. Teachers have expressed fear that by sharing their observations and suggesting an assessment, they will upset the family and make things worse for the child. They worry that the family will feel guilt and sadness. Teachers don't feel they have the professional expertise or training to make these judgments. They can't find the right words to help the family understand. Teachers are also worried about themselves—that families will be angry or dismissive, that families will retaliate against the teacher or the school, that families won't acknowledge the teacher's expertise, and, certainly, that families won't appreciate all the extra-special time the teachers have put in to understand and respond to the child. Most of all, teachers fear that they will not be heard and that the child will not get what she needs.

But teachers (and administrators) are also highly motivated to share their observations and concerns with families. Teachers have high hopes for what comes out of these discussions with families. They hope that

- Families will be able to enlist outside resources.

- Families will feel supported and be able to parent their child more successfully.

- Teachers will gather useful information and concrete strategies to help the child in the classroom.

- Everyone will be on the same page about how to support and appreciate the child.

Aside from the feelings of teachers, there are realities that can add stress to the teacher-family dialogue about a challenging child. There is often little or no time for families and teachers to communicate. Sometimes, a school administration does not support this kind of honest dialogue between teachers and families. Sometimes a family is under too much stress to take in, much less act upon, information about a child. Often the child behaves so differently at home and at school that families and teachers do not believe each other is accurate in their observations or descriptions. Cultural differences can hinder the development of trust and effective communication. Power dynamics can also get in the way of trust and communication. If the family perceives the teacher as having too much power, they might not share their honest reactions. If the family perceives the teacher as having little or no power or expertise, they will not listen. Add to this list the huge emotional task parents have of processing and responding appropriately to the difficult information a teacher has to share. It becomes clear why teachers are so afraid of these interactions. It also explains why these relationships *are* often challenging and bumpy.

Understanding these pressures and challenges helps a teacher have reasonable expectations of the relationship, of the family, and of themselves. You begin to understand that you can only do what you are able to do in light of the challenges above. You learn that no matter how much you care and how perfectly you communicate, the family still has their own difficult personal journey to take. You can't make the journey unnecessary. You can only walk along side in as much of a professional, honest, and caring way as you are able.

If you look back over the story of Angie's and Mike's relationships with Danny's and Michelle's parents, you will notice a number of things. Angie and

Mike did a lot of thinking about those relationships. There was a purpose and a focus to their thinking. They were trying to understand the child-rearing philosophies of Danny's and Michelle's parents and how the parents viewed their children. The teachers wanted to be honest, but they also wanted to share information in a way that would build the dialogue and the partnership. In some respects, Mike and Angie set the pace and agenda. And in some ways, they let the parents set the pace and agenda. In this way, Mike and Angie walked alongside the parents' journey. They didn't try to control it. They didn't get frustrated when the parents didn't agree, and they didn't take it personally when parents weren't happy with them. It is important to understand the journey families might take so that you can learn not to take personally the reactions that families have along the way.

In an article she wrote for families, "You Are Not Alone: For Parents When They Learn Their Child Has a Disability," Patricia McGill Smith commented,

> The day my child was diagnosed as having a disability, I was devastated—and so confused that I recall little else about those first days other than the heartbreak. Another parent described this event as a "black sack" being pulled down over her head, blocking her ability to hear, see, and think in normal ways. Another parent described the trauma as "having a knife stuck" in her heart. Perhaps these descriptions seem a bit dramatic, yet it has been my experience that they may not sufficiently describe the many emotions that flood parents' minds and hearts when they receive any bad news about their child. (Smith 2003, 2)

While Smith is referring to receiving the news that a child does indeed have a disability, in our experience, parents can begin to have intense emotional reactions as soon as teachers raise a question, concern, or suggest an evaluation. This level of reaction makes sense. Children represent optimism and hope for the future to us. To watch an infant learn to think, communicate, express himself, and unfold as a unique individual is to watch a miracle. Parents can't help but relate that miracle to the child himself and assume the child has unlimited potential. The assumption of potential is linked with some of the strongest feelings of love and adoration the parent has ever experienced. And all of it—loving their child, knowing their child, having someone from outside give them feedback about their child—are such new experiences in the early childhood years. No wonder parents react to teachers' feedback in ways that may dismay and overwhelm the early childhood professionals trying to help.

In her article, Patricia McGill Smith goes on to describe many common reactions families have to the news that a child may have a disability (or, we would argue, on learning that any developmental questions or challenges exist). Not surprisingly, the list describes the common reactions people have to any trauma or grief. The list of reactions includes denial, anger, blame, grief, loss, fear—especially fear for what this means about the child's future—as well as guilt, confusion, powerlessness, disappointment about the child, rejection of the child, or rejection of the people trying to share the information.

Take a moment to contemplate that list. Imagine each emotion, where it might come from, and what form it might take. Understand that whatever public reaction the families reveal to you, underneath, they may be experiencing some of these reactions as well. These reactions may be reverberating in their relationship with each other and in their families in complicated, unsettling ways. Once you spend some time walking in the families' shoes, it is much easier to understand why they often seem difficult as you try to problem solve with them about their child's challenges. You see how unreasonable it is to expect that they would quickly process the information you share and respond in effective ways. Having reasonable expectations for how families respond when you share difficult information is key.

It is also key to have reasonable expectations for how long it might take families to act on your information or to see what you see. With these reasonable expectations, you can create effective approaches for how to communicate and partner with families. These same reasonable expectations can also foster a sense of appreciation for families whenever they do take in information and act upon it. Their ability to take in difficult information and do something about it is a strength you can reflect back to them. If ever there were a period when families could benefit from having their parenting strengths pointed out to them, this period is one of them.

Some families would find all of the thought and planning that Angie and Mike put into their conversations with parents a bit of overkill. "If you honestly look at the child through a supportive lens," they might say, "then don't worry so much about when you suggest a referral or exactly what you say or where the families are at emotionally. Your strength-based, supportive approach comes across however you communicate. We don't need our hands held. We're grown-ups. Don't worry so much about our reactions. Just be caring and honest, and we'll be okay."

In our work at The Little School, we have walked the journey with families who have made statements very similar to the ones above. From our side, they did seem to need some hand-holding, understanding, and reasonable pacing. We believe our suggestions provide the best likelihood for assessments happening as quickly as possible. They also will lead to the best use being made of the information contained in the assessments. But we also believe these families communicate an important point. Just because families might have emotional reactions to what we share doesn't mean we shouldn't share what we observe. In that sense, teachers do need to let the adult members of families be "grown-ups," and we have to be grown-ups too.

You don't have to do everything right all of the time to stay in a trusting partnership with families. If you get the big picture right, you can make all sorts of mistakes and the family-teacher partnership will survive. What professional behavior is included in this big picture?

- Observe and engage the child through a nonjudgmental developmental lens that includes his sensory profile.

- Share that information in an honest, caring way with the child's family.

- Understand and accept the family's reactions and don't take it personally.

- Honestly engage with the information they share with you and include it in your work with their child.

- Accept the decisions families make even when they differ from your advice.

- Continue to problem solve with them about how best to help the child thrive at home and at school.

- Value and appreciate their child and their parenting.

Be aware that the teacher-family relationship is not the only relationship that is affected when a child has challenges. Families have described in poignant detail how relationships with grandparents and other extended family members can become charged. These extended family relationships may become a source of pain and conflict when a child does not conform to the expectations of relatives or relatives don't understand the child. Parents of other children, including other families in the school community, can also become a source of pain through no fault of their own. Well-meant comments or questions can trigger a storm of emotions in parents of children with challenges. Simply watching how easy it is for other parents to interact with their children can be heart-wrenching. Everyday activities such as grocery shopping, playing at a playground, or attending a birthday party can be nightmare experiences and another source of anxiety. Stress occurs in marriages, in sibling-to-sibling interactions, and in the relationship of the parent to the nonchallenged siblings.

The family of a child with challenges doesn't have an easy road to walk. Be compassionate and understanding of families. Let them have their reactions. Even the most difficult reactions serve a purpose. How could any family get through the challenging task of raising a child without a healthy dose of denial, for example? A little denial allows a family to keep going and to continue to have a positive view of their child until they have figured out how to have a positive picture that includes a disability, impairment, or challenge.

Sometimes, a parent has to leave the first early childhood setting that raises issues and try another to be able to hear a school's input. Danny's parents saw his challenges, but they were also convinced that, in a more structured setting, his challenges might disappear. Sometimes a change of schools *is* the solution for a child. More often, parents who have left The Little School program thinking we were the problem (or who have arrived at our program thinking we were the solution) have discovered that their child still has challenges. But having made the choice to move schools, they felt ready and able to act in their child's interests. They could see their child more clearly. Although leaving a school does delay a formal assessment, it also provides parents with the tools and information they need to act more effectively as their child's advocate.

Teachers sometimes think an assessment and intervention will be a "magic bullet" that will begin a child on the road to recovery (and to being more manageable in the classroom). But not all children are accurately diagnosed and not all specialists are created equal. A label or a diagnosis is often necessary for a child to receive services. But that doesn't speak to the effect a diagnosis can have on a family. In a support group for families of children with challenges, a parent asked if others had found that getting their child diagnosed or "labeled" was helpful. People in the group were clearly ambivalent. On one hand, a "label" gave them a direction, something to explore and learn about. What they learned researching the diagnosis sometimes really helped them understand, accept, and support their child. Just as often, the diagnosis itself paralyzed them. The label was too painful, too limiting, and didn't seem to help them make sense of their child.

As an early childhood professional, it is not easy to walk this road with families. It is not necessarily easy to be on the receiving side of denial, rejection, or the many possible reactions of families. So have compassion and understanding for yourself as well. Forgive yourself when a family tells you that you were too harsh in how you shared information—or that you were too gentle. Be kind to yourself when a family tells you that you waited too long to share your concerns—or that you jumped the gun too quickly. Don't be surprised when a family tells you that your observations weren't detailed enough, or that you didn't really listen to them. Be ready to have compassion for yourself when a family tells you that you were too alarmist—or that you weren't alarmist enough. You will hear all of these things. We certainly have. And we understand that sometimes a family's feedback is part of the process that they are going through, part of the journey.

Each time a family gives us feedback, we also reflect and try to see the grain of truth in what they are saying. We do this because we know that we are not perfect. We know we have a lot to learn. And however much we learn, we know that we will keep making mistakes and continue to learn from them.

* * *

In this chapter, we have tried to present the emotional journey that parents take when their child has challenges. There is an emotional journey of the teacher too. Factors such as lack of time, school setting, and policies, to name a few, can make the teacher-family partnership challenging. In an authentic partnership, the teacher's job is to be honest, nonjudgmental, and accepting of the parent's insights and decisions. It is also important that the teacher be compassionate toward herself; the journey is difficult for everyone.

Often, families of children with challenges can feel isolated, especially from other parents. Schools can help families connect with each other. In the next chapter, you will read how to create a school and classroom environment where all families feel their needs are being met. You will learn how to empower families to help other families. A supportive environment can help transform families of children with challenges from isolated individuals to engaged advocates of their child and other children.

Chapter 12

Creating an Inclusive Community of Families

Some of the families of children with special needs who have graduated from our program have bittersweet memories of their time there. The child may have thrived and the family-school partnership may have been very positive. But if these families felt that the other families in the school did not embrace their child, did not accept and understand her differences, then the bitterness of those memories seems to last forever. For a long time, the fact that families were so affected by other families' reactions was confusing and frustrating to us. We had worked so hard in partnership with them on their child's behalf. And yet our hard work was diminished by something we felt we had no control over—the behavior of other families.

Over time, we came to realize that this universal human need for connection and belonging was so important that we couldn't act as though it were something beyond the scope of what we thought about when developing our program. If we wanted to create a successful inclusion program, we had to figure out how we could help the adult community embrace the children of special needs and their families. Even though the adult members of families had not signed on to be our students, we had to figure out how to teach them about being members of an inclusive community. And we had a feeling it wasn't going to be easy.

—Leslie, Todd, and Cassie

Remember when the other families in the class were upset about Danny's aggression? What helped them stay relaxed and open-minded even when they knew their child might be hit? What helped them eventually share the same pride in his progress as his teachers and parents?

And what made a mother in Michelle's class willing to set up a regular play date between her child and Michelle, even though her daughter was developmentally ahead of Michelle in so many ways? Surely her daughter would have gotten more out of play dates with peers more developmentally similar to her?

The culture of an inclusive family community would include one in which families

- Care about and support the school's mission to serve all children.
- Care about and support each child, regardless of developmental profile or challenging behavior.
- Care about and support each other.

Creating an inclusive family community is similar to creating an inclusive classroom community. If you treat children a certain way and meet their needs, they will respond to your modeling, coaching, and encouragement by treating other children in an inclusive manner. In a similar way, creating an inclusive family community consists of steps that include meeting the individual needs of the families and helping them see their roles in the wider community. Here are the four steps in the process:

1. Build goodwill.
2. Create community among families.
3. Create a shared vision of the value of inclusive classrooms.
4. Empower families to support other children and families.

Creating an inclusive family community starts with building a trusting, authentic, responsive relationship with each individual family. The goodwill generated from that positive relationship helps families be open to your vision of the value and importance of inclusion. Building family community—in other words, building personal connections among families—brings out the natural empathy humans feel toward others whose experience they understand. Giving other families specific tools to support children with special needs and their families helps empower parents to act on their empathy.

Building Goodwill

The first step in creating an inclusive community is to build goodwill. The following sections suggest some ways you can do this. You will notice that building goodwill with a parent is much like building trust and a relationship with a child.

Building Goodwill through Building Authentic Relationships

How do we get to know the important details about a parent? What sets him apart as unique? What is important to him? What strengths and what vulnerabilities does he bring to the school environment? What aspects of life experience, family, and culture have shaped the beliefs and attitudes that will determine how he responds in the program setting? With children, we have time each day to get to know them using our good observational skills. To get to know parents, we have to spend time with them, hang with them, talk to them. For the harassed teacher, the busy administrator, or the harried administrative assistant, doing so may not seem like a high priority. Nevertheless, when you make the time for getting to know them, you realize doing so is the most important thing you could be doing.

Knowing a parent or family creates the foundation for the positive partnership you will forge with them about their child *and* about the school and classroom. Just as colleagues work better together when they know where each other is coming from, so professionals will respond more successfully to family concerns and enlist parent support if they know where the families are coming from. Aside from getting to know a family, how else can you build goodwill?

Building Goodwill through Individualizing

A parent who trusts you will follow you anywhere. Teachers and schools create trust when they listen and respond to a parent's concerns. Just as we individualize to children's needs in a classroom, we can, within reason, individualize to parent's needs as well.

What might such individualizing look like? Here's an example from an everyday issue at all schools: lateness at drop-off time.

> Tony was a new parent in the school. She seemed to like the school and her son, Trey, was really enjoying it. But Trey regularly came an hour late to school. He would often come when the other children were starting to clean up the room, and he'd be frustrated at missing open choice. The teachers consulted Mary, the director, who decided it was time to get to know this new family. Mary caught Tony one morning and asked her to join her for a cup of coffee.
>
> As Mary and Tony relaxed and chatted about whatever came into their heads, Mary learned some details about Tony's life. She was a single mom with four children. She had a large extended family, many of whom were teachers and ministers, and they all belonged to the same church. Tony had a lot of respect for education, which was second only to religion in terms of what she wanted to offer her children. She was working hard to make sure each of her children got what they needed. Currently, her four children were in four different schools. Her second child was autistic. The best program for him could only be reached by bus, and Tony had to make sure he got to the bus stop every morning. In the logistics of her life, there was just no way that Tony could get Trey to school on time.
>
> Mary started looking around for reasonable solutions. She discovered that a parent in another class dropped his older child off at school right near the bus stop where Tony dropped her older son. When the dad, Samuel, heard about Tony's dilemma, he offered to meet Tony at the bus stop every day and drive Trey to school with his daughter.

Here's another example. This is an even trickier challenge, because it involves pickup time.

> Nina was supposed to be picked up at 12:30 every day, right before nap. Every day, Nina's dad, Ali, arrived at 1:00 or 1:30. Every day, Nina would worry. And inevitably, Ali arrived right in the middle of naptime with a loud greeting and big hug for his daughter. The children who had just fallen asleep would wake up, and the resentful, frustrated teachers would start the process of getting them back to sleep. The teachers had spoken to Ali numerous times about his lateness and now felt their relationship with him had turned decidedly sour.
>
> They decided to focus on building a positive relationship with him. They learned that he was a jazz musician. They had some great conversations with him about music. They asked him if he was late because he was working so late at night with his gigs.
>
> "No, that's not it," he said. He explained that in his birth country, time was looked at very differently from the way it was in American culture. His home culture believed that time wasn't something that should control you or your life. Family, relationships, music, being in the moment, and being attuned to your world were the most important things in life. Ali didn't agree with the importance of being at a specific place at a specific time. He could never understand or get used to our culture's emphasis on moving quickly to meet the demands of an artificial system of minutes and hours.
>
> The teachers were dumbfounded. It made so much sense! Why were they so uptight about time? The next day, when he woke the children up again, the teachers remembered why. But what Ali had shared inspired them to find a way to make things work for everyone.
>
> Parents had the option for a 12:30 p.m. or 6:00 p.m. pickup. The teachers asked Ali if he could pick Nina up at 6:00 instead. He said he couldn't afford the cost, and he wanted to spend the afternoons with his daughter. The teachers asked the director if she would make an exception for Ali and Nina. Then they presented a plan to Ali. If Ali didn't arrive by 12:30, the teachers would put Nina down to rest. When he arrived, if Nina wasn't finished resting, he could hang out quietly with her at her mat. And he would only have to pay for one more hour a day. The new system worked great. Nina knew just what to expect. Ali hung around more. And all of the children and teachers looked forward to his visits.

Most programs address lateness with a clear policy and steep fines. Sometimes that works, and sometimes it doesn't. Part of the premise of a relationship-based program is that you recognize the whole person, not simply the *student*, *teacher*, or *parent-at-our-school* part of them. In reality, most parents or caregivers are late because of the challenges built into their daily lives. All the rules and fines we create won't change those. Many large institutions need to have clear rules to function. But sometimes we have more flexibility than we think, even in the most bureaucratic setting.

Many in early childhood might reasonably object. "We don't have time to do all that talking and thinking for each family" and "If you let one parent slide by, everyone will take advantage."

The simple truth is this: what works better for the family also works better for the program. Families are more likely to be on time when you help them come up with a solution that addresses the actual cause of their lateness. Even more than that, the family recognizes your commitment, dedication, and flexibility. They experience firsthand the value of an individualized approach. You have built a bank of understanding, trust, and goodwill. You can draw upon that goodwill to help create a supportive community for families of children with special needs.

Building Goodwill through Responsiveness to Concerns

As professionals, we all know the best way to respond to the concerns of a family:

- Listen authentically.

- Acknowledge or reflect what you have heard.

- Share your knowledge or perspective if appropriate.

- Problem solve together if appropriate.

- Get back to the family with solutions or responses as appropriate.

It is easy to see how using these steps to respond to family concerns will naturally build trust and goodwill between program and family.

Teachers also know how hard these often are to put into practice. Their defensive hackles come up quickly, especially when a parent questions their teaching or is concerned about another child in the class. To learn how to create a positive, inclusive family culture, it is essential to learn how to respond effectively to a family's concerns about the classroom, the children, and their stated or unstated concern about getting what their own child needs.

For those of us who have worked in inclusive classrooms, the following questions will be familiar:

- If you are spending so much time with the child with special needs, will *my* child get enough attention?

- Will the child with special needs physically hurt my child?

- Will my child pick up less mature or negative habits from the child with special needs?

- How can you guide my child toward the learning challenges he is ready for if this child with special needs is ready for so much less?

Addressing Adult Assumptions

Adults often confuse children with developmental challenges and children with behavioral challenges. They may assume that children with special needs are aggressive or have behavioral problems. Similarly, they may assume that children with behavioral problems are children with special needs. It is important to help families separate these two categories. Many children with a variety of developmental profiles have behavioral challenges. And many children with special needs do not have any behavioral challenges at all. All groups—children with developmental challenges, children with behavioral challenges, and their families—deserve an inclusive, supportive community. Because they all deserve support and because families often have concerns about both groups of children, we sometimes refer to both groups when we discuss different points in this chapter.

Giving families printed articles with research-based information is one useful way to respond to these familiar questions. But responding to a family's questions with information about their own child is likely to pack a more powerful punch. Make sure you share the many ways in which their child is learning and growing. Collect more documentation if you need to—photographs, videos, and narratives of what happens throughout the day. If this documentation includes a positive or at least a neutral picture of the child with special needs, all the better. Make sure you let the family know you are aware of any challenges their child is having, and be ready to talk about the child in a thoughtful way. By doing this, the question of whether the child is getting what she needs in your classroom can be answered with a resounding yes! This is a clear case in which simply using best practices leads directly to setting up an inclusive community. Families can be generous to other people's children when they know that their own children are getting what they need.

To respond fully to the questions above, you not only will have to talk about the child but also about your teaching practices and the other children in the class. Listen carefully and identify the family's specific concerns. Then address them honestly. Honesty is the key if you want families to support your inclusive classroom. Most families don't need things to be perfect, but they do need to know you are willing to give them the straight story. If a child is aggressive, be ready to share your plan to keep the other children safe and help the aggressive child make progress. If you feel it's all right for a child to experience a little aggression as another child grows, be ready to explain how coping with a reasonable amount of aggression helps build resilience and advocacy skills. Be ready to share how and when you will evaluate your plan for the aggressive child's progress.

What if you don't have a plan in place and you are not sure that you are adequately responding to the situation? Be honest and professional at the same time. A family will always respect you for saying, "Great question. Let me think about it so I can answer you thoughtfully." Such a response buys you time to consult your director, colleagues, and other resources. Just make sure you do get back to the family. It is your responsiveness more than the specifics of what you say that builds goodwill.

Many of the suggestions in this chapter can work in family child care as well. The challenge of family child care is the small size of the community. Bad feelings between two parents or families can poison the atmosphere for everyone. Your advantage is that you have more daily contact with families than most classroom teachers. As you talk to families every day, coach them to look at the challenges of their own child and other children in a positive way. Explain how everyone learns social lessons when a child struggles.

Here are some examples of the kind of language that helps parents learn how to be supportive and inclusive:

- "Now that Maggie's bigger but can't talk as well as the other girls, she's been showing her frustration by pushing them. I give her a firm limit each time, but I know the pushing will stop when she starts talking more. You should see how she uses her new size to help the others, though. She pushes them in the wagon outside forever, and they say "More, Maggie, more."

- "It is true, Anthony can't play or talk as well as Jevon can. But they really seem to enjoy playing together. I think it is giving Jevon a chance to be the leader. His play with Anthony is helping him develop his leadership skills."

- "I know Noah is getting tired of hearing Katie cry. We all are. I keep telling him, 'She is just finding a way to feel comfortable in this new place. Let's try to figure out what makes her comfortable.' Noah figured out that Katie is calmer when we turn the lights off and just use natural light. We also have her spend time in the other room so she gets a break and the other children get a break too."

- "You're worried Gabriela is going to start screaming like Bobby does? When Bobby has a tantrum, we talk about how he is still learning how to handle disappointment. We ask the other children how they handle it and make a list. When Bobby calms down, we talk about the list so he knows some other choices next time. One time today, Bobby was about to scream and your daughter said, 'Bobby, want me to tell you the things on your list so you don't have to scream?'"

Don't wait for parents to make comments before you start coaching. You can write similar things about the day on the daily message board:

- The children helped Bobby make a better choice when he got upset today. Everyone felt good!

- The children figured out that Katie likes the lights off. She was much calmer. Good for them, and good for Katie!

- Bea is talking more! Maggie is strong enough to lift Bea! Corey wants to share her food with both of them! They all have their challenges with each other, but don't we all?

Communication is key! Find multiple ways to help parents see what is happening through your eyes.

Creating a Community of Families

Once you have established goodwill and a feeling of connection with the families in your program, you can begin to help them connect with each other.

Helping Families Understand Each Other

There are many ways to create connections between families. Surprisingly, one opportunity comes when parents have concerns and questions like the ones mentioned in the family child care notes. As you talk with families about their own child's experience in the classroom, you can also begin to give them an eye into the experience of the child with special needs and his family. Offering this point of view begins to forge a connection between the concerned family and the child with special needs. Remember that all families have a right to privacy. You should never share anything personal about a family or child. You should never share a diagnosis or say that a child sees a specialist unless that child's family has given you permission. But you do not need to share the fact that a child has special needs to help families understand the child more. Consider a school policy that allows teachers to share with all families the goals a particular child is working on. You can also share the strategies the teacher is using to help that child reach those goals.

Think back to Danny's and Michelle's goals and strategies. Most of them would not have given other parents a clue about specific identification and special needs. And yet they would have let the parents know how hard the teachers (and Danny and Michelle) were working. Speak to the families of children with special needs about what information you can share with other families about their children. Danny's mother, for instance, most likely would have appreciated having other families know that she felt very bad about her son's aggressive behavior and was working very hard to change it. A parent hearing this might be likely to feel empathy, and a good discussion might ensue between the two families.

If you have a child in your classroom who is similar to Michelle, you might share with a parent that the girl is ready for a friend but that it is hard for her to find one in the hustle and bustle of the classroom. This way, you help the parent understand why the girl might need playdates. If her parents give you permission to share that they are looking for a regular playdate for their daughter, another parent might be responsive.

These kinds of conversations actually create opportunities to use all four of the steps for building a supportive community:

1. *Build goodwill* by sharing honest information.
2. *Create a community* by helping families understand another child's and family's experience.
3. *Communicate your vision* by the way you communicate about the children and your classroom practices.
4. *Empower families* by letting them know ways they can be helpful to another family.

Creating Opportunities to Get to Know Each Other

There are many ways to create a parent or family community. Community happens naturally when families have time to spend together and get to know one another. As a program, you can offer families the time and space to be together. The rest is up to them.

Offering families time and space may require the kind of creativity a relationship-based program demands. Be clear about what you are after. If your objective is to provide a place in which families might get to know each other better, the place has to be easily accessible, one in which families would naturally find themselves or have a reason to seek out. The place has to invite relaxed conversation, but it doesn't need to be big or fancy. It can be as simple as a couch and a chair facing each other in the hallway with a lamp, a plant, and a sign saying, "Hot coffee available in the kitchen." At least some of your parents would be happy to rest there at the end of a long day and visit with others while kids play with a few simple toys in baskets left there for the purpose. This same lounge might also be a good place for families and teachers to visit casually with each other.

For busy families, finding time to get together might take even more creativity. Think about the families of children in your program. Which of these events would be most likely to encourage attendance?

- A presentation about parenting or child development.
- An event in which children and their families do an activity together.
- An event centered on children sharing what they are learning in the classroom.
- A project, such as sprucing up the playground.
- A just-for-fun potluck meal or picnic.

There are hundreds of different ways to bring people together. Your job is to think of creative ways that would appeal most to the families in your program. Then stand back and see what happens. Many a fast friendship has been forged while painting a wall together.

Why are personal connections to each other valuable? Remember the description of the emotional journey families take when they have a child with special needs? It can be a hard and lonely road. If families find themselves comfortable enough to share their stories with others in the community and find supportive, receptive ears, how much easier might that road become? People tend to be receptive when they are making a personal connection with someone. In general, people tend to be more sympathetic and supportive to people or human situations that they have been personally exposed to. One heart-to-heart conversation is likely to have more positive impact on a family's support of your inclusive program than all of the articles on your library shelf, even if those articles have definitive research about how valuable inclusion programs are for children.

Creating a Shared Vision of the Value of Inclusive Classrooms

As we wrote earlier, in a culture of inclusion, families care about and support the program's mission to serve all children. Families care about and support each child, regardless of developmental profile or challenging behavior. And families care about and support each other.

Earlier in this chapter, you read how you can use a parent's concerns about children with challenges to help him understand these children and the challenges they face. People have an innate desire to care for children. People also seem to have an innate propensity to avoid or shy away from what they don't understand. It helps families care about and support each child if they gain an understanding of each child. They also become more supportive through their encounters with the *families* of children with challenges. Both of these methods bring families to greater understanding through personal means. There is another personal relationship that will also influence a family's sense of the value of inclusion.

We are referring, of course, to the teacher-family relationship. As in so many other ways, you provide the model for how families view and approach children with challenges. Families should be exposed to your excitement about each child and the interactions that occur between children in your classroom. Families should learn from you the ways in which all of the children are learning from each other. You should never underestimate your influence on families when you share information in a professionally articulate, enthusiastic way. Some teachers are more easily articulate. Some find enthusiasm easier to convey than the right words. Some use methods other than words. There are so many wonderful tools these days, and they get less expensive and easier to operate all of the time. You can post children's dictations, drawings, and photographs of their work around the school, on a Web site or blog, or as e-mail attachments. Video and audio are other effective ways to help families literally see and hear the classroom. But don't simply present these media. Link them to the value of an inclusive classroom and a supportive community.

Most children have some arena that is challenging for them. Most children have a time during their preschool years that is bumpy, when they can use some extra support. As families hear you speak with such compassion about bumpy times or even bumpy children, they come to understand that a relationship-based, inclusive environment will meet their child's needs whenever and however they occur. As this understanding grows, families become more interested in supporting an inclusive environment. If every child has special needs at some point, then a program that serves children with special needs will be more than equipped to meet every child's needs, whatever they may be.

There is an important way to create a shared vision of an inclusive community that goes beyond the personal. Whether a small family child care or a large, complex early childhood center, every program needs to clearly convey to families its vision, mission, and approach. This vision, mission, and approach should be boiled down into some simple language that can be understood by everyone on staff. Families should hear about it before they ever decide to place their children in the program. After joining the program, they need to be exposed to its mission in numerous ways. It should be

- Highlighted in written materials parents receive when they enter the program.
- Evident in the environment, whether in written statements posted on the walls or visible through the kind of setup, art, or documentation you share when families walk through the space.
- Supported by research that has been translated into easy-to-understand handouts, pages on your Web site, or entries in your program's blog.
- Reinforced by respected guest speakers who share your same message.

Whenever families and staff meet with each other, whether in individual parent-teacher conferences, school-family meetings, events where families are invited into the classroom with the children, or playground cleaning workdays, the program's values, mission, and approach should be evident in what people say, what happens, and how families experience the event. If you say you are a program that wants everyone to feel comfortable and included, make sure that is true whenever and wherever you have family events. Are there chairs for older grandparents who can't stand for too long? Accommodations for late arrivals? If someone is hard of hearing, have you thought of how to include him? Have you thought about how to support the child who doesn't have anyone from her family show up? Experiencing your vision will bring to life the written information you have shared with parents.

Empowering Families

The old saying "Knowledge is power" can be applied to the process of community building. You can provide some of that knowledge, but the real power begins when families start sharing experiences with each other.

Offering Useful Information about Children

The first universal principle, *We are more same than different*, can be applied to families as well as children. You know that children learn best when they are involved learners who can construct their own knowledge. Families, too, will be most invested in an inclusive, supportive community when they have an active role in creating it (Davis-Kean and Eccles 2005, Keyser 2006).

One of the reasons a teacher or program needs to find an appropriate way to share information about children with challenges is because people are uncomfortable when they don't know what to do. If families know that a child like Michelle is most likely to answer them when they get right down to her level and look in her eyes, they are more likely to want to talk to her. If they have tips for how to have a child like Danny over for a playdate without his going wild and wrecking the house, they are more likely to reach out for the playdate. Most of this kind of empowerment can be accomplished simply by sharing the goals and strategies for individual children. Sometimes it can be accomplished by having families help out in the classroom and learn how to interact with specific children by observing how you relate to them.

Encouraging Families to Offer Useful Information

You might also want to encourage families of challenging children or children with challenges to share relevant information with other families as it comes up. Again, they don't need to share a diagnosis or go into complex explanations. Encourage families to provide only the information that is needed for the child to have successful encounters. When a child is invited over to play, a parent might say, "She is really shy at first and might hide in a corner. But if you just leave her alone, she'll come around and have a good time." Or before a birthday party, "My son loves birthday parties, but he can get revved up with all of the stimulation. Is there a quiet place where I can take him to help him calm down?" Or when they pass in the hall and the child doesn't answer the other parents' greeting, "She doesn't always take in what people say unless they are close and look at her. And then sometimes you need to wait a few seconds." This will take a lot of practice and a lot of courage on the families' part, but it will be worth it.

Sometimes families may wish to write a letter to the other families in a class before school even starts. The letter describes their child's interests and favorite things as well as her challenges and invites other families to approach them with questions. The underlying message is "Our child is like any other child, and it is okay to ask for any information you need to feel comfortable with her." This is a useful approach if the child's challenges are obvious, such as a wheelchair.

Helping Families Respond to Their Own Children

Even when families want to be supportive, they don't always know how. At The Little School, families often ask us what to say when their child says that a child is a baby because she can't talk or another child is bad because he hit someone else. When families approach you, give them language to use with their own children, much like the language offered throughout this book. Let them know how they can be helpful to the child or the situation. Even when families haven't asked, if you know their children are going home talking about an issue, be proactive. Write a letter to families telling them what is happening in the classroom, and what they can say to and do with their children to support your goals in the classroom. If you do this regularly, families will learn a lot of specifics, and they will also learn that your program is a dynamic place, full of lovely moments as well as challenging moments. Again, if you just talk about the life of the classroom, you are not breaching confidentiality.

In Danny's story, all of the parents in the program started out concerned about his aggression and ended up feeling proud of his progress. This might sound difficult to believe. And yet we authors have seen that very phenomenon over and over again after parents start out with concerns. It doesn't always work. It sometimes takes a long time to work. And it is often hard work along the way. But it happens often enough that we want to give you one more story about parents rallying around an aggressive child.

Lester was the bright, verbal, imaginative child of effective, likable parents. He was highly impulsive, physically gangly, invasive, and he drooled constantly. He was also physically and verbally aggressive toward other children. His verbal expression was characteristically graphic and imaginative: "I am going to throw you under a car so it will flatten you and your eyeballs will pop out." The other children were terrified of him. They had nightmares about Lester, didn't want to come to school because of him, and complained loudly to their families about him. And the families complained loudly to us.

One day, we had a meeting with the children. We explained to them that Lester got scared a lot, and when he got scared, he tried to help himself by being scary himself. We went around the circle, and the children all shared what scared them. Then Lester himself shared. Lester and the children agreed that when Lester got scary, the children would know he was scared and go get a teacher to help him. Before we sent the children home, we wrote up what happened in a letter to the families. We asked the families to review the circle conversation with their children and let their children know that Lester was a child just like they were, and they could help him learn to keep kids safe.

By playing a role in Lester's development, children and families felt empowered and became consequently invested in Lester's development. From then on, we all grew together.

Empowering Families

We used many strategies to help Lester grow. But families always felt it was their messages to their children about Lester that made the difference. They took a personal interest in him and were proud of his progress. How different that was from their initial reaction! We suspect that throughout their child's schooling, those families never again looked at difficult children the same way. Part of an inclusive mission is to help parents and families become invested in the growth and development of *all* children and to give them the lifelong tools to apply to that investment.

You want to do more than empower parents and families to support specific children. You want to empower them to be cocreators of your vision of an inclusive community. They might have ideas that you haven't thought of.

Some ideas might sound as if they would take a lot of work, but maybe a parent has more energy than you do! Give families opportunities to volunteer and be involved. Create times or places in which people can communicate with each other about the vision of the program and family community. Below are some specific ideas about encouraging a supportive, inclusive family community. There are many, many more ideas, limited only by your creativity and the creativity of the families in your program:

- Ask a veteran parent to share stories about the benefits of inclusion as part of family meetings, and even informally, when she talks to other parents.

- See if there are families who would like to plan an event for the entire program community about inclusion—they can share what they've learned, and how they've learned it. Some families of children with special needs may want to share how inclusion is beneficial to all of the children and make themselves available for questions.

- Send out a letter at the beginning of the year reminding families how hard it is for new families to join an established group and make some suggestions for how to reach out. Again, this benefits everyone, including families with challenged or challenging children.

- Make a bulletin board for families to share their hopes and desires for the kind of community they would like to create with each other. Provide sticky notes and pens. Maybe they want to hear from other families about good parenting books or parks or activities. Maybe they want to start a babysitting exchange. This provides a forum for families of children with special needs to make their requests known without singling them out. And it meets the needs of every other family in the same way.

- Bring together families across different classes who might be able to support each other in particular ways—a potluck for the families of adopted children or a discussion group for the families of children with special needs. Again, if affinity groups occur around a range of topics, families of children with special needs won't feel singled out in getting a much-needed forum to talk with and hear from other families in similar circumstances.

- To create a greater understanding of the diverse circumstances of families, have them share their stories in newsletters. See the example on page 229.

- Have families who have finished the program create a short handbook for other families about how they (and their children) can gain the most from an inclusive program. Try to get families with children with special needs and families of typically developing children to work on it together. The handbook can cover topics like "How to ask questions of other parents" or "Do I take my concerns to the school or the parent?"

The Challenges and Rewards of Creating an Inclusive Community

For every positive story like Danny's, Michelle's, or Lester's, there are stories of a community that did not rally around a challenged child and whose families did not receive empathy and support from other parents.

Charlie and his family fell into that second category. They joined a class that had been together for a year. Charlie had identified special needs. His family very much wanted playdates with children and parents outside of school to build their son's social skills and interests, but they didn't feel comfortable up front telling parents about Charlie's differences. When they hinted at them, other parents just weren't responsive: they felt that Charlie's parents were hiding something from them, and this got in the way of their empathy. We gently encouraged Charlie's parents to reveal more, and they tried. But they had not reached a place within themselves of feeling comfortable talking openly about Charlie to other parents they didn't know well. Charlie progressed, but Charlie's family never got to experience a supportive parent community within The Little School during his time there.

After Charlie graduated, Charlie's parents continued to grow too. They took over leadership of a support group for families of children with special needs within our preschool and helped found a support group for parents in their school district. One year, we decided to run a series of personal parent narratives in our monthly newsletter to increase people's awareness and sensitivity toward other families in our diverse school community. One parent wrote about being the parent of an adopted child of a different race and the questions she wished people didn't ask. A gay father wrote about his family and the questions that people *could* ask. And Julia, Charlie's mother, stepped forward and offered to write about being part of the parent community as a parent of a child with special needs.

Enrolling our child with developmental challenges at The Little School was truly a life-changing experience for our family. Three and a half years into our son's life, we had never been able to leave him somewhere, walk away, and know that he would be understood, supported, and treated with respect. The Little School was not only a new beginning for our son, but also for us as parents. Having spent two years trying to understand and overcome our son's challenges, we had learned to navigate the world with him in a way that made our life, and our parenting, different than those of most people we knew. We had tried to stay "below the radar," so to speak— avoiding conversations that brought out our differences and trying our best to fit in to other people's version of life. The Little School, we hoped, would give us the chance to be more open, and therefore better understood, appreciated, and respected for our differences.

Our son had been diagnosed before he was two years old with challenges that included delayed speech, slow auditory processing, difficulty regulating his arousal levels, low muscle tone, and significant social delays. He did not fit neatly into a box with a label, so we did not use one. We worked around the clock with him in therapy and at home, and by the time he was ready to begin life at The Little School, his language was above average, and on good days, during the short periods of time people saw him at drop-off and pickup, he seemed like a fairly typical three-year-old. We knew, however, that it wouldn't take long for people to start noticing something different going on.

Before we arrived for the first day of his class, we connected on the phone with another parent of a child with special needs. We were desperate for advice: Should we tell the parents in our son's class about his challenges? How much should we tell? Have other parents done this? Our ultimate question was this: Would telling the parents of our son's classmates about his challenges pave the way for more support and understanding, or would it cause people to back off?

We ran through all the things we could say: "Our son has perfect hearing, but he often doesn't hear when people speak to him." "Our son can get overstimulated, so sometimes he will throw things or wreck a child's project, but he's really not aggressive." "Our son is just learning to see other kids as fun and mostly likes to be with adults—we'd really like to get him on some playdates." We worried that parents who hadn't encountered children like our son would find these statements confusing, implausible, or even scary. After much thought, we decided to take some time to get to know people and see our son react to the environment before telling them about his differences. While this may have not been the best decision, the alternative felt just too scary and confusing, and we were somewhat paralyzed. Saying nothing was clearly the safer road for us.

Our reluctance to share information about our son's differences gradually lessened over time as we discovered that the more we communicated with other parents, the more they felt invited to communicate with us about our child. We have come to realize that sharing is often educating, and that when people shut down, turn away, or seem disinterested, it can often be because they lack information and are confused or uncomfortable about our family's differences. We still to this day encounter parents who have taken actions to prevent their child's association with our son, nervous that something negative will come from it. We now view this not as hostility, but as a natural reaction we all have to both protect and do what is best for our child.

If we can put ourselves in the company of people who strive to understand and even seek out diversity and who want their children to do the same, we find that talking about differences is much easier. If we aren't fortunate enough to have such a community, then we have to work hard to try to create one. When people start to understand how our son sees and relates to the world differently, it can interest them in learning about how we are all different, and that, in turn, can lead to greater acceptance, empathy, and curiosity. So now we are much bolder about talking openly with people we don't even know about how our son is different, hoping that somehow we're making a positive impact in people's ability to recognize, adapt to, and embrace differences.

Many parents of children with challenges face the same dilemma we did upon entering The Little School. The identity of kids with special needs is kept private until the parents choose to share information about their child. We would like to encourage all parents to be curious about the individual differences among all children in their child's class and to try to view a noticeable difference as something to embrace. Asking thoughtful questions of other parents about their child and showing interest in how you can help your child to understand their child better is a great way to reach out and offer support. And support is something most parents of special-needs kids will never turn away.

—Julia
Charlie's mom

Clearly, this parent had grown a lot. And she was willing to share her growth to benefit others. She continues to share by allowing us to use her piece in this book. After Julia wrote her newsletter article, she got several e-mail replies from parents. Some of them were from parents who had been in her son's class. They expressed empathy for what she had gone through and appreciation for what she had written. Parents said she had opened their eyes. She got support as well as validation. She even finally got that offer for a play-date! Here are a few of the e-mails she received:

Julia, I have been meaning to e-mail you to say thank you. It was wonderful reading your write-up last week in the newsletter. I really appreciated you sharing with us your experience as a mom, parent, and family. I actually sent it to my very close friend who has a son who is three. He has many of the same issues that you describe, and I was wondering if I could give my friend your contact information. After reading what you wrote, she would really like to connect with you.

Hi Julia. I am a new mom at school, and I wanted to thank you for your honesty and sharing of yourself and your family. It was so refreshing and real to read. Every family has something that challenges them somewhere in their family, but not everyone is willing to admit that. I was really moved by your candor and sharing and your experience. I hope to cross paths with you at some juncture.

Wow . . . what an amazing article. Thank you from the bottom of our hearts for sharing your story. Your story will make it easier for the next family, and so on . . . and so on . . . and so on. . . .

I just wanted to say that your article for the newsletter was pretty amazing. I appreciate your openness and candidness. It sure gives me a lot to think about as a parent and as a member of two educational communities. Thanks for taking the time to write.

Wow, Julia . . . brilliantly written . . . educational and illuminating. . . . Hope your family is enjoying the Holidays. Would love to set Charlie and Sean up for a playdate when you guys have time.

So yes, it can be difficult to attempt to create an authentic culture of inclusion among parents. It requires you to enter the messy arena of adult social relationships. It asks you to stretch people's attitudes while showing respect for and building connection with them. But when you have a chance to affect not only the lives of the children in your care but also the lives of their families and all the children they will come across, isn't it worth it?

• • •

In this chapter, we discussed the creation of a relationship-based, inclusive parent community. We shared four methods for its creation, as well as examples, suggestions, and pitfalls. Just as the creation of an inclusive, relationship-based classroom and staff environment allows each child to have a more successful experience, so, too, does the creation of an inclusive parent community.

In the next chapter, we step back and take a look at the broader picture. How does the attempt to support individual children through relationship-based, inclusive education change how we look at teachers and children? How does it change how we define the field of education itself?

Chapter 13

Why Inclusion? Future Directions in Early Childhood Education

In this book, we have tried to share our experience of relationship-based inclusion at The Little School. We have tried to show how this approach to teaching grew out of a typical classroom setting and flowed from basic best practices. We have demonstrated how it helps build a way of knowing and supporting all children. And perhaps most important of all, we have tried to suggest that inclusion is about opportunities and connections much more than it is about challenges and solutions. We focused on stories from the classroom to bring to life our belief that inclusion is something more than just a means of serving children with special needs.

We have also taken care to acknowledge that inclusion can mean different things to different people. Some practitioners feel that inclusion works best when it focuses on mastering techniques of therapeutic intervention (Odom 2000). Others see it as a source of significant change for the whole field of education (Bricker 1995). We would like to suggest that these perspectives can fit together.

Just as children must be seen in the layers of their context—from local to global—our work in the classroom must also be recognized as part of a larger picture. We came to learn about inclusive practices because we wanted to address local circumstances: the growing number of children in our program who needed specific support. But we came to write this book because as we shared our locally gained knowledge with others, we saw that the entire field of early childhood education has become more and more preoccupied with responding to children's challenges.

As a result of our experience in the world outside our program, we now feel that the process of individual successes translating to global educational change is an important part of inclusion itself. Perspectives and practices that work for one child in the classroom will also have an impact on the larger field of education itself. This model of inclusion comes from basic best practices, focuses on individual support, and sees all children as possessing strengths and challenges. We can't help but feel that it has natural potential to improve the overall quality of early childhood education. But it remains primarily a means of mastering effective and proven techniques of therapeutic support.

Let us revisit some of the key points from our approach and consider what they may imply about teaching and education in general.

Rethinking the "Typical" Child

Families and teachers of all children are often perplexed by the question of whether a child is typical, normal, or healthy. The idea of *typical* and *atypical* development deepens this kind of thinking. It suggests two kinds of children: *normal* and *other*, and a clear, fixed line dividing them. Intervention can reinforce this divided view of children. When adults decide that a child needs an assessment, evaluation, or regular course of therapy, it is natural to see that child moving across a clear line between *normal* and *special* children.

Early childhood professionals should not minimize the real differences between children or the challenges that can come from these differences. In our experience, children with Down syndrome, cerebral palsy, severe autism, or other disabilities have significant developmental differences from children without assessed challenges. But even children with these differences share strengths and challenges with other children. It is becoming clearer and clearer to us through our experience that many "typically" developing children experience challenges of the same quality, on the same continuum, as children assessed outside developmental norms. The diagnoses or therapeutic goals that many children acquire are in some ways institutional necessities—they allow children to be moved through health care and educational systems. They may say less about who a child really is and how she differs from peers than we once thought. These diagnoses can also preserve a segregated population and a narrow view of children.

We feel that the broader educational value of inclusion rests on an understanding that we have expressed throughout this book: we are more alike than different. Our similarities are more profound than our differences. An individualized, strength-based view of children, one that comes from a commitment to deep observation, appreciation, and reflection of each child, allows teachers to see and foster the connections between children. It is this understanding that has helped us serve a surprisingly wide range of children in the same educational community. But we have come to believe that it does more than that. Inclusion, without ignoring reality, redefines what a child or even a person is. In looking beyond categories and diagnoses, in seeing all people's individuality in rich detail, we create a more inclusive image of childhood.

Rethinking the "Typical" Teacher

Teachers so often feel that they have to know the answers. It can seem as if they must have insight and techniques for every possible situation if they want to gain and keep the trust of families or supervisors. When children or families feel at a loss, they want an immediate answer. And goodness knows, early childhood educators sorely want to show enough expertise to feel respected by their peers, family, and society itself. A teacher must be someone who can inspire trust and confidence and who can manage the type of environment that many find overwhelming. It is no wonder that people so often buy into what teacher Tim Gillespie (2001, 4) calls the narrative of the "super teacher"—unflappable, infinitely competent and skilled, and never at a loss for answers or plans.

This is one reason why educators feel so overwhelmed by children who are different or challenging: they make teachers feel as if they don't know everything. These children leave teachers searching for answers where they most want to have them but least often do. When we at The Little School first took on the challenge of working with children with special needs, we, too, were afraid that we would fall on our faces when we wanted most to excel. We had to make a commitment to operating outside our comfort and expertise.

Although this seemed at first like the biggest challenge of inclusion, it turned out to be one of the deepest and broadest benefits. Inclusion inspires a vision of the teacher as a constant work in progress. When you accept that you will feel your way with each child, make mistakes, and learn from families, colleagues, and from the child herself, you begin to free yourself from the pressure to be a perfect, finished practitioner. You begin to welcome surprises, accidents, false starts, and dead ends. They not only help you find the right recipe for supporting an individual child, they also contribute to your process of learning and discovery. Not knowing all the answers becomes the *key* to success, not a threat to success.

Teachers who embrace struggle also present a problem-solving, curious model of education to students. Reflecting deeply, taking in as much detailed information as possible, cultivating real curiosity, breaking challenges into steps, sticking with things even when they seem overwhelming—all of these are fundamental tools of learning. Teachers who know all the answers can be intimidating. (And teachers who are overwhelmed or disorganized can be discouraging too.) But teachers who hold a core of knowledge and expertise, yet constantly push themselves to gain new insights and skills show children the way to lifelong satisfaction in the learning environment. As we tried to show throughout this book, learning to slow down and focus on relationships becomes the core of teaching. When challenges are truly complicated or intense, even the slightest breakthrough or progress becomes a celebration. Surely children, and the larger field of education, need to learn this from teachers like you as well.

Embracing challenge and moving away from the drive to be perfect fosters a strength-based view of teachers. We have focused on a strength-based view of children throughout the book. But it may be even more important to focus on your own strengths as a teacher than on the children's. Teachers can have such high expectations of themselves and be inclined to focus on what they see as their failings or weaknesses. Children learn from observing patterns and relationships in the people around them (Siegel 1999). It is hard to know just how much they learn from observing the way teachers treat themselves. With each new research study on learning, educators are becoming more aware of how crucial it is to place emphasis on their own strengths. You need to balance the drive to do well with accepting that you can always do better.

Through our work at The Little School, we have found that this strength-based view of children and the acceptance of individual challenges have helped us redefine our image of teaching. They give us the tools to build a more multi-dimensional definition of our role. We can then offer children a commitment to a lifelong journey of development, an enthusiasm for the unknown, a balance of structure and exploration, and a positive, patient, and forgiving view of ourselves.

Finally, we hope inclusion can do for the community of teachers what it is doing for the community of children: soften the sense of two separate populations. Inclusion pushes us beyond divisions between regular and special education teachers—those who know about *education* and those who know about *special needs*. We don't mean to suggest that the two disciplines should become one or that teachers do not need to study or learn therapeutic techniques. The knowledge of the special education and therapy professions play a vital role in the evolution of inclusion and in ensuring its quality.

But we do hope that as teachers learn to help as many young children as possible participate in the same classroom communities, they will acquire a broader base of knowledge and skills to serve all children over time. Special education teachers would learn more basic best educational and developmental perspectives and practices. And teachers who today choose to learn general educational skills would receive much more specific training on how to serve children with a wide variety of differences.

A New Definition of Education

If inclusion can help unite regular and special education students and teachers into a more unified community, then we feel it can also help bring both these branches of education under the same roof. This, as you will recall from chapter 1, is the fundamental definition of inclusion. In child care centers, preschools, elementary schools, and beyond, we already see dramatic change from just a generation ago: kindergarten classrooms with paraprofessionals to support individual children, child care centers with parent support groups and networks of consulting therapists, second grade teachers who do physical and sensory activities before asking the students to sit down to morning meeting. There is no single template for how inclusion can affect the structure of education or the nature of teaching, but we do see growing collaborations and connections between what used to be separate fields.

In fact, inclusion dictates that there be no one blueprint. Throughout this book, we have stressed that inclusion relies on individual goals and strategies for individual children, families, and programs. The same is true for inclusion education. The model of individual responses to individual circumstances must also apply to how we adapt inclusive practices to each local school, district, or community. This is not a new idea. The democratic reforms in public school in the 1960s, driven by thinkers such as Vito Perrone and Patricia Carini and the Reggio Emilia philosophy, all started with the same idea: quality education must grow in a unique way out of the details of each local community (Carini 2000, Malaguzzi 1998, Perrone 1991). Inclusion adds a systematic, organized way of tailoring classroom practice to individual children, collaboration among adults, and improvement in the quality of individual programs. As more and more students, teachers, families, administrators, and legislators question the current emphasis on unified standards for all, inclusion adds vital support for the argument that education must be an individualized craft.

That being said, the priorities of inclusion can and should have some broad implications on how educators create early childhood programs. As we showed in the stories of Danny and Michelle, addressing the needs of individuals and groups highlights the universal need for more teachers. A commitment to effective support of all children should filter up to the question of teacher-to-child ratios and effective staffing at all levels of education. Even though this book starts from the idea that you may need less special education training than you think to serve children with special needs, it has also called for better ongoing support and training of all teachers. It is no secret that early childhood education has been badly undervalued in our society. But the growing incidence of children with assessed special needs is not just an education issue. It is one of the major public health concerns of our time. Because inclusion brings together the worlds of education and public health, we feel that it should double the amount of time, energy, and resources our society at large devotes to early childhood education.

We hope we have showed that effective inclusion will not only improve how much staffing and training teachers and programs have in the future but what kind of training and support teachers will receive. Our relationship-based approach to local teaching can guide how the field of education can best improve: through relationships. A growing commitment to inclusion should strengthen the relationships between teachers and administrators, between schools and therapists, and between the different branches of the educational community.

In teacher credential and college degree programs, the worlds of *regular* and *special* education remain somewhat separate. Special education students learn volumes about atypical development but very little about effective curriculum theories or best practices. Early childhood education students learn about child development and practice but very little about children with special needs, sensory integration, or therapeutic practice. As teachers who have spent time in both early childhood education and special education graduate programs, we three have been surprised to find how little either discipline addresses the kind of work we do in the inclusion classroom or how little each discipline collaborates with the other. We feel strongly that the widespread adoption of inclusion suggests a higher level of partnership between regular and special education training. We hope that on some small level, books like ours can begin to fill the gap.

Ripples on the Water

As much as we want to share our feelings about education at large, we understand that the challenges of working with all children, including those with special needs, is your main concern. We have learned a great deal of detailed information about these challenges as we work with teachers, care providers, and administrators across the country.

We have learned that for many in the field of *mainstream* early childhood education, the growing number of children with challenges has fostered uncertainty and apprehension. Teachers sincerely want to know how to serve the needs of all of the children in their care. And when they are uncertain, it creates a sense of helplessness. In fact, we see that a certain culture of learned helplessness has settled into the field of early childhood education around children with challenges.

We have also seen that when teachers find ways to respond to challenges and learn how to serve the needs of children who once overwhelmed them, they begin to feel a sense of empowerment. Each small triumph or fragment of progress raises a teacher's spirits, builds pride and determination, and, perhaps most important, becomes a tool for working with all children. As teachers collect these experiences with individuals, they go on to work more successfully with everyone.

We would like to think that the big impact of inclusion education would be such a huge collection of triumphs, skills, and confidence-building experiences that can slowly transform this culture of learned helplessness into a culture of learned empowerment. Although we don't assume that inclusion will act as some sort of large-scale, magical elixir for all of education, we cannot ignore the link between individual growth, small local changes, and change in the larger world of education.

In this way, inclusion links with the growing movement to see teachers as researchers (Cochran-Smith and Lytle 1999). Teachers traditionally have been viewed as people who receive clinically proven theories and methods from experts and put them into practice. In this model, global ideas filter down into local practice. We hope that this book helps to show that the opposite can be true as well: local successes ripple out to the larger community. We believe that some of our practices can be adapted to your work—be it a part-time nursery school, family child care, public preschool, or kindergarten inclusion classroom. We also believe that as you read and reflect on the ideas in this book and tailor them to your local circumstances, you will add to the contributions that inclusion is making to education in general. A best-practices, practitioner-developed therapeutic model, working with and from important research and theories, can help continue to bring teachers more respect as creators as well as consumers of educational philosophy.

Do we devote much of our time to carrying banners for large-scale change, to influencing how teachers are trained, or to public policy? Probably not, although this must be part of our work. Inclusion must always be primarily about getting it right for each child in the classroom. But the little insights, innovations, and inspirations that start in classrooms do indeed ripple out to society at large.

We can and do make a difference by helping one child at a time.

References

Ayres, A. Jean. 1979. *Sensory integration and the child.* Los Angeles: Western Psychological Services.

Bowlby, John. 1982. *Attachment.* Volume 1 of *Attachment and loss.* New York: Basic Books.

Boyle, Coleen A., P. Decoufle, and M. Yeargin-Allsopp. 1994. Prevalence and heath impact of developmental disabilities in U.S. children. *Pediatricts* 93 (3): 399–403.

Bricker, Dianne. 1995. The challenge of inclusion. *Journal of Early Intervention* 19 (3): 179–194.

Bricker, Dianne. 2000. Inclusion: How the scene has changed. *Topics in Early Childhood Special Education* 20 (1): 14–19.

Bronfenbrenner, Urie. 1979. *The ecology of human development: Experiments by nature and design.* Cambridge, MA: Harvard University Press.

Caine, Renate N., and Geoffrey Caine. 1994. *Making connections: Teaching and the human brain.* New York: Addison-Wesley. Quoted in Witmer 2005, 224.

Carini, Patricia F. 2000. A letter to teachers and parents on some ways of looking at reflecting on children. In *From another angle: Children's strengths and school standards*, ed. M. Himley and P. Carini, 56–64. New York: Teachers College Press.

———. 2001. *Starting strong: A different look at children, schools and standards.* New York: Teachers College Press.

Cochran-Smith, Marilyn, and Susan L. Lytle. 1999. The teacher research movement: A decade later. *Educational Researcher* 28 (7): 15–25.

Davis-Kean, Pamela. E., and Jacquelynne S. Eccles. 2005. Influences and challenges to better parent-school collaborations. In *School-family partnerships for children's success*, ed. Evanthia. N. Partikakou, Roger P. Weissberg, Sam Redding, and Herbert J. Walberg, 57–76. New York: Teachers College Press.

Dewey, John. 1916. *Democracy in education: An introduction to the philosophy of education.* New York: Macmillan.

Division for Early Childhood and the National Association for the Education of Young Children. 2009. Early childhood inclusion. Joint position statement. Washington, DC: Division for Early Childhood and the National Association for the Education of Young Children. http://www.dec-sped .org/uploads/docs/about_dec/position_concept_papers/PositionStatement _Inclusion_Joint_updated_May2009.pdf.

Gillespie, Tim. 2001. Stories and the teaching life. *The Quarterly* 23 (4): 2–6.

Glasser, William. 1998. *Choice theory: A new psychology of human freedom.* New York: Harper Perennial. Quoted in Witmer 2005, 224.

Goleman, Daniel. 1997. *Emotional intelligence: Why it can matter more than IQ.* New York: Bantam Books.

Gray, Carol. 2000. *The new social story book.* Arlington, TX: Future Horizons.

Greenspan, Stanley I., and Serena Wieder. 2006. *Engaging autism: Using the floortime approach to help children relate, communicate, and think.* Reading, MA: Perseus Books.

———. 1998. *The child with special needs: Encouraging intellectual and emotional growth.* Reading, MA: Perseus Books.

Heymann, Jody S., Kate Penrose, and Alison Earle. 2006. Meeting children's needs: How does the United States measure up? *Merrill-Palmer Quarterly* 52 (2): 189–215.

Katz, Lilian G., and Sylvia C. Chard. 2000. *Engaging children's minds: The project approach.* Stamford, CT: Ablex Publishing.

Keyser, Janis. 2006. *From parents to partners: Building a family-centered early childhood program.* St. Paul: Redleaf Press.

Koplow, Lesley. 1996. Why homeless children can't sit still. In *Unsmiling faces: How preschools can heal,* ed. Lesley Koplow, 219–229. New York: Teachers College Press.

Kranowitz, Carol S. 1998. *The out-of-sync child: Recognizing and coping with sensory integration dysfunction.* New York: Perigee Books.

Little School. 2004. *Relationships: The key to teaching and learning in the early years.* DVD. Directed by David Summerlin. San Francisco: Little School.

MacLean, Paul. 1990. *The triune brain in evolution: Role in the paleocerebral functions.* New York: Plenum Press.

Malaguzzi, Loris. 1998. History, ideas, and basic philosophy: An interview with Lella Gandini. In *The hundred languages of children: The Reggio Emilia approach—advanced reflections,* 2nd ed., ed. Carolyn Edwards, Lella Gandini, and George Forman, 49–97. Norwood, CT: Ablex Publishing.

Odom, Samuel. 2000. Preschool inclusion: What we know and where we go from here. *Topics in Early Childhood Special Education,* 20 (1): 20–27.

Osgood, Monica G., and Lauren Blaszak. 2003. Sample individual IEP program outline. Wharton, NJ: Celebrate the Children. http://celebrate the children.org/Pages/sampleIEPs.html.

Perrone, Vito. 1991. *A letter to teachers: Reflections on schooling and the art of teaching.* San Francisco: Jossey-Bass.

Perry, Bruce, and Maia Szalavitz. 2007. *The boy who was raised as a dog and other stories from a child psychiatrist's notebook: What traumatized children can teach us about loss, love, and healing.* New York: Basic Books.

Piaget, Jean. 1971. The theory of stages in cognitive development. In *Measurement and Piaget,* ed. Donald R. Green, Marguerite P. Ford, and George B. Flamer, 1–11. New York: McGraw-Hill.

Schön, Donald. 1983. *The reflective practitioner: How professionals think in action.* New York: Basic Books.

Siegel, Daniel. 1999. *The developing mind: Toward a neurobiology of interpersonal experience.* New York: Guilford Press.

Smith, Patricia McGill. 2003. You are not alone: For parents when they learn their child has a disability. *NICHCY News Digest* 20 (3): 2–6, http://www.nichcy.org/informationresources/documents/nichcy%20pubs/nd20.pdf.

U.S. Congress. 1990. *Americans with Disabilities Act.* 101st Cong., 2nd sess. Public law 101–336. *U.S. Statutes at Large* 104 (1990): 369–378.

U.S. Congress. 2004. *The Individuals with Disabilities Education Improvement Act.* 108th Cong. Public law 108–446. *U.S. Statutes at Large* 118 (2004): 2647–2808.

U.S. Department of Education. National Center for Education Statistics. 2007. *Preprimary enrollment.* Washington, DC: U.S. Department of Commerce.

U.S. Office of Special Education Programs. 2000. *History: Twenty-five years of progress in educating children with disabilities through IDEA.* Washington, DC: U.S. Department of Education. http://www.ed.gov/policy/speced/leg/idea/history.pdf.

Vygotsky, Lev S. 1978. *Mind in society: The development of higher psychological processes.* Cambridge, MA: Harvard University Press.

Williams, Mary S., and Sherry Shellenberger. 1996. *How does your engine run? A leader's guide to the Alert Program for self-regulation.* Albuquerque: Therapy Works.

Witmer, Miriam M. 2005. The fourth R in education: Relationships. *The Clearing House* 78 (5): 224–228.

The Language of Inclusion

How do you build a truly inclusive classroom community? When we examine the attitudes we communicate in the very words we choose each day, we can build new attitudes and understanding. The examples below demonstrate the language used in an inclusive classroom.

In general, when you speak to children, stress how everyone

- Is learning different things at different times.
- Has different things that make them feel comfortable or uncomfortable.
- Has something to teach others.
- Runs into problems.
- Has the ability to solve problems that come up.
- Has the ability to do things that make others feel good and safe.
- Feels good when they make others feel good.

Language Examples to Promote Understanding and the Development of a Caring Community

Helping Children with Arousal and Regulation

- You like to play superhero with your cape. And you want Ken to be a bad guy. Does Ken like being the bad guy all the time? Hmm, what can we do? We can't make our friend Ken unhappy, and you both want to be the good guys. Good friends often like to be the same thing. Let's make up something you both could fight against. No one likes to be the bad guy all the time. It's too scary.

- You are learning to keep each other safe when you are playing a very exciting game. That game makes our engines very excited, and then they run super fast and are hard to control. What can we hit that won't get hurt?

- When you are playing a fighting game, I notice it's really hard not to hurt someone. Lots of kids are learning this! See if we can try shadow fighting, where we don't really touch one another. I'm glad you can remind each other to not really touch.

- Many of the kids are working on learning to play exciting games without hurting one other. You are feeling so angry with each other right now. Let's talk about this problem at meeting time. I'm sure our friends will have good ideas about how to make it work better. When you feel better, I bet you will have some good ideas too.

- That game gets kind of scary. Your hearts are beating very fast, and there is a lot of yelling. When a game gets too scary, kids learn to say "Time-out!" until they feel safe again and ready to play some more.

- Elena is very good at remembering to call "Time-out!" when the game feels too rough. She will help you remember to keep the game fun. If you can't remember to listen to Elena, I will need to ask you to take a break from the game until your engine can stay at a comfortable speed for listening to your friends. That's the way to keep the game fun.

- When that happened, it made me very scared, and my engine started going very fast. Then I yelled and got you very upset. Let's both take some deep breaths before we solve the problem. I need to calm my engine down!

- Brandee is very upset. Louise, can you bring the calming box over? I'm hoping we can find a calming card that will work to help Brandee feel better.

- I'm glad you went to the calming corner when that game got uncomfortable for you, J.T. Will you tell the kids at meeting time how good it feels to take a break? Maybe others can learn from you. You have been working so hard to take care of yourself when you are having big feelings!

Explaining Children's Differences

- Cara uses a wheelchair to move around because it helps her legs work differently. Yes, her legs can move, but her muscles can't stay strong enough to hold her up. . . . That's the only thing that works differently for Cara's body. When she was born, she learned everything that you did, but when you learned to walk, Cara learned to use a wheelchair to move around.

- Sonya wears the earphones because some sounds really make her feel uncomfortable. In our class, we work together to help one another feel safe and comfortable.

- I gave Travis a lap weight because that helps him to sit and listen. I notice you do well when you sit with your legs in the tailor-sitting position without a lap weight. Corrie does best when he sits on a big block. Liang sits in the plastic cube chair so she can be in a chair that holds her in place. Everyone needs different things to help them stay and participate. I'm so glad everyone is learning what works best for themselves.

- Holly is learning to ask for things instead of grabbing them. You are working on writing your name. We are all learning different things.

- Jung likes to hold a fidget in his hands during meeting time. It helps him to listen and pay attention. See how he can play with it but still look up and listen. Fidgets help some people to stay in their spot and be part of the group. Other people may get distracted by having something in their hands during meeting time. You can tell a fidget is distracting someone if he needs to pay attention to the fidget instead of the group.

- Robert is learning to keep people safe when he is scared, angry, or upset. The teachers will help him. You have already learned to use words to solve problems. I'm so glad you are in his class. He will learn a lot from you, I'm sure.

- When Santiago goes into a crowded place like the bathroom, he gets a big "uh oh" feeling inside him. The noise hurts his ears, and getting bumped makes him feel very uncomfortable. I am going to send him into the bathroom with just one friend who can take good care of him while he is learning to manage those big "uh oh" feelings. What gives you a big "uh oh" or scared feeling?

Encouraging Children to Support Each Other's Differences

- Wow! Reggie likes to play on the slide with you! You are really fun to play with. Reggie is just learning that playing with kids is fun. I think he will learn a lot from you! You know how you are learning letters? Reggie knows all about letters. I bet he could teach you! Friends can learn a lot from each other!

- You like to play games with your friends about good guys and bad guys. Max likes to play games about going on train rides. I wonder how we can put your ideas together? You have so many great ideas. I can tell Max feels safe with you and wants to learn from you. That's pretty amazing! Usually he only likes to play alone!

- Yes, Marco is working on telling us what he wants. His mouth is learning to form words so they can be understood. I'm so glad you are able to look at him and give him extra time to talk in the best way he can. You are a great friend!

- Necie gets very upset when her mom leaves. She is learning to feel safe at school. I remember when it used to be hard for you to say good-bye to your dad. What helped you feel safe? Oh, reading a book helped you? Necie, your friend Justin thinks a book might help. Oh, Justin, will you get a tissue for Necie so she can wipe her nose? Thanks. I'm so glad kids take such good care of each other in our class.

- Monique likes to give her friends big hugs. When she gives hugs, she feels really close to her friends. Big squeezes make her body feel good. What makes your body feel good? Gentle hugs, tight hugs, or waving hello? I'm glad you are teaching each other what makes your bodies feel safe and happy. I wonder who else likes big squeezes? Let's play the squeezing game on the cushions over here, so no one gets hurt. Shall we make everyone into a sandwich/pizza/burrito/pancake with the pillows?

- Ana was sitting in the window looking very sad. She told me she really wanted to play with you. Can you think of a way to make Ana feel happy? Wow—when you invited Ana to play, she looked so happy. You sure are good at making your friends feel happy!

- Yes, that was very scary when Mai yelled so loud at you. She is learning to keep our ears safe when she is upset. You are learning to listen to her quieter words when she is asking you to try her play idea. Good friends can teach each other a lot.

- We all have things that make us feel uncomfortable. In our classroom, we will try to help everyone feel safe together.

Samples of Social Stories

Social stories, as you read in chapter 8, are a tool to help children master specific challenges. They use text and images in a homemade book format to lay out a challenge and solution sequence for a child to review over and over.

As reviewed in chapter 8, these are the steps we use to make a social story:

- Set the scene.
- List relevant positive things about the child.
- Share the child's goal in child-friendly and manageable terms.
- Point out what the child is doing that works better and/or outline the desired action. Make the goal sound appealing and attainable.
- Summarize by acknowledging the child's efforts.

Following are some examples of the text of social stories teachers at The Little School have made to support children through specific challenges. You can see that the language is very simple. The text and accompanying pictures use simple, concrete, repetitive language and images.

Sample Social Story #1: All about Me

This social story was developed by Cassandra Britton and The Little School teacher Barbara Chu to help a child who was experiencing challenges with impulse control and social connections. As you can see, the teachers focused on a sequence of self-awareness concepts. The first three are very simple, fundamental, and intrapersonal—they focus on Simon himself. The story then goes on to lay out a sequence of interpersonal concepts, again flowing from simple to more complex. Each line of text appears on its own page with an accompanying photograph of Simon at school, engaged in the activity described.

All about Me

My name is Simon.
I go to The Little School.
I have a lot of friends.
I am learning to keep my friends safe. My friends are learning too.
I am learning to keep toys safe. My friends are learning too.
I am learning to help my friends. My friends are learning too.
I am learning to make my friends laugh. My friends are learning too.
I am learning to take good care of my friends. My friends are learning too.
I am learning to solve problems safely with friends. My friends are
    learning too.
I am learning to give safe touches. My friends are learning too.
I can make up fun games my friends like to play.
I can join fun games my friends make up.
I am learning to Stop and Think, especially when I am excited and my engine
    is very high. My friends are learning too.
I can have fun with my friends. I am learning to be such a good friend. That
    makes everyone happy.

Sample Social Story #2: Amazing Grace

This social story was developed by The Little School teacher Jetta Jacobson to support a child who was experiencing challenges with gross motor exploration. Grace opted out of play at yard time, spending more and more time on the bench. When she did climb, swing, run, or pedal, she often became frightened and anxious and stopped abruptly. Jetta and her coteachers made a copy of the book for school and one for Grace to read with her family at home. She asked to read the book daily and often jumped up and down in excitement when her teachers read it to her. After the book project, Grace became much more relaxed and active in the yard.

Each page of text was accompanied by a photograph of Grace demonstrating the action described. In this way, the process of creating the social story became part of the support itself. The line "Shake it! Shake it! Shake it!" was borrowed from a favorite class song, showing how familiar and comfortable elements can be woven into this versatile tool.

Amazing Grace

Amazing Grace is a big, strong, and smart girl!

Grace is brave. She tries new things.

Grace balances with no hands!

Amazing Grace climbs so high! She goes all the way to the top!

Amazing Grace, she climbs so high! She likes to shake it in the sky! Shake it!
    Shake it! Shake it! Shake it!

Amazing Grace has strong arms. She hangs from the monkey bars!
    Amazing Grace hangs her feet on the bars!

Amazing Grace goes to the top of the slide!

Amazing Grace can ride a bike all by herself!

Amazing Grace has lots of fun ideas. Her friends like to play with her!

Appendix B

Supporting Children's Sensory Systems

Types of Sensory Input

The following lists provide brief and simple ideas for using sensory integration concepts to support all children in your program. Chapter 3 contains background and an overview of sensory integration. More detailed examples of sensory-based teaching can be found in chapters 5 through 9.

Proprioceptive Input

- Input into the muscles, ligaments, and joints that process unconscious knowledge of where the body is in space.
- Can help children with low arousal become more alert and engaged.
- Can help children with high arousal become calmer and more organized.
- Calming and organizing for anyone, regardless of profile.

Vestibular Input

- Input into the inner ear that processes body's unconscious relationship with movement and gravity—works with proprioceptive sense to keep track of where the body is in space.
- Contributes to raising arousal level and mobilizing muscle tone.
- In the right amounts can support attention, organization, and processing.
- When not coupled with enough muscle work (proprioceptive input) can be disorganizing.

Tactile Input

- Input into the skin of the entire body that gives the body an unconscious sense of general comfort or discomfort. Works with the proprioceptive sense to keep track of where the body is in space.

- Light touch can be very destabilizing for those who are oversensitive.
- Deep, firm touch or compression is calming and organizing for those who are sensitive to light touch or those who need a lot of touch to feel comfortable and connected with their bodies.

Auditory Input

- Input of sound through the ears (hearing).
- Sometimes a child can have trouble hearing things.
- Sometimes a child can hear well but have trouble processing the incoming sounds.
- Sometimes a child can hear things most people screen out. She has trouble figuring out what is the most important thing to pay attention to because she is distracted by the fish tank, a plane flying overhead, or someone talking in the next room.
- Sometimes a child can hear some but not all pitches. As a result, speech from others may sound fragmented and hard to comprehend.

Visual Input

- Information taken in with the eyes and processed in the brain.
- Sometimes a child can have a visual impairment (problem with his eyes) and have trouble seeing.
- Sometimes a child can have visual processing challenges in which the brain has trouble interpreting information from the eyes.
- Sometimes a child may have difficulty with depth perception, affecting the quality of her movement, making her clumsy or hesitant.
- The vestibular system supports muscle tone, and sometimes vestibular issues affect quality of eye movements.
- Sometimes visual challenges or visual processing challenges can affect a child's ability to scan her environment, read visual information or social cues on the faces of others.
- Sometimes visual processing difficulties can make it hard for a child to distinguish differences in shapes/letters/numbers on a page.
- Sometimes visual difficulties can make it difficult for a child to distinguish the main picture from the background on a page.
- Sometimes visual sensitivities can make a child feel overwhelmed and need to shut down if an environment is too visually cluttered or bright (fluorescent lights can be especially irritating).
- Sometimes visual difficulties can make it difficult for a child to decode or navigate a cluttered play area or a fast-moving playground.

Auditory/Visual Input

- All children benefit from a multisensory approach in which, for instance, verbal input is paired with visual information.

- Some children benefit from a reduction in one or all kinds of input. For these children, having fewer inputs helps them to pay attention.

- Some children benefit from both reduction of stimulation and multi-sensory pairing. So a teacher might want to use fewer words and pair them with a gesture (see examples below).

Working with Children Who Have Sensory Processing Challenges

- Remember that children with physical challenges may be more emotionally reactive. They might need to be soothed before they can engage or they might need to be aroused to engage.

- Remember that making things more predictable, with clear structure and expectations and lots of warnings about what to expect, helps children to cope with their challenges.

- Affect is a great tool to get children engaged and aroused.

- Music is a valuable tool to get children engaged, aroused, or soothed and is also a helpful learning channel. Convey important information through songs.

- Tuning in to their bodies is helpful for all children. It is especially helpful when children have become disregulated. Paying attention to breathing can be both calming and arousing.

General Sensory Support Strategies

- Create some class rituals to help the children regain calm when the class becomes disorganized. For example, a teacher at our school introduced a simple call and response Swahili chant. When the children hear it, they have to repeat it back in exactly the same pattern. Using this musical method to refocus is very effective. Some teachers use a silent gesture, such as raising their hand. When the children see the teacher making the special gesture, they all make it as well.

- Maintaining some vestibular inputs in the indoor environment is helpful for children who need more movement to get aroused. A rocking chair is the simplest indoor item. Sit and spins don't take up much room. Ball chairs are becoming very popular in classrooms.

- Have items that provide tactile and proprioceptive input. Restuff your stuffies with beans or flax seeds to give them weight and heft. Create tight nooks for children to crawl into. Have pillows available.

- Look at the visual stimulation children are receiving. How much is on your walls? Does it look organized and calming? Or is it chaotic, which might overstimulate children? Ask the same question of your overall room environment.

- Consider the sound and lighting of your room. Egg cartons make cheap sound insulation. Lamps with covers create calming ambient lighting. Putting tennis balls on the ends of chair legs cuts down on a lot of excess noise.

- Have nooks or calming corners. Whatever you call them, have quiet places in the classroom that one or two children can retreat into.

- Offer easy tools to reduce stimulation, such as headphones that muffle the noise but allow some sound through.

- Provide visual cards for communication tools. Is there a visual symbol a child can show if he needs to use the bathroom, if she angry, if he is hungry?

- Give children water bottles to suck on and stay hydrated. Some programs even offer chewing gum. Various commercial and therapeutic chewies also help children who seek lots of oral input to stay organized.

Practical Sensory Supports to Embed throughout the Day

Arrival

- Give a big hug to children who like or need proprioceptive input.

- Provide a quiet greeting and quiet area for children who like to start their day with low input.

Transitions throughout the Day

- Post a visual schedule for the day that the class can refer to at each transition.

- Teach the children a song that identifies or helps with transitions. One classroom we know uses the tune "*Frere Jacques*," changing the words to suit each transition. "First we play, first we play, then we clean, then we clean. Now it's time for meeting, now it's time for meeting. Let's all meet. Come sit down."

- A proprioceptive component embedded in transitions helps to organize and calm. For example, ask children to stack chairs or push a heavy piece of furniture to put it away as they transition from cleanup to meeting or snacktime.

- For some children, standing in line is very difficult. Try leading some stretches that involve proprioceptive input—pushing our own hands against each other, stretching our arms high, leaning to one side. If a child has a hard time staying in line, send her to the end, or hold her hand in the middle of the line. Some children have a hard time staying organized in a crowded bathroom. Send these children to small spaces like bathrooms a few at a time.

Open Choice

- Create a simple, clearly defined visual environment that embeds clues about how to use the area. For example, an activity placed on a table mat suggests the activity stays on the mat. A circle taped on the floor suggests that the floor activity stays inside the circle.
- Always include a sensory activity using materials like playdough or water that children can freely explore.
- Try to have an activity that involves the entire body and offers proprioceptive input. Most gross-motor activities do. If you don't have much space, have some weighted stuffed animals or dramatic play props; some pillows, chair, or couch a child can dive into; something low that children can jump from. Remember that if you give children the chance to move around a lot, they might get very aroused. Hanging from bars, climbing, lifting, or pushing objects is calming and organizing.

Circle Time

- Provide different seating options, depending on the needs of the group. Some children participate best from a cube chair; some, sitting on a crunchy cushion; some need a visually defined area. Sitting on the floor is very hard for children with weak trunk muscles, tight hamstrings, or high need for movement. Rocking chairs, ball chairs, placements that offers walls to lean on, or just a big block as a seat are also good options to provide. Also consider a lap or shoulder weight for children who need more proprioceptive input. Experiment until you see improvement.
- Offer fidgets if they help children to pay attention. A fidget can be any item that is small, has an interesting feel to it, and is easy to manipulate. Discuss with your group the idea that different things help people to listen and learn. Experiment with fidgets for everyone, and see who is helped and who is distracted. Take fidgets away from those they distract in a nonpunishing way, and notice other sensory supports these children might enjoy. Everyone appreciates sensory supports!
- Choose your language, affect, and gestures carefully to keep the children engaged but not overstimulated.
- Use calming, organizing techniques, such as breathing together or calming fingerplays, between or at the end of songs or activities.

Snacktime or Mealtime

- Place children next to peers they feel comfortable with and who do not overstimulate them.

- Make sure tables and chairs fit snugly.

- Experiment with ball chairs, rocking chairs, and lap or shoulder weights for children who seem distracted by their disorganized bodies.

- Build calming rituals, such as a calming song, to center the group members before they eat together.

- Seat children in small groups or in quiet places to facilitate relaxed eating.

- Seat children who are restless close to the teacher so she can reach them and put a calming hand on them if needed to help them tune in to the group.

Outdoor Time

- Establish clearly defined areas that offer different, essential body-movement opportunities.

- Ideal outdoor activities include swings, monkey bars, bikes, and sand and water play.

- Keep outdoor groupings manageable in number so things do not become too chaotic or loud.

- Use sound-muffling headphones outside with children who are sound sensitive.

- Provide a bridge for children who have a hard time outside figuring out what to do or how to connect with other children. Scaffold symbolic play so many children can join. Try organized or semi-organized play, such as Freeze Tag, Duck, Duck, Goose, or hide-and-seek.

Appendix C

Suggested Resources

There are many more books, Web sites, and organizations devoted to the topics below than we could review or include. This list is not intended to be definitive or comprehensive. These are resources with which we are familiar or that we use ourselves. Each of them can lead you to explore further.

Inclusion

Bowe, Frank. 2004. *Making inclusion work*. Upper Saddle River, N.J.: Prentice Hall.

California Map to Inclusive Child Care: http://www.cainclusivechildcare.org/camap/

Daniels, Ellen R., and Kay Stafford. 1999. *Creating inclusive classrooms*. Washington, DC: Children's Resources International.

The Division for Early Childhood: http://www.dec-sped.org

Klass, Perri, and Eileen Costello. 2003. *Quirky kids: Understanding and helping your child who doesn't fit in—when to worry and when not to worry*. New York: Ballantine Books.

Partnerships for Inclusion: http://www.fpg.unc.edu/~pfi

San Francisco Center for Collaborative Early Childhood Teacher Education: http://sfececenter.org

Relationship-Based Education

Bainer, Claire Copenhagen, and Liisa Hale. 2007. *Second home: A day in the life of a model early childhood program*. St. Paul: Redleaf Press.

Bos, Bev. 1990. *Together we're better: Establishing a coactive learning environment.* Roseville, CA: Turn the Page Press.

Carter, Margie, and Deb Curtis. 2010. *The visionary director: A handbook for dreaming, organizing, and improvising in your center,* 2nd ed. St. Paul: Redleaf Press.

DeVries, Rheta, Betty Zan, Carolyn Hildebrandt, Rebecca Edmiaston, and Christina Sales eds. 2001. *Developing constructivist early childhood curriculum.* New York: Teachers College Press.

Duckworth, Eleanor. 2006. *"The having of wonderful ideas" and other essays on teaching and learning,* 3rd ed. New York: Teachers College Press.

Meier, Daniel, R., ed. 2009. *Here's the story: Using narrative to promote young children's language and literacy learning.* New York: Teachers College Press.

Paley, Vivian G. 2004. *A child's work: The importance of fantasy play.* Chicago: University of Chicago Press.

Raikes, Helen, and Carolyn P. Edwards. 2009. *Extending the dance in infant and toddler caregiving: Enhancing attachment and relationships.* Baltimore: Brookes Publishing.

Singer, Dorothy G., and Jerome L. Singer. 1990. *The house of make-believe: Children's play and the developing imagination.* Cambridge, MA: Harvard University Press.

Sensory Integration/DIR

Biel, Lindsey, and Nancy Peske. 2005. *Raising a sensory smart child: The definitive handbook for helping your child with sensory integration issues.* New York: Penguin.

Greenspan, Stanley. 1995. *The challenging child: Understanding, raising, and enjoying the five "difficult" types of children.* Reading, MA: Addison-Wesley Publishing.

Heller, Sharon. 2002. *Too loud, too bright, too fast, too tight: What to do if you are sensory defensive in an overstimulating world.* New York: Harper Collins.

The Interdisciplinary Council on Developmental and Learning Disorders: http://www.icdl.com

Kranowitz, Carol S. 2006. *The out-of-sync child has fun: Activities for kids with sensory processing disorder.* New York: Perigee Trade.

Brain Development

Committee on Integrating the Science of Early Childhood Development. 2000. *From neurons to neighborhoods: The science of early childhood development.* Washington, DC: National Academy Press.

The Dana Foundation: http://www.dana.org

Greenspan, Stanley. 1997. *The growth of the mind: And the endangered origins of intelligence.* Reading, MA: Addison-Wesley Publishing.

Siegel, Daniel, and Mary Hartzell. 2003. *Parenting from the inside out: How a deeper self-understanding can help you raise children who thrive.* New York: Tarcher Putnam.

Diversity and Identity

Derman-Sparks, Louise, and the A.B.C. Task Force. 1989. *The anti-bias curriculum: Tools for empowering young children.* Washington, DC: National Association for the Education of Young Children.

Gonzalez-Mena, Janet. 2008. *Diversity in early care and education: Honoring differences,* 5th ed. New York: McGraw-Hill.

Social Relationships

Corsaro, William. 2003. *We're friends, right?: Inside kids' culture.* Washington, DC: Joseph Henry Press.

Kemple, Kristen M. 2004. *Let's be friends: Peer competence and social inclusion in early childhood programs.* New York: Teachers College Press.